NOMOS XLI

Yearbook of the American Society for Political and Legal Philosophy

GLOBAL JUSTICE

Edited by

Ian Shapiro, *Yale University*
and
Lea Brilmayer, *Yale University*

NEW YORK UNIVERSITY PRESS · *New York and London*

NEW YORK UNIVERSITY PRESS
New York and London

Library of Congress Cataloging-in-Publication Data
Global justice / edited by Ian Shapiro and Lea Brilmayer.
p.   cm. — (Nomos ; 41)
Includes bibliographical references and index.
ISBN 0-8147-8119-5 (cloth : alk. paper)
1. Justice. I. Shapiro, Ian. II. Brilmayer, Lea. III. Series.
JC578 .G56 1998
320'.01'1—ddc21   98-40144
                    CIP

New York University Press books are printed on acid-free paper,
and their binding materials are chosen for strength and durability.

Manufactured in the United States of America
10 9 8 7 6 5 4 3 2 1

CONTRIBUTORS

BRIAN BARRY
Law and Political Science, Columbia University

LEA BRILMAYER
Law, Yale University

CHARLES JONES
Political Science, University of Western Ontario

JOHN KANE
Politics and Public Policy, Griffith University

LIAM MURPHY
Law, New York University

DEBRA SATZ
Philosophy, Stanford University

SAMUEL SCHEFFLER
Philosophy, University of California at Berkeley

IAN SHAPIRO
Political Science, Yale University

HILLEL STEINER
Government, University of Manchester

INTRODUCTION

IAN SHAPIRO AND LEA BRILMAYER

It is commonplace to observe that we live in an era of increasing globalization. Public and academic commentary alike are replete with discussions of the accelerating international mobility of capital, the increasing number and activities of international organizations like the UN, the IMF, the World Bank, and various transnational judicial forums, the growth of such regional organizations as the EU and NAFTA, and the information revolution that renders the idea of a "global village" vivid at the level of individual television sets and computer screens. Globalization may well be in its infancy, yet its impact to date must be judged dramatic when compared with any previous era in human history.

Although globalization is proceeding at multiple levels, it would be a mistake to assume that it is moving humanity, however gradually, in the direction of a single world government. The globe continues to be divided up into nation-states, of which there are considerably more than there were before the Soviet empire's collapse. As this event underscores, there are centrifugal forces at work in the world along with centripetal ones. There are powerful ideologies in the world—most obviously but not only Islamic fundamentalism—that are hostile to globalization due to antipathy for American consumer culture that it is taken to represent. There also are efficacious political movements in countries like Canada and the United Kingdom that seek substantial local autonomy—if not outright secession. Indeed, as the example of the United Kingdom indicates, it is too simple to ask whether globalization is increasing or decreasing, because sovereignty is being disaggregated in multiple ways. At the same time as control over some decisions is moving from Westminster to Brussels, authority over other matters is being devolved to regional parliaments in Scotland and Wales. We are evolving toward a world in which authorities and jurisdictions overlap in increasingly complex and intricate ways, perhaps more like Europe before the rise of the nation-state system and less like the world most of us have known in the twentieth century.

Questions about global justice are at least as pressing in this environment as they ever have been. Globalization has done little, if anything, to promote justice, if this is understood to require substantial redistribution from rich to poor. The world's few wealthiest countries continue to control and consume the vast bulk of its resources while billions live below the poverty line. Indeed, since the mid-1970s, globalization has contributed to the growth of inequality within the wealthiest countries. Although capital mobility has increased, that of many sectors of employees has not. Particularly those in the advanced countries who lack the wherewithal to adapt to the technological revolution have watched their incomes erode as industrial jobs have moved away and they have been forced into the low-paying service sectors of the economy. As several contributors to this book note, this makes it difficult to regard questions about global justice as pertaining simply—or even principally—to relations among rich and poor nations. The effects of globalization are differently distributed within nations as well as among them. Plausible arguments about global distribution are bound to be sensitive to this reality.

One response to it is to insist that individuals, rather than corporate entities of any sort—be they families, communities, or nations—are the appropriate subjects for all claims about justice. This is the tack taken by Brian Barry in our opening chapter. He offers a spirited and wide-ranging defense of cosmopolitanism against the views of Michael Walzer, Will Kymlicka, Charles Taylor, David Miller, and others who have argued for one or another form of deference to the autonomy of nations and states in the name of justice. The touchstone of Barry's normative scheme is the well-being of individual human beings, and putative claims on behalf of states and nations must be evaluated by how well or poorly they do in reference to that criterion. Indeed, national boundaries are of only contingent moral significance for Barry. In his view, a particular constellation of them can be defended only if the possible alternatives are likely to be worse from the standpoint of the well-being of those whose lives will be affected by them. The only form of nationalism that passes Barry's test is a kind of "civic nationalism"—marginally more robust than Habermas's "patriotism of the constitution"—that would, among other things, be geared to undermining politicized forms of group identity and achieving distributive justice for entire populations within a nation's borders. Beyond this, the division of the world into autonomous nation-states is seen by Barry to be a regrettable evil insofar as it stands in the way of the sorts of international redistribution that would be likely to promote global justice.

Exploring the cosmopolitan logic further, Debra Satz argues in chapter 2 that it should lead to the rejection of even Barry's "civic nationalism." In her view, "there are no relationships among conationals, based merely on their being conationals, that can justify substantial inequalities among the countries of the world." Whereas Barry thinks it appropriate that he has obligations "to contribute to the old age pension of somebody I have never met and have no particular interest in who lives in Rotherham, but not to the pension of somebody equally distant to me who lives in Rennes," on the grounds that "I belong to the same scheme of social insurance as the first but not the second," Satz demurs. That the optimal basis for an insurance scheme is the existing nation-state is a dubious proposition for Satz; she sees it as contributing to the existence of a world in which billions go without any social insurance whatsoever. Although Satz recognizes that some forms of obligation may be limited to conationals, risk pooling and redistribution to secure the basic necessities to ensure survival and freedom from domination are not among them. In a global economy, we are too deeply implicated in one another's economic fortunes (or misfortunes) to countenance such a view, she argues. Satz believes that Barry's requirement of redistribution from wealthy to poorer countries to the point that they can set up functioning liberal democracies of their own is insufficiently demanding; it will not free people from the possibility of domination that she regards as a requirement of cosmopolitan justice. In any case, Satz sees Barry's endorsement of civic nationalism as militating even against the redistribution that he advocates, since it allows the arbitrary exclusion of persons, regardless of their economic and political circumstances.

Samuel Scheffler presents a different perspective on cosmopolitanism in chapter 3 by focusing on the distributive consequences of endorsing the idea that subgroups of the world's population—most commonly but not always national subgroups—might develop special responsibilities to one another that take precedence over their general responsibilities to humankind as a whole. Scheffler believes that most of us are unwilling to relinquish the thought that we have special responsibilities to members of particular groups, even when living up to these responsibilities undermines the legitimate demands of global justice. Yet attempts to defend special responsibilities are vulnerable to what he describes as the distributive objection, because they provide the wealthy with a kind of moral tax shelter. They provide the well-to-do with a justification "for channeling their time, energy, and other resources into rewarding relations and associations and away from people who are needier. Simply by entering into such relations and associations, one acquires special responsibilities to one's associates, and within limits, these responsibilities then take priority over, and thus serve to shield one from, the claims of others for assistance." Scheffler considers several possible lines of response to the distributive objection but finds them all wanting.

He is thus left with a conundrum. On the one hand, he describes the impulse that gives rise to special responsibilities as "so fundamental that I cannot imagine any argument powerful enough to overturn it." On the other hand, this impulse and the imperatives to which it gives rise run into the distributive objection, which maintains that "such responsibilities confer additional advantages on people who have already benefited from participating in rewarding groups and relationships and that this is unjustifiable whenever the provision of these additional advantages works to the detriment of those who are needier." Thus stated, Scheffler does not believe that there is any solution to the conflict between the general responsibilities imposed on us by the requirements of global justice and the special responsibilities that people create out of their interactions and relationships.

This conclusion suggests to Scheffler that the problem needs to be reconceptualized. There is a tendency to see commitments to the generalized responsibilities commanded by global justice and the special responsibilities to those with whom one is locally affiliated as emanating from different moral schemes, such as the cosmopolitan and communitarian ones discussed by Barry. Scheffler challenges this dichotomous thinking on the grounds that most of us feel the pull of both general and special responsibilities. Accordingly, he sees the challenge not as determining which of these responsibilities should win out over the other. Rather, it is to come up with institutions and practices that can make them jointly realizable. Scheffler suggests, in conclusion, that repudiating the legitimacy of special responsibilities might be unwise even for those with strong cosmopolitan predilections. Globalization, he notes, is taking new forms at century's end. The principal distributive divide is less between rich countries and poor countries, as Satz contended, and more between a wealthy—globally distributed—cosmopolitan elite and the rest. Members of the wealthy elite do not have particular commitments to one another and are unlikely to assert the priority of their special responsibilities. Rather, appeals to special responsibilities are more likely to be made "as part of the identity politics with which the movement toward global integration finds itself increasingly in conflict. The function of such claims may be not to justify resistance to the idea of global justice but, rather, to call attention to the interests of those whom the movement toward global integration has left behind."

Although John Kane does not take issue with this conclusion, in chapter 4 he registers skepticism of Scheffler's account of the tensions between general and special responsibilities. Scheffler's model presents global responsibilities as preexisting and subsequently modified by the special responsibilities that people accumulate as by-products of the relationships they choose to develop. The reality, Kane points out, is typically the opposite. People initially develop a sense of their local commitments to kith and kin, with the claims of general responsibilities taking a back seat if they are given any weight at all. Accordingly, he is doubtful that Scheffler's model captures the nature of the conflict between local commitments and the demands of global justice and is skeptical that that attending to it will make those with strong local affiliations more likely to take seriously the claims of global justice. Kane also is skeptical of Scheffler's formulation of distributive objection so as to cast suspicion on all special responsibilities and interpersonal commitments that operate to the detriment of needier third parties. He points out that this is an exceedingly strong constraint, since virtually every commitment we make is arguably to the detriment of some needier third party. How are we to determine "the level above which spending on one's own children becomes illegitimate," he asks, "because it reduces the amount that we would otherwise have available to discharge our alleged general responsibilities toward needier people?" Such a strong constraint seems less likely to win converts to the notion that we should find ways of reconciling our general and special responsibilities, since most people would not affirm the assumptions about obligations to others.

Whereas Kane thinks that Scheffler takes too little account of the pull of special responsibilities, Liam Murphy thinks he underestimates the demands of global justice—at least in some contexts. In chapter 5 Murphy distinguishes two classes of qualitatively different relationships of special responsibility: those— such as immediate family relationships—whose scope is rather narrow and those—such as compatriot relations—whose scope is considerably broader. In his account, defending special relationships with respect to the former does not substantially threaten global justice, whereas affirming the priority of special relationships among compatriots is notably more constraining. The wider the scope of special responsibilities is, he argues, "the more likely we are simply to reject the claimed responsibility" in the name of global justice. But Murphy thinks it is important to note that "the more compelling claims of special responsibility are those of narrow scope," suggesting that in practice the tensions between claims of general and special responsibility might often not be as troublesome as Scheffler supposes. Murphy's argument treats broad claims of special responsibility as inherently suspect, without reference to Scheffler's distributive objection. This is a significant reconceptualization, because he demonstrates that the distributive objection itself has the potential to generate perverse implications that few defenders of global justice would want, on reflection, to endorse.

Is the tension between global justice and broad scope claims of special responsibility as unproblematic as Murphy suggests? That is Charles Jones's question in chapter 6. Jones evaluates one version of the claim of patriotic loyalty, dubbed *compatriot favoritism*, from the standpoint of the claims of global justice. The tension he identifies emanates from the fact that whereas justice revolves around the idea of impartiality, it is in the nature of patriotic commitment to be partial to one's favored compatriots. In the course of exploring this tension, Jones distinguishes his account of impartiality from what he regards as the two chief—but implausible—rivals: Godwin's first-order impartialism and Bernard Williams's antijustificationism. He considers various arguments that might be adduced in compatriot favoritism's defense, ranging from appeals to the specific characteristics of one's country, to the particular vulnerability of compatriots to one another's actions, to the value of intimacy to the development of a mature moral perspective, and to the appeal to agreement about basic values. All these arguments are found wanting in key respects. Jones also takes up the problem of conflicting loyalties, arguing that compatriot favoritism is unable to respond to this difficulty. Moreover, he argues that even if a version of compatriot favoritism could be ethically justified, it would not constrain the claims of global justice in ways that commentators such as Alasdair MacIntyre, George Fletcher, Daniel Bell, Richard Rorty, and others have argued that it would.

Despite their disagreements, Barry, Satz, Scheffler, Kane, Murphy, and Jones agree that the claims of global justice are not

extinguished by more local commitments, be these to family,
community, or nation. This leaves open the question of what the
claims of global justice actually are. Do they refer to bundles of
basic rights, essential to a tolerable existence, or are they better
understood in relative terms as a proportionate share of the
world's resources, somehow measured? Much of the discussion
of these issues in recent decades has been framed by Rawlsian
assumptions or, rather, an extension of those assumptions to a
global frame of reference by such theorists as Charles Beitz and
Thomas Pogge.[1] Hillel Steiner takes up both these arguments in
chapter 7 and shows them to be wanting as a basis for a plausible theory of global justice.

Instead of a Rawlsian framework, Steiner argues for a neo-
Lockean one, in which Locke's use-rights to the common are explicitly theorized on an international basis. Just as it is permissible in a Lockean scheme for individuals to appropriate natural
resources provided "as much, and as good" remains available to
others in common, in his view we should think of those who appropriate global resources for themselves—usually, but not always, nations—in a similar way. Steiner's proposal is for a global
fund in which those with monopoly control of territorial sites
containing natural resources are bound to contribute taxes
equal to the value of the resources they own and everyone on the
planet then has a vested right to an equal share of the fund's
proceeds. The global fund "is thus a mechanism for ensuring
that each person enjoys the equivalent of enough and as good
natural resources." He shows that this proposal exhibits a number of advantages over the going alternatives, most important,
that it does not require taking a position on the moral legitimacy of nations or on the domestic policies of governments on
the rate at which, or purposes for which, natural resources are
consumed. Any political entity that enjoyed monopoly control of
a territorial resource would be bound to pay the tax. Beyond
this, the theory is silent on how the political entity in question
would distribute the costs of raising the relevant for the tax internally, whether it would choose to turn resources into produc-
tive mines or religious shrines, to pool them, or to let them be
privately owned by its citizens. As a result, although formidable
problems of measurement and enforcement remain, Steiner

manages to avoid some of the practical difficulties confronting the neo-Rawlsian theories that he rejects.

Whether one is a neo-Rawlsian, like Beitz and Pogge, or a neo-Lockean, like Steiner, serious practical obstacles must be confronted in the pursuit of global justice. The highly inegalitarian global distribution of wealth is protected and reinforced by the political division of the world into sovereign nation-states that differ greatly from one another in their political power and over whom no international authority is binding. Given this reality, it is difficult to imagine any of the proffered schemes for global redistribution making much headway. This does not mean that the different schemes, and the debates to which they give rise, are without interest. One might reasonably think it important to make clear what global justice requires in principle even if it cannot be realized in practice in the foreseeable future. Alternatively, one might believe that even if entire schemes of global redistribution will never be implemented, theoretical reflections about what they require might still affect practical politics at the margins, nudging things in the right direction. Even if this hope seems too sanguine, one might judge it worthwhile to articulate conceptions of global justice that tend to undermine the legitimacy of the status quo, even in the knowledge that one's proposals will probably never be implemented. Nonetheless, the question arises whether there are not more fruitful ways to proceed if one's goal is to move in the direction of articulating arguments about global justice that might actually influence outcomes. The supposition that there may be informs our concluding chapter.

In chapter 8, Lea Brilmayer develops a view that she distinguishes from neorealist accounts that eschew all interest in the moral point of view, as well as the version of classical realism that limits the obligations of statesmen and stateswomen to serve their nation's interest. Although her view contains a normative component, it is not one that need entail obligations to outsiders. The realist morality that interests Brilmayer is a kind of long-run consequentialism emphasizing that "in order to be truly ethical, realist diplomats should take a hardheaded look at the long-term effects of what they are doing, rather than acting on narrow moralistic principles." This can sometimes commit them to employing morally unattractive means for the pursuit of legitimate ends and to opposing those who insist on morally attractive means regardless of the consequences. A realist's opposition to economic sanctions or endorsement of nuclear deterrence can be viewed, she argues, in this light.

Although there is nothing intrinsic in the international context that favors the realist approach, in practice Brilmayer argues that it is often more compelling there. The lack of third-party enforcement of legal and moral rules in the international context means that situations are more likely to arise in which, for instance, supporting a perpetrator of evil such as the shah of Iran must be weighed against the institution of an even worse regime if one's support is withdrawn. "Internationally, there are more cases (and, more important, more plausible cases) in which the consequentialist stakes are high, that is, when following deontological moral rules risks serious harm to others." The anarchic character of the international system means, in short, that there is more likely to be divergence on the ground between the imperatives of deontological and consequentialist moralities. Accordingly, one can act with less confidence in stock moral recipes and rules there than in the domestic political arenas, at least in countries that are reasonably well governed. It is the lack of a good and strong political system in the international realm that increases the likelihood that well-intentioned actions will backfire, paving the proverbial road to hell. In that arena, statesmen and stateswomen must act in the knowledge that others cannot be counted on to behave according to principle and that they have a moral duty to factor the considerations that follow from this fact into their calculations about how to act. It is this duty, Brilmayer argues, that lies at the core of the moral vision of realism. It is cynical to the extent that it assumes people cannot generally be expected to act as they should. It is fatalistically resigned to the fact that sometimes "immoral" means may be required to avoid the lesser of two evils. It relies on a strongly consequentialist conception of the duties of leadership. And it scorns the self-indulgence of idealists who keep their deontological hands clean, regardless of the consequences for others.

NOTE

1. Charles Beitz, *Political Theory and International Relations* (Princeton, N.J.: Princeton University Press, 1979); Thomas Pogge, *Realizing Rawls* (Ithaca, N.Y.: Cornell University Press, 1989).

1

STATISM AND NATIONALISM: A COSMOPOLITAN CRITIQUE

BRIAN BARRY

–Persecution, says he, all the history of the world is full of
it. Perpetuating national hatred among nations.
–But do you know what a nation means? says John Wyse.
–Yes, says Bloom.
–What is it? says John Wyse.
–A nation? says Bloom. A nation is the same people living
in the same place.
–By God, then, says Ned, laughing, if that's so I'm a nation
for I'm living in the same place for the past five years.
So of course everyone had the laugh at Bloom and says he,
trying to muck out of it:
–Or also living in different places.
–That covers my case, says Joe.
–What is your nation if I may ask? says the citizen.
–Ireland, says Bloom. I was born here. Ireland.
   The citizen said nothing only cleared the spit out of his
gullet and, gob, he spat a Red bank oyster out of him right
in the corner.[1]

I. INTRODUCTION

A simple—some would say simpleminded—way of thinking
about international morality is that what ultimately matters is

12

the well-being of individual human beings. With this as our touchstone, we will have little difficulty in concluding that the global distribution of income is very bad, since a billion of the world's population live in conditions of degrading poverty, condemned to watch helplessly as their children die of malnutrition and easily preventable diseases while another fifth engross the lion's share of the world's wealth.We shall also have to recognize, if we take that as our starting point, that many of the world's states do an extremely poor job of improving the well-being of those who live in their territory. Some are criminal in the elementary sense that the military or civilian forces are either officially or unofficially (with official connivance) engaged in torturing and killing parts of the population on the basis of their ethnicity, political views, or economic status. Others are corrupt to the core: those running them are concerned only with extracting as much from the country as they can, at whatever cost to the inhabitants. Yet others are incompetent to such a degree that they fail to perform the basic function of a state: guaranteeing security of person and property according to known laws.

These indisputable facts would seem to call for a large-scale transfer of resources from rich countries to poor ones and would also suggest that the most despicable governments should be subjected to international pressure (up to and including military intervention) to mend their ways or renounce their power. Yet the persistent tendency of recent theoretical work in international relations and political theory is hostile to such conclusions. The dominant paradigms in these disciplines may be described as statism and nationalism. The connection between these two approaches is complex, and one of my objectives in this chapter is to tease out their relationships. But in practice, they come together in suggesting that redistribution and intervention are far more morally problematic than one might imagine from what I have said so far. Against this, I wish to defend both my starting point, which I call cosmopolitanism, and the implications that I have drawn from it. No doubt, the insights of statism and nationalism must be absorbed, but doing so will still leave intact robust conclusions favoring international redistribution and intervention.

I shall start by laying out the leading ideas of statism and nationalism (section II). I shall draw attention to the difference between popular nationalism and academic nationalism and argue that there is a disjunction between what the academic nationalists defend and what the popular nationalists do. This is, I suggest, an especially acute problem because academic nationalists typically have particular nationalist causes that they wish to support by their theoretical labors, and these ought to be an embarrassment to them. In section III, I discuss the implications of statism and nationalism for redistribution and intervention. I shall be especially concerned with the way in which nationalist theorists commonly endorse the same conservative conclusions as those reached by statist theorists, despite the apparent conflict between the two doctrines. I shall then introduce more formally the notion of cosmopolitanism and ask in section IV how it squares with statism. I shall argue that a "morality of states" cannot be a self-contained morality. It can be defended only by showing how the interests of states conduce to the interests of individuals. But once it is put in a form compatible with cosmopolitanism, it ceases to have strong antidistributive or antiinterventionist implications.

The remaining two sections focus on the relations between nationalism and cosmopolitanism. Nationalism presents more of a challenge to cosmopolitanism than does statism in as far as it appears to set up a conflict between two objectives that a cosmopolitan can acknowledge. If a nation is an ethical community for its members, that is a good for them, but what if that is inconsistent with the redistribution and intervention that cosmopolitans endorse? I shall argue that there is no such conflict. Most nationalism entails unequal citizenship and is thus incompatible *ab initio* with cosmopolitan morality. Any nationalism that passes this test will also be compatible with the kinds of redistribution and intervention that a cosmopolitan wishes to see. Ultimately, the only form of nationalism that a cosmopolitan can endorse without heavy qualifications is one that rests on the conception of a nation that Leopold Bloom was struggling toward in his lunchtime encounter with the anonymous "citizen" and his confrères. In defining a nation as the same people living in the same place and in claiming membership of the Irish nation (though not ethnically Irish), Bloom had the root of the matter in him. With only a few years to go until the centenary of Bloomsday, the difficulties that perplexed Bloom have scarcely been brought closer to resolution.[2] I shall have a stab at defining a workable concept of civic nationalism in the sixth and final section.

II. STATISM AND NATIONALISM: THE BASIC IDEAS

Statism is (for reasons that are easily understood) a doctrine popular with governments, regardless of their other ideological commitments. It is also strongly established among theorists of international relations, especially in the United States in the form of "realism" and its offshoots. For some, such as Hans Morgenthau, it was a way of exploiting intellectual capital by bringing the traditions of European statecraft to the unsophisticated "idealistic" Americans. For others, such as Kenneth Waltz, it promised the possibility of an a priori science of international relations, of a kind that Hobbes aspired for domestic politics.[3]

Although this influence is often not acknowledged, Hobbesian ideas are fundamental to statism. Hobbes argued that, in the absence of a sovereign authority with the power to enforce its laws, individuals have a right to do whatever they judge necessary for their self-preservation. He himself pointed out that anyone who doubted that such a state of nature could exist had only to look at relations between sovereign states to find an example. It should be recalled, however, that Hobbes postulated a large number of "Lawes of Nature, dictating peace" that, if observed, would tend toward "the conservation of men in multitudes."[4] Their applicability was limited, since the obligation to adhere to them existed only when this could be done safely. Even so, Hobbes claimed that a conscientious adherence to them would reduce the level of conflict and have a beneficial effect on the survival prospects of everybody. So, "he that having sufficient Security, that others shall observe the same Lawes toward him, observes them not himselfe, seeketh not Peace, but War; & consequently the destruction of his Nature by Violence."[5]

Hobbes devoted only one paragraph in *Leviathan* to international relations, and in this he explicitly extended the application of the laws of nature from individuals to states: "the Law of Nations, and the Law of Nature, is the same thing. . . . And the same Law, that dictateth to men that have no Civil Government, what they ought to do, and what to avoyd in regard of one another, dictateth the same to Common-wealths."[6] The notion of a morality of states develops this idea: some of the norms of international morality adhere to the letter of Hobbes's "laws of nature," such as the maxim that *pacta sunt servanda*; others, such as the prohibition on aggressive (as against defensive) war are plainly in the spirit of them. However, the equivalent of Hobbes's "right of nature" carries through also to the international case: ultimately, a state may and must do what is (in the judgment of those running it) necessary for its survival, and international morality must be understood as containing a universal escape clause to accommodate this, as Hobbes pointed out.[7] Susan Strange has written of the morality of states with characteristic acerbity that "the mutual interest of all governments in their own survival sustains a whole set of conventions that could be summed up as 'dog does not eat dog.'"[8]

Is the morality of states a morality at all? If universal egoism counts as a morality, then so does its statist analogue, for it too prescribes impartially for all. Philosophical egoism says that I should pursue my interests and everybody else should pursue theirs; it is not to be confused with selfishness, which says that I should pursue my interests and so should everybody else. Again, we might follow David Gauthier and argue that a set of precepts functions as a morality as long as it sets constraints on action, even if the source of those constraints is long-run self-interest.[9] In that case, too, the morality of states will count as a morality.

There are disagreements among statists that I have elided in this stylized version of statism, but it is not as protean a doctrine as is nationalism. For my purposes, the most important distinction to be made is between the kinds of claim that nationalists typically make and the kind of case typically made for nationalism by academics sympathetic to it. The nationalism of real-world nationalists characteristically has two elements, often described as blood and soil. Less poetically, the first is the identification of a nation or people as a descent group; the second is the claim that there exists a certain national territory or homeland which the members of the descent group are entitled to control. Let me take up the two points in order. It is notorious that almost anything may serve to differentiate those who see themselves as belonging to one nationality from others. But why should phenotype, language, religion, or place of residence (among others) serve as markers of nationality in some cases and not others? The answer is that for almost all real-life nationalists, a differentiating feature serves as a marker of nationality when it is thought to coincide with a distinctive descent group.

This does not necessarily entail that the members of an ethnically defined nationality (as we may call it) actually believe in the myth of a common ancestor. But it does mean that the nation is thought of as a sort of extended family. A revealing illustration of this way of thinking was the common reaction in Britain to the Unilateral Declaration of Independence by Southern Rhodesia (now Zimbabwe). Although, it was conceded, the whites represented by the government were engaged in an illegal last-ditch effort to maintain a racialist regime, they were nevertheless our "kith and kin" (as the phrase went) and should, for that reason, not be subjected to sanctions by the British government.

The implication of this conception of nationality is that the way in which one acquires a nationality is by birth. Others may be able to become "naturalized citizens" of a state, but they do not thereby become members of the nation. Thus, for example, Germany automatically accepts as citizens those who can prove German ancestry, even if they are completely innocent of German language or culture, and this provision is no more than a formalization of the characteristic conception of nationality. Even in countries that do not define citizenship (nationality in the legal sense) by descent in this way, such as Britain and France, the conception of the nation as a descent group is still popular. Thus, there is a widespread view that the descendants of immigrants from the Indian subcontinent or the Caribbean cannot really be members of the English nation (though perhaps they can aspire to being British) and that the descendants of immigrants from North Africa cannot really be members of the French nation.

The second aspect of nationalism that has been and continues to be so influential in the real world is that to each nation there corresponds a national territory, or national homeland, to which it has some sort of legitimate claim. There are a variety of bases on which such a claim may be advanced. The basis may be theological (God gave the land of Israel to the Jews) or quasi theological (it is the manifest destiny of the white man to dispossess the native population in the American West). It may be geographical: Ireland, being an island, is "naturally" one country, and the boundaries of Italy are "naturally" created by the Alps. But by far the most popular basis is some notion of historical entitlement: Slobodan Milosević said that Serbia is where Serbs are or where Serbs are buried, thereby including Kosovo as part of the national homeland, despite its almost entirely non-Serbian population. Typically, the boundaries claimed for the national state enclose the largest territory that the national group at any time in history had within its control.[10] "Nearly every East-Central European nation has, within its historical and cultural repertoire, a memory of a 'Greater' homeland, along with tragic stories of how the borders were truncated to their present location."[11]

It is important to recognize that the claim to national self-determination that flows from this conception of the national territory is not based on the wishes of the current occupants of the territory. Rather, the idea is that the nation should have its national territory even if this creates substantial areas occupied by homogeneous national minorities that could form independent states or be attached to some other state. Thus, the demands made by representatives of nationalities at Versailles were based on claims to a historic national territory, usually including substantial minorities. Of course, these claims could not all be satisfied simultaneously, because there were rival claimants to the same areas. They inevitably had to be cut back, but the result was a compromise between these historic claims, not a drawing of boundaries designed with an eye to minimizing the extent of national minorities.

The logic of blood and soil nationalism suggests that the consent of the inhabitants of the national territory (or however much of it the national group can secure) should not be necessary for the state's legitimacy. If, however, there is to be a plebiscite, what is to be consulted is "the people" considered as a single entity—the inhabitants of the state whose boundaries are to be validated—rather than "people" considered as individuals. The plebiscite is "won" as long as a majority of those in the territory vote in favor of a state with those boundaries, a condition that will normally be fulfilled as long as the members of the nationality claiming the territory form a majority within it. Howard Adelman has set out these ideas as follows: the validity of a demand for "sovereign statehood" has "two conditions." "First, the majority of individuals within a designated political jurisdiction must consent to a state as representing the will of the people. Secondly, the majority of the people within the state jurisdiction must identify themselves as a distinct nation."[12]

Adelman ingenuously deploys this biconditional to explain why it is all right for Quebec to secede from Canada if there is a majority for doing so within the boundaries of the existing province but not all right for smaller areas within Quebec to secede from it, even if they contain homogeneous populations that do not wish to be part of an independent Quebec. "The people" is a predetermined group to be treated as if a majority can speak for the whole, even if it is manifestly divided. The implication is, of course, that whoever determines the area in which the vote takes place can to a large degree determine the outcome. Thus, Irish nationalists would like to have a plebiscite with the whole island as the unit. Unionists insist that the legitimacy of Ulster within the boundaries created by partition in 1921 is demonstrated by the presence of a majority within that area in favor of the status quo. Similarly, plebiscites on the boundaries proposed by the Treaty of Versailles made no provision for those who would have preferred different boundaries to see if they could get a majority within some alternative set of the borders.

Lea Brilmayer has argued that nationalism of this stripe satisfies the requirements of a morality. What we have are claims of entitlement of a recognizable kind: "nationalist claims typically take the form 'we are entitled to thus-and-such because it was taken from us wrongly,' or 'because we have suffered injury for which this is the only possible reparation,' or 'because God intended us to have it,' or something of that sort."[13] Hence, she suggests, nationalist claims "are general in that they rest on the assumption that any group that has a good moral claim to a particular resource is entitled to fight for it, and should be given it. It does not offend the principle of generalizability when nationalists deny that their opponents have good claims." For "the general principle [is] that groups with good claims should fight for them."[14] As with the morality of states, I shall leave until later an assessment of the quality of this morality. My purpose at present is simply to lay it out and contrast it with the kind of nationalism typically advanced by academics sympathetic to nationalism.

This academic kind of nationalism differs from blood and soil nationalism in two respects. In place of making nationality a matter of descent, something that people can do nothing about, it makes it a matter of will: nationality is conceived of as a matter of identification rather than birth. And in place of historical (or other) entitlement to some specific territory, it puts at the center of the moral claim of a nation a claim to *some* territory in which it can pursue its ends. Ideally, on this view, there would be no national minorities. The existence of national minorities may have to be accepted reluctantly, but ruling over them is not to be seen as an essential part of the national project. This form of nationalism can easily be seen to be universalistic. For its ideal is that every nation should have a state and every state should contain one and only one nation.

The value of a national state is similarly expressed in universal terms. Nations, it is suggested, are good for their members by providing them with the indispensable conditions of flourishing. The fundamental idea here, which manifestly has its roots in the German romantic nationalism of the nineteenth century, is that human beings require immersion in a language and culture in order to thrive. This gives meaning to their lives, prescribes values, and provides them with an everyday morality to live by. Ideally, people should grow up as the bearers of such a language and culture, spend their whole lives within it, and raise their children in such a way that they have the will and the capacity to maintain it. A nation, understood as a collection of people unified by language and culture in this way, needs a state to create the institutional framework within which the common language and culture can be protected and the common values pursued through a variety of public policy measures.[15] A weaker version allows that subunits (cantons, provinces, states) in a federal state may—on condition that they control linguistic and cultural issues—provide a satisfactory alternative to an independent state.[16] Either way, the notion is that a political authority must have sufficient autonomy to embody, as it were, and to protect the distinctive language and culture of its people.

It is not controversial, I take it, that a lot of nationalisms bear no relation to this picture. The antagonism between Serbs and Croats in the former Yugoslavia or between Protestants and Catholics in Northern Ireland, for example, has nothing to do with language and culture and everything to do with the competing demands of groups defined by descent. Religion is in both cases a marker but is no more than that: it is not what the conflict is about. But it is important to recognize that language can also function, like religion, as a marker for descent groups. Among the things people acquire by descent is their mother tongue, as it is revealingly called—the language they learn from their mothers (or, we had better say today, parents). Thus, even if language serves to differentiate a national group, it may well still be common descent that, for the members of the group, makes it a nation. They may, in other words, think that what matters is their being "kith and kin." The significance of the common language is that to be a native speaker of it correlates highly with membership in the relevant descent group. It is worth bearing in mind that Herder, who can be cited as a source for the linguistic-cultural interpretation of a nationality, connected language indissolubly with the idea of a nation as a kind of extended family.

Let me give these general remarks a bit more of a point by applying them to the causes that animate the theoretical efforts of the two best-known academic defenders of nationalism, Charles Taylor and Michael Walzer. Taylor has for many years constituted himself an indefatigable spokesman for francophone nationalism in Quebec, presenting its case to an international audience of political theorists whom he assumes to be temperamentally skeptical of its pretensions. Although not in favor of Quebec's complete separation from the rest of Canada, he supports the renegotiation of the Canadian constitution to give the province more autonomy, and he has defended the language policies of successive Quebec governments. This defense leans heavily on the idea of the state as the protector of language and culture. But it is, I suggest, very doubtful that the phenomenon to which he gives his support bears any very close resemblance to the phenomenon on the ground. This puts him in an analogous position to those who argued that in principle public ownership admits greater equality and concern for the general good than capitalism and then used this claim (which is certainly arguable) to support the Soviet Union, despite its oppressing workers, giving immense privileges to the *nomenklatura*, and creating environmental disasters far worse than those produced by Western European capitalism.

To put it bluntly, one would have to be suffering from clinical paranoia about the insidious power of the English language to have imagined that the survival of the French language in Quebec depended on the existence of a law making it, for example, a criminal offense to display a shop sign in any language except French. What, then, is the significance of language legislation, given that the French language is in no danger of dying out in Quebec? I suggest that this kind of language legislation is effective in achieving its purpose precisely because it is gratuitous. Its function is exactly the same as that of the annual "marching season" of the Orange Lodges in Northern Ireland. The point of marching, with drums and fifes playing and flags waving, through Roman Catholic areas is to put the minority community in its place—and that place is an inferior one.

Naturally, the form taken by the assertion of superiority corresponds to the fault line between the communities. In Quebec it is language, so the mode of assertion employed is linguistic. In Northern Ireland it is history. The Protestants are the descendants of colonial settlers (mainly Scottish), so the mode of assertion is the commemoration of military successes. The Apprentice Boys' March in Londonderry, for example, celebrates the time when the apprentice boys of Londonderry shut the gates against the (Catholic) foe and thus saved the day. This was, admittedly, three centuries ago, but that counts for nothing in a country where graffiti bearing the legend "Remember 1640" are not treated as a joke.

Taylor is undeniably correct in claiming that it is not a violation of a fundamental human right to be prevented from displaying a shop sign in the language of your choice. In the same spirit, we might say that it is not a violation of a fundamental human right to have people marching past your front door celebrating past victories of their tribe over yours. Both are, if you like, symbolic politics, but Taylor claims to be a specialist in symbolic politics. *Kristallnacht* was a way of indicating to Jews that if their windows could be broken with impunity, so could their bodies. Many took the hint, and the rest were successfully cowed. Similarly, if a Quebec government was prepared, as at one point it was, to invoke a provision in the constitution that allowed it to override decisions of the Supreme Court (the so-called notwithstanding clause) in order to reinstate its shop signage law, this was bound to have sent a strong message that constitutional protections were not to be counted on in Quebec. This message has indeed been received by the Anglophone community, and their pervasive sense of insecurity has led many of its members to leave in the last thirty years.

Taylor himself has recently conceded (at least implicitly) the inadequacy of the alleged instrumental justification (*survivance*) for Quebecois demands to be *maîtres chez nous*. For he has picked up the fashionable idea of a "politics of recognition" and proposed its application to the case of Quebec.[17] However, he has concentrated his attention on the relation between Quebec and the rest of Canada, claiming that at the heart of Quebec's demands is the desire for recognition as a "distinct society" in Canada. What he averts his gaze from is the "politics of recognition" within Quebec. What is to be recognized there is the superior position of the francophone ethnic group.

The case of Michael Walzer is perhaps even more curious than that of Charles Taylor, since it is at least possible to make some case for a connection between the linguistic-cultural conception of nationality and the actuality of politics in Quebec. The same cannot be said for Walzer's object of special concern, the state of Israel. Walzer's partiality toward Israel is familiar enough. Yet the cultural interpretation of nationalism espoused by Walzer is totally unsuitable for the purpose of defending the creation or subsequent history of Israel.[18] It is possible to make sense of Israel quite straightforwardly on the blood-and-soil conception of the nation and its legitimate claims. Thus, Israel's fundamental "law of return" takes exactly the same form as the German one. All that is required in either case is proof of descent. And the justification for the dispossession of the existing Palestinian population is very hard to provide without invoking historical/theological grounds. (The suggestion sometimes made that the creation of Israel constituted reparations for the Holocaust fails to explain why the Palestinians should be singled out to pay such a high cost, since they had nothing to do with it.) Moreover, the cultural conception of the nation presupposes some existing language and culture which is be preserved and nourished by a national state. Yet this does not fit the case of Israel in the least. The object of its founders was to make a decisive break with the Jewish culture of eastern Europe, from which most of them came. The language, modern Hebrew, was an artificial creation: it was designed deliberately to put the members of the new state on an equal footing, since everyone would have to learn it.

It might be said that now, at any rate, there is a distinctive language and culture shared by Jews in Israel and that the state can be presented in the framework of cultural nationalism as the protector of that. But this cannot be squared with the treatment of the national minority of Palestinians ("Israeli Arabs," in the official terminology). Those who belong to this fifth of the population do not serve in the army, and hence are denied benefits attached to that; they are prohibited from living in most of the country, which is "Jewish land"; the public services in the areas in which they live are of a lower standard than those in the rest of the country; they are not protected against job discrimination; and they are actively excluded by state policy from a share in the running of the major institutions.[19] None of this is necessary to ensure that Israel is the home of Jewish culture. But, as in Quebec, it falls into place if we think of the situation as one in which the majority supports a system of ethnically defined first- and second-class citizens in accordance with the legally prescribed definition of Israel as a Jewish state. It again illustrates the disjunction between what nationalists do and what their apologists among the political theorists defend.

III. STATISM AND NATIONALISM: THE
MAIN IMPLICATIONS

Statism is in essence a doctrine that endorses the status quo among states, almost regardless of what that is. The United Nations, as a trade union of states, endorses the territorial integrity of existing states and supports their resistance to secessionist movements such as those of Biafra and Katanga. However, its policy follows the realist line advocated by Hobbes. According to him, it is wrong to seek to overthrow a sovereign, but rationality demands that allegiance should be transferred from a sovereign that has been deposed to whatever political authority can promise effective protection. Similarly, a secessionist movement that manages to gain permanent control over a territory will be admitted to the club by the other states, as in the case of Bangladesh.

Statism has no theory about the way in which the boundaries of states should be drawn. It simply takes them as given. This is, on the face of it, surprising, since the United Nations is officially dedicated to securing the "self-determination of peoples." The phrase occurs in its charter and recurs in both the international human rights covenants of 1966. However, it has never been understood to imply that any group claiming to constitute a "people" has a legitimate right to secede from an existing state. Rather, the only application has been to decolonialization. In practice, then, self-determination amounts to the doctrine that colonies have a right to become independent states. (A colony for this purpose had to be separated by saltwater from the colonial power, thus avoiding awkward questions about land empires such as the Soviet Union.) The statist bias is plain in the interpretation of this right:

> UN state elites adhered persistently, though not consistently, to the principle of *uti possidetis juris*, which required that states, on attaining independence from colonial rule, retain their colonial borders. The new right to self-determination, therefore, legiti-

mated certain new *states* while denying legitimacy to various *peo-ples* who came into conflict with those states.[20]

Just as the United Nations is actually a trade union of states, so the only form of national self-determination it recognizes takes the state boundaries created by the colonial powers as its units, however arbitrary they may be. Moreover, even where the international community is forced to recognize the irretrievable breakdown of an existing state, as in the former Yugoslavia, it simply attaches itself to the next political unit down from the original state. Thus, the only kind of self-determination encouraged by the international community in the former Yugoslavia was "the right of the citizens of the individual Yugoslav republics to decide democratically within the framework of existing frontiers . . . whether and to what degree their republics should be part of a Yugoslav state."[21] A perverse consequence of this rule is, incidentally, that a state concerned about secession should avoid letting the potential seceders have the kind of political autonomy enjoyed, for example, by the Alto Adige in the German-speaking South Tyrol in Italy, since the international community will be more willing to countenance the secession of such an autonomous region than to accept the breaking up of a unitary state.

Since statism shares with blood and soil nationalism a kind of moral collectivism, both interpret plebiscites as a way of legitimating preset borders. Hence, colonial territories can vote on whether they want independence, and a majority in the whole area in favor is taken as sufficient to validate the independence of a state inheriting the colonial borders, even if it is clear that the majority is drawn from only one section of the territory. In Yugoslavia, the same approach was applied to the individual republics. Thus, it was held that the independence of Bosnia was validated by a majority vote among those living within the existing boundaries. That the majority did not include the Serbian third of the population was not regarded as a problem of legitimacy: "the people" within the borders had spoken.

The fundamental norm of the morality of states is the legal equality of all states. However unequal they may be in power and wealth, states acknowledge no superior legal authority, so that the binding force of international treaties has to rest on the consent of the parties. A state is a state if it is recognized by other states. Even if it is incapable of performing the elementary functions of a state within the area notionally under its jurisdiction, it is still supported by the norms of international morality against incursions by better-organized neighbors and would-be secessionists within.[22] Dog does not eat dog, let us recall.

The idea of state sovereignty is invoked to rule out coercive intervention by one state in the internal affairs of another. Thus, "Article 2-7 of the United Nations Charter . . . precludes UN intervention in 'matters that are essentially within the jurisdiction of any state'."[23] *A fortiori*, unilateral intervention is excluded. As far as redistribution is concerned, the hardest norm concerning international distribution promulgated by the United Nations goes with the grain of statism and is explicitly anti-redistributive. This declares that states are entitled to be sole beneficiaries of the natural resources in their territory and those in the sea and in the seabed around their shores, now extended to a two-hundred-mile limit. Although the norm is obviously most advantageous to resource-rich countries with long coastlines, such as Canada and the United States among the rich countries, and among the middling ones Brazil and Chile, it was supported by third-world countries.[24] It is an index of the hegemony of statist ideology in international gatherings that even resource-poor and landlocked countries did not propose the cosmopolitan alternative of treating national resources as a common possession of mankind.

Peter Jones has pointed out that there is a flat contradiction between the different articles of the United Nations International Covenant on Economic, Social and Cultural Rights (1966). Thus, article 11, "'recognizing the fundamental right of everyone to be free of hunger,' commits the state parties to taking measures 'to ensure an equitable distribution of world food supplies in relation to need.' On the other hand, . . . Article 25 provides that 'Nothing in the present Covenant shall be interpreted as impairing the inherent right of all peoples to enjoy and utilise fully and freely their natural wealth and resources'."[25] In practice, it is clearly the second that has won out.

Even though third-world countries would like transfers to them from rich countries, it is significant that they are most enthusiastic about forms of transfer that do not disturb the statist paradigm. Thus, the New International Economic Order promoted by the "Group of 77" in the late 1970s had as its centerpiece an increase in the price of primary commodities to be brought about by some combination of restricting production and stockpiling.[26] This would have required the cooperation of the Western countries, which was not forthcoming. In any case, it would have been a highly inefficient way of bringing about a relatively small transfer (the peculiarity of oil was not adequately appreciated) and would have made the worst-off countries—those lacking natural wealth—even worse off. Despite this, it became the prime third-world policy in virtue of its turning what was in effect aid into import income—thus putting it (on conventional statist principles) beyond reach of any external body's discretion. The mode of transfer currently in vogue is similarly statist in the same sense: the cancellation of debt. It is worth observing that this also does nothing for the poorest countries: even the collective insanity that gripped the world's bankers as they desperately sought homes for petiodollars after 1975 did not mean they were prepared to lend money to Bukina Faso and similar resource-poor countries.

To complete the picture, it is necessary to acknowledge the existence of aid provided either directly by countries or through bodies such as the World Bank. Much bilateral aid fits perfectly in the statist paradigm, since it is motivated by the perceived security or commercial interests of the donor country. As far as the rest is concerned, the two most salient features are the lack of a hard norm (comparable to that stipulating national sovereignty over natural resources) mandating contributions, and the small amount of aid in relation to the national incomes of the rich countries. Thus, the United Nations norm that official aid should amount to 0.7 percent of GNP is a mere aspiration, with no mechanism to ensure compliance, and the actual performance falls far short, with most of the wealthy countries failing to get even half way. Nor is aid unequivocally welcomed by potential beneficiaries. The statist ideology has no more vociferous adherents than the governments of third-world countries—the more so, the less their regime can bear international scrutiny. It is true that the practice of attaching to aid conditions (either about the nature of the regime or the way in which funds are to be used) does not violate the norm of nonintervention because withholding aid is technically a nonbenefit rather than a sanction.[27] Nevertheless, it constitutes a challenge to the ideology of statism in that it subjects states to outside judgment.

Nationalism in both the forms I have discussed is equally opposed to intervention and redistribution. Blood and soil nationalists assert absolute collective ownership rights over the national territory and tend to resent fiercely external criticism of their internal affairs, including their treatment of "their" national minorities. The academic theorists of nationalism converge on the same answers. Thus, Walzer insists that if the members of a nation are living in accordance with their "shared understandings," they are in a condition of justice *for them,* so any external interference is unjust. Indeed, there is not even any legitimate basis for external criticism. As far as international redistribution is concerned, Walzer denies that there can be any such thing as international distributive justice, since there is no international community united by shared understandings of the meanings of goods.[28] This, however, appears to presuppose states that are the home of a nation. What of the rest? "It is of the essence of nationalism . . . to be a revolutionary doctrine calling for the destruction of existing states and the construction of new ones with different boundaries, and thereby upsetting existing legal frameworks," as Margaret Canovan has remarked.[29]

Despite this, academic nationalists tend to write as if their doctrine could provide an underpinning for statism, taking existing state boundaries as given. For example, here is Mary Bethke Elshtain:

> The nation-state model may have emerged historically as a Western invention of the Treaty of Westphalia in 1648 but this form has been embraced worldwide. Aggrieved people want, not an end to the nation-state, or to sovereignty, or national autonomy, but an end to Western colonial or Soviet or other external dominance of their particular histories, languages, cultures and wounded sense of collective identity.[30]

What has to be observed is that the Treaty of Westphalia created (and to a large extent indeed ratified) a system of states, not nation states, and that scarcely any of those states emerging from Western colonial or Soviet domination are nation states. The point is "that very few nation-states have ever existed. What for the most part existed have been multi-national states, dominated by a hegemonial nation."[31]

We can see in David Miller's recent book *On Nationality* the curious process by which nationalist premises are deployed as a basis for the derivation of statist conclusions.[32] According to Miller, nations should be able to work out their own fates without outside interference and cannot make claims on other nations for resources because it is up to them to redistribute internally to deal with poverty. But even if we accept this for nations (and I shall challenge it later), it seems bizarre that Miller should deploy it to explain why wealthy Western countries should not intervene in the internal affairs of states in sub-Saharan Africa (on the ground that this would be a violation of national autonomy or "self-determination") and why they have no obligation to provide economic aid (on the ground that this would be a violation of collective responsibility).[33] Many of these countries do not make contact at any point with the requirements necessary to trigger the values of national autonomy and national responsibility. These include Angola and Rwanda, which Miller cites specifically as suitable applications of the principle of national autonomy, and Somalia, which is cited as an illustration of the way in which this principle of national responsibility relieves rich countries of an obligation to aid poor ones.[34]

Manifestly, the nationalist idea here has been transformed into the doctrine of state autonomy and state responsibility, which is assumed still to apply even if the state is riven by internecine conflict between opposing groups and the government is in essence a gang of looters intent on squeezing what it can out of the population at whatever cost to the future of the country. Contrary to what Miller so confidently claims, only practical considerations (which may sometimes be powerful) weigh against intervention and economic aid where states are so radically defective in providing their citizens with the minimum of physical and economic security. Miller regards it as a decisive objection to cosmopolitanism that it results in this conclusion. I urge it as a decisive objection to his own particularistic theory that it results in its denial.

Since Miller has in recent years become an avowed disciple of Walzer, we should not be surprised to find the same statist distortion of nationalism in his work. Walzer falls into a long tradition of communitarian thinking about nations that has been encapsulated by Anthony Smith as follows: "Because of its communal individuality, the group should be free of external interference and internal divisiveness to frame its own rules and set up its own institutions, in accordance with its needs and 'character'."[35] This "ideal of the *volonté generale*," as Smith describes it, is rarely realized in any actual state. Yet it is surely evident that state autonomy can be justified within this theory only when the state does embody some sort of national consensus. Despite this, Walzer has argued for a "legalist" paradigm that corresponds precisely to what I am calling statism. International relations should, according to Walzer, operate on the "morally necessary" assumption that there is a "fit" between government and community.[36] Admittedly, Walzer draws the line at genocide and slavery, but this too does not mark a break with statist morality, since there are international conventions outlawing these.[37] The clear implication of Walzer's argument is that we are to overlook the fact that scarcely any countries in the world are the homes of historic communities with shared values of the sort that he posits, but are, rather, the site of conflicts both within and between ethnic groups. We are instead to make a presumption that is to be overridden only when it is violated in the most gross terms possible.

For a final example of the same curious phenomenon, I turn to Will Kymlicka's *Multicultural Citizenship*. Kymlicka departs from the Walzer/Miller variety of cultural nationalism and follows Taylor in emphasizing that control over a political subunit may be adequate for the appropriate degree of collective autonomy. But he buys into the standard academic nationalist notion of immersion in the national culture as a supreme good. According to him, it is an essential context for the development of a capacity for individual autonomy. It is by virtue of this that he feels entitled to give his book the subtitle *A Liberal Theory of Minority Rights*.

If he were to carry through consistently the notion that group autonomy is validated by its contribution to individual autonomy, Kymlicka would surely have to say that only national minorities with liberal cultures can make a valid claim to collective autonomy, since they are the only ones that contribute to individual autonomy. Instead, he says that "both foreign states and national minorities form distinct political communities, with their own claims to self-government" and that this rules out intervention even when the political community violates elementary liberal prescriptions.[38] (Like Walzer, he makes an exception only for slavery and genocide.) But where does this unconditional claim to national independence come from? It can arise only if we refuse to take the fundamental human right to be to live in a liberal society and instead say that it is to live in an integral national culture, whether liberal or illiberal. This is, of course, a total capitulation to the doctrine of romantic nationalism, and an abandonment of liberalism.

Kymlicka pursues a curious mode of argument to get to the conclusion that national minorities in liberal states should be permitted to pursue illiberal courses. He starts from the fact that Western countries would not invade Saudi Arabia with a mission to clean things up along liberal lines and uses this as a basis for arguing that national minorities should similarly be able to oppress women, deny religious freedom, and generally behave in a barbarous fashion, as long as that is what their culture tells them to do.[39] There are, manifestly, many reasons for not invading Saudi Arabia, including a sensible reluctance to take on the formidable military hardware that the governments of the West have been busy selling to the Saudi government for the last twenty years and the same unwillingness to take over the administration of a country (for an indefinite period) that led to the abrupt termination of Operation Desert Storm. (It could plausibly be argued that the international community had an obligation to intervene forcibly in the internal affairs of Iraq under the terms of the genocide convention.) None of the reasons for the unwillingness to take over Iraq (or, *a fortiori*, Saudi Arabia) provides any basis for saying that a country committed to liberal values should permit national minorities to behave illiberally.

If we want to clear our minds about the validity of some principle, we should surely focus on a case in which its application is as straightforward as possible. It seems to me absurd to argue, as Kymlicka does, from what one might say about a case involving coercive international intervention to what one should say about a case in which a court can prevent sex discrimination or religious persecution by making an enforceable judgment. There is a straightforward conflict between the values of group autonomy and liberalism here, and a cosmopolitan is bound to say that the latter should take precedence.[40]

Kymlicka seeks to cover the nakedness of his commitment to liberalism by saying that "liberal reformers inside the culture should seek to promote their liberal principles, through reason and example, and liberals outside should lend their support to any effort the group makes to liberalize the culture."[41] But the experience of those who have sought to air liberal principles even quite cautiously in Saudi Arabia shows just how empty a concession to liberalism this is. Presumably we would no more invade Saudi Arabia to enforce freedom of speech than we would to enforce any other liberal measures. By Kymlicka's cock-eyed reasoning, this suggests that national minorities should similarly be allowed to prohibit liberal propaganda, thus nullifying his gesture toward liberalism. It is very unusual for a society that contravenes other fundamental liberal precepts not to place severe restrictions on freedom of speech. And it could no doubt be said truthfully of most cultures in the world that suppression of dissent is an integral element in them.

Kymlicka would allow liberal states to withhold economically advantageous deals (such as membership in NAFTA or the European Union) from illiberal states as a way of putting pressure on them to reform. And he says that "obviously" there are analogies with national minorities that enjoy political autonomy in a certain area. However, since political subunits in a state do not have tariff barriers with the rest of the country, this seems a good deal less than obvious. Such economic pressure should not, Kymlicka says, extend to "a total embargo or blockade." It is not at all clear to me why only a "total" embargo or blockade is ruled out, since the underlying distinction is apparently intended to be between "incentives and coercion."[42] Why, then, should any sort of embargo or blockade be permissible? Many people are prepared to support economic sanctions but not forcible intervention in certain cases. This makes sense if one accepts the legitimacy in principle of forceful intervention but is convinced of the pragmatic case against it. (I shall point out the weakness of this position in the next section.) Conversely, if there really is a principle such as Kymlicka enunciates to rule out military intervention, I cannot see why it legitimates pressure (as distinct from proselytizing—wherever the government does not prohibit it) in any form. Kymlicka's proposal to allow pressure in some forms but not others seems to be pure fiat.

In practice, Western governments are clearly inclined to follow through the logic of Kymlicka's noninterventionism all the way and sign trade deals with countries whose records are notoriously poor, such as China, Malaysia, Indonesia, Turkey, and Saudi Arabia. Indeed, Kymlicka's chosen example of a country that should be left to its own devices, Saudi Arabia, provides an ironic footnote. So far from the British government threatening not to sell weapons to Saudi Arabia unless the government behaved better, it was the Saudis who threatened not to buy weapons from Britain in 1996 unless it deported Mohammed Al-Masari, a dissident (not, incidentally, a liberal one), who had been deploying the fax machine as a way of getting around censorship. And the British government, explicitly acknowledging that it was responding to economic pressure, agreed. Only a court decision to the effect that the British government had not found a safe place for him to go prevented it from summarily deporting him. Respect for "cultural diversity" could scarcely be carried forward more slavishly.

IV. Cosmopolitanism versus Statism

Cosmopolitanism is supported by a few moral and political philosophers, such as Charles Beitz, Thomas Pogge, and Peter Singer.[43] It is also probably the working creed of officials in some United Nations agencies such as UNICEF and the WHO, and NGOs such as Amnesty International, Oxfam, and Green-peace. How great its resonance is with the publics of Western countries is not easy to tell. However, I believe that citizens are less blinkered by the statist vision than are their governments. The widespread support for NGOs such as those I mentioned (and many others dedicated to similar causes) is one sign. During the unfolding tragedy of Bosnia, moreover, Western public opinion was constantly ahead of governments in favoring more forceful intervention to stop the bloodshed and halt or reverse "ethnic cleansing."

In Britain, the scandal created by the government's lying to Parliament about its policies on arms sales to Iraq arose because ministers feared that the actual policy of authorizing large-scale sales to such a brutal regime would be unpopular with the public. There were close links (in which money changed hands) between Conservative politicians, civil servants in the Ministry of Defense, and the major arms firms, so the whole business was corrupt. But I am prepared to believe that in addition the ministers involved genuinely believed that they were pursuing the national interest by authorizing contracts for the arms industry and that this justified them in misleading the public, who would object on the basis of "sentimental" (that is, principled) humanitarian convictions about the external obligations of the United Kingdom. Another encouraging sign of cosmopolitanism thinking in Western countries was the refusal of a large part of the French population to fall in behind Jacques Chirac's attempt to invoke nationalist sentiment in supportof the resumption of nuclear testing.

A cosmopolitan is, by definition, a citizen of the world. But this should not be misunderstood. Cosmopolitanism is a moral outlook, not an institutional prescription.. The first people to call themselves cosmopolitans were the Stoics, who already belonged to a state that encompassed the whole of the civilized world (and some bits that were not, such as Britain). The point for them was to indicate that they were, in the first instance, human beings living in a world of human beings and only incidentally members of polities. It is this spirit that animates contemporary cosmopolitanism, which is a moral stance consisting of three elements: individualism, equality, and universality. Its unit of value is individual human beings; it does not recognize any categories of people as having less or more moral weight; and it includes all human beings. I believe that the logic of cosmopolitanism entails that the interests of future people have as much significance as those of contemporaries, but I shall not make much of that here.

Utilitarianism is the simplest form of cosmopolitanism, since it says that we weigh the interests of everybody on the same scale ("everybody to count for one and nobody for more than one") and recommend whatever actions, policies, laws, or political institutions have the prospect of satisfying interests most in the aggregate. In practice, utilitarians have been remarkably unforthcoming about the international implications of the doctrine, with the exception of Peter Singer. However, my reason for starting from utilitarianism is to insist that it is not the only, or indeed the most, common form of cosmopolitanism. Both Beitz and Pogge, the other philosophers I mentioned, take John Rawls as their starting point and support (in broad terms) a global version of Rawls's theory of justice. This means that they are committed to universal civil and political rights and the redistribution of material resources for the benefit of those with the least, wherever on earth they may be living. This seems to me in broad terms the most plausible version of cosmopolitanism, and it is the one whose implications I shall investigate here. Within a state, cosmopolitanism of this form is commonly called liberalism by political philosophers, though I suspect that we underestimate how far this usage is a term of art peculiar to us. We could extend the usage of liberalism in this sense so that it coincided with what I am here calling cosmopolitanism. But since the emphasis in this chapter is international, I believe that it will be more perspicuous to talk about the implications of cosmopolitanism.

Because it is defined in terms of a moral stance rather than (as with statism and nationalism) an institutional nostrum, there is a good deal of room for dispute about the institutions that would be best adapted to bringing about the cosmopolitan vision of a just world. "What is crucial to the cosmopolitan attitude is the refusal to regard existing political structures as the source of ultimate value."[44] I would extend that to *all* political structures: the value of any political structure (including a world state) is entirely derivative from whatever it contributes to the advancement of human rights, human well-being, and the like. I leave aside on this occasion nonhuman animals and the environment, but adding them would not change the basic point that political structures have no independent value.

An exceptionally vivid illustration of the way in which statism conflicts with cosmopolitanism is in their treatment of the notion of terrorism. One of the few things that the trade union of states can happily agree on is the evil of "terrorism," defined so as to include only violence not carried out by or with the connivance of state authorities. Benjamin Netanyahu's book, *Fighting Terrorism*, has been described as "rich in unintentional ironies," and one of the richest is surely his "defin[ing] terrorism as the deliberate and systematic assault on civilians to inspire fear for political ends."[45] On this definition, Israel—one of the cheerleaders in the cry for the suppression of terrorism to be put at the top of the agenda—would have to be regarded as one of the major perpetrators of it, having begun its existence with massive exercise in "ethnic cleansing" by terror, and subsequently assaulted many thousands of civilians in the Occupied Territories and (directly or by proxy) Lebanon for every one of its own civilian population to have suffered from a terrorist attack. The other great champion of the fight against terrorism, the United States, might well have to count as the major sponsor of terrorism in the world by virtue of its financial, military, and diplomatic support of Israel and a whole series of right-wing regimes in Latin America (such as those of Bolivia, Chile, El Salvador, Haiti, Guatemala, Brazil, and Argentina) and elsewhere (for example, Greece under the Colonels). Jonathan Glover, who defines state terrorism as "cases [in which] those who use violence for political purposes are those in power or their agents," concludes, surely correctly, that "even a casual study of state terrorism shows that it totally dwarfs unofficial terrorism in its contribution to human misery."[46] This is the authentic cosmopolitan note in that it assesses actions by their effects on individual human beings and refuses to assume that actions of the same nature have different moral significance according to whether or not a state is behind them.

I take it to be straightforward that no cosmopolitan can regard the morality of states as a self-contained morality. Here,
surely, cosmopolitanism reflects common sense. There would
have to be something crazy about giving a value to states as
such. Nationalism can, of course, explain why (some) states have
value for their members. But the only way in which pure statism
itself can be defended is by arguing that it constitutes a convention whose general observance is more conducive to individual
interests than any alternative arrangement could be. The most
plausible candidate for a mediating premise connecting cosmopolitan premises to statist conclusions is that "international
peace may be best served in a system in which there is a convention of respect for the autonomous domestic jurisdiction of
states."[47] However, as Charles Beitz has remarked, one may
doubt the truth of this or reject the assumption that peace is
worth having at any price.[48] Statism has not, after all, resulted in
peace, so the possibility that some alternative could do better
can scarcely be ruled out. In some cases, the international recognition of boundary realignments could have reduced conflict,
since the alternative was not peace but warfare.[49] And if "peace"
means leaving tyrants with a free hand, that is a high price indeed.
    Even in the existing state system, the consequences of letting
things take their course may be so horrendous that military intervention is worth trying. Saying this is not to deny that such
action is always fraught with risks, as the misadventures of the
United Nations in Somalia illustrate all too clearly. It is also necessary to acknowledge that action by individual states is seldom,
if ever, going to be disinterested and that humanitarianism may
be a cloak for commercial or strategic interests. Economic sanctions avoid some of the objection to force, especially if organized
internationally, but they are not without drawbacks of their own.
They carry with them the inevitable drawback that a regime that
is indifferent to the suffering of its subjects will not be deterred
by economic sanctions so long as it can deflect their ill effects on
them. The case of Iraq illustrates this.

    The UN has imposed sanctions on Iraq that are cripplingly effec-
    tive. But it is not Saddam Hussein who is suffering. It is the sick,

the weak and the poor. . . . A study has confirmed the finding of the World Health Organization that half-a-million Iraqi children under the age of five have died as a result of UN sanctions—ten times more than [the total number of people who] were killed during the entire Gulf war.[50]

The UN General Secretary, Boutros Boutros-Ghali, raised "the ethical question of whether suffering inflicted on vulnerable groups is a legitimate means of exerting pressure on political leaders whose behaviour is unlikely to be affected by the plight of their subjects."[51]

A major drawback to both military intervention and economic sanctions in the current statist system is that decisions are taken in an ad hoc way, and this is equally true whether the action is unilateral or taken under the auspices of the Security Council. A cosmopolitan must, I believe, wish for the development of an international system of adjudication. Jonathan Glover has argued that respect for human rights might become a condition for being a member in good standing of the "society of states."

> There should be international courts to which human rights complaints could be brought against states (by, or on behalf of, individuals as well as governments). The European Court of Human Rights is a possible model. Acceptance of the jurisdiction of such courts, and the provision of access to their investigators, could be regarded as a test of a country's fitness to participate in the international community. It could perhaps be a condition of membership of various international bodies (in the way that Spain, Portugal and Greece would not have been able to join the European Community while under dictatorships). It might also be made a condition for such things as eligibility for loans from the World Bank or the International Monetary Fund.[52]

All this represents an attempt to shift the "morality of states" in a cosmopolitan direction while leaving intact the key institutional feature of statism, the absence of an authority superior to states. Although I have emphasized that cosmopolitan morality does not commit its adherents to any particular institutional arrangement, including a world state, it seems clear that the present system is incapable of dealing with such vital issues as global warming, the loss of biodiversity, and pollution. Even when international agreements are solemnly signed, there is no mechanism to enforce their observance, and states are notoriously failing to meet the obligations they have accepted. Similarly, most states are officially committed to observe the conventions on human rights, but there is no way of ensuring that they adhere to their undertakings. Proposals of the kind put forward by Glover are a step in the right direction, but the ultimate objective should be, I suggest, the creation of an international legal system that takes precedence over those of individual states.

Similarly, the cosmopolitan ideal in relation to the global distribution of income is a system of income tax that is levied at the same rate on people with the same income, regardless of where they live. (As with federal income tax in the United States, this would leave it open to states to add their own income taxes for their own purposes.) Its recipients should be poor people, again regardless of their place of residence. But this requires an international tax collection system. Cosmopolitans therefore inevitably fall back, within existing institutional constraints, on recommending redistribution from rich countries to poor ones. But they cannot regard that as the whole story, even in the state system, because they cannot be indifferent to the way in which the benefits of the transfer are distributed in the recipient country. Thus, cosmopolitan support for international redistribution with states as the units must always be conditional. If whatever resources are supplied to a country will find themselves in Swiss bank accounts belonging to members of the government, the case for aid will disappear. But by the same token, a strong prima facie case for international intervention to displace this government then exists.

V. COSMOPOLITANISM VERSUS NATIONALISM

Proposals for the international enforcement of human rights and for international redistribution (especially in the form of an individual tax and transfer system) are liable to run into objections from nationalists, as we saw in section III. However, I wish to maintain that, to the extent that nationalism has these implications, it is incompatible with cosmopolitanism anyway. The only two forms of nationalism acceptable from a cosmopolitan standpoint can be combined without any incoherence with intervention and redistribution and, indeed, require them in order to be morally defensible. One case is that of the ethnically pure state, which (I argue later in this section) is tolerable only as a last resort. The other, which I shall take up in the next and final section, is civic nationalism.

Let us begin by returning to blood and soil nationalism. I have accepted Lea Brilmayer's argument that claims to a national territory can count as moral claims, since they fall within the recognizably moral genus of claims based on entitlement. I cannot, however, accept her suggestion that contemporary political philosophers are at fault in not taking such claims seriously. On the contrary, my complaint is that those sympathetic to nationalism, while talking a different language, are in fact acting as a front for blood and soil nationalism.

According to Brilmayer, both philosophers and the world community should take seriously claims to national territory and seek to "adjudicate the merits."[53] But can we imagine an international tribunal reaching a verdict on such competing claims that would not be utterly arbitrary? What kind of evidence could be adduced by the parties? The claim that God gave the land of Israel to the Jews would presumably be supported by reference to the Pentateuch. The claim that Italy obviously constitutes the peninsula up to the Alps (thus incorporating the South Tyrol) would, I take it, be supported by the production of a large relief map. The claim that greater Serbia includes Kosovo would be supported by wheeling in a barrowload of history books. But what on earth would the court do in the face of other people who denied the existence of God or claimed that He had been misreported, rejected the obviousness of the conclusions to be drawn from studying the map, and argued that the concerns of those currently living in an area should take precedence over claims based on past occupation by members of some other descent group? Brilmayer suggests that the adjudication problem is difficult but that this does not make it any the less worth addressing. In my view, however, it is more like asking philosophers and lawyers to rule on the question of whether or not the number seven is orange.

In any case, claims to national territory of the kind that Brilmayer asks us to take seriously do not articulate with cosmopolitan premises. "Thus, for example, the People's Republic of
China insists that Tibet was historically part of China and not an
independent political entity; the Baltic states, it was alleged by
the Soviets, joined the Soviet Union of their own free will."[54]
Suppose both of these claims to be true. So what? A cosmopolitan cannot accept that these facts can tell us anything morally
significant. The barbarity of Chinese rule over Tibet in recent
years would not be one whit extenuated by a past history of Chinese suzerainty over Tibet, even if it could be shown to have extended for thousands of years. And if the Baltic states had a
good case for independence, it would not have been affected by
anything their political leaders had done in 1940, any more
than the case for Irish or Scottish independence could be re-
futed by pointing to a treaty ratified by representatives of both
sides some centuries ago.

Leaving aside the theological/geographical/historical basis of
nationalist claims, let us ask how nationalism fares from a cosmopolitan point of view, considered simply as a claim that each
nation should have a state. The obvious objection is that in practice any territory that includes one national group almost invariably will also contain members of at least one other. This is a for-
mula for a system of first- and second-class citizens, which is fundamentally contrary to the equal citizenship to which
cosmopolitans are committed. What has been said of the Yugoslav successor states may be generalized to many ex-colonial
and ex-Soviet states.

> While these republics were indeed premised on a vision of "gov-
> ernment of the people, by the people, for the people," they did
> not imagine the "new birth of freedom" envisaged by Lincoln.
> Instead they manifested a different ideology, of government of
> one kind of people, by that kind of people, for that kind of peo-
> ple, at the expense of all others in the state who are not so fortu-
> nately situated. Hardly a vision of undominated equality, what
> these constitutions defined and were meant to implement was
> and is a system of permanent discrimination and inequality, of,
> by, and for the majority, the ethnically defined "nation" or
> *narod*.[55]

often been pointed out) an analogy between secession and divorce. The aspect of the analogy I want to press is this. Studies are taken to show that divorce has bad effects on children, but all they actually show is that children of divorced parents do less well on various criteria than children of intact marriages. But this does nothing to establish that those children do worse if their parents divorce than if they do not. Whatever characteristics of a marriage result in its breaking up are presumably bad for children whether it actually breaks up or not—and the impact may well be worse if it does not.[66] Similarly, things may have degenerated to the point at which the creation of ethnically pure states is better than a continuation of the status quo. But that is to say only that it is less bad than a very bad alternative.

There are some cases in which, tragically, the creation of ethnically pure states appears to be the only alternative to bloodshed and repression with no foreseeable end. For example, the de facto partition of Cyprus (accompanied by "ethnic cleansing") has created peace in that troubled island and would presumably have been recognized by the international community if Greece did not have the twin diplomatic advantages of a large and influential population of Greek descent in the United States and membership in the European Union. The vicious policies of the Turkish government toward the Kurds and of the Serbs toward the Kosovars create strong cases for independence, as does the subjugation of the Palestinians. And it is hard to see any solution now for the conflict between the Hutu and Tutsi except for the United Nations to sponsor a massive population movement so that all the Tutsi finish up in one area and all the Hutu in another, with a frontier between them manned by United Nations forces.

It is important to recognize, however, that the objections to ethnically pure states from a cosmopolitan viewpoint are not confined to the costs of bringing them about. The optimistic picture of an ethnically pure state as one that is bound to have equal citizens is far from accurate, as Zygmunt Bauman has pointed out.

Philosophical well-wishers on both sides of the liberal/communitarian divide all too often courteously close their eyes on the realities of those "minorities" whose cause they are prompted to advocate by their laudable sympathy for the left-behind and deprived. Frequently the reality, when contemplated at close quarters, and particularly from inside, does not look exactly prepossessing. More often than not the *survivance* postulate turns into an awesome weapon of subjugation and tyranny, exercised by the acclaimed or self-proclaimed guardians of the "community" (ethnic, racial, religious) and its traditional values in order to exact obeisance from their hapless wards and to stamp out every inkling of autonomous choice.[67]

Charles Taylor's defense of Quebec government policies illustrates this:

> The collective goal is not only that francophones be served [by government agencies] in French but that there still be francophones there in the next generation . . . . It cannot be translated into rights for existing francophones. Indeed pursuing it may even involve reducing their individual freedom of choice, as Bill 101 does in Quebec, where francophone parents must send their children to French-language schools.[68]

And again, even more bluntly: "Political society is not neutral between those who value remaining true to the culture of our ancestors and those who might want to cut loose in the name of some goal of individual self-development."[69] Obviously, French will go on being spoken in Quebec as long as enough people choose to speak it and encourage their children to speak it. What Taylor is talking about here is imposing a "collective goal" held by "political society" on those who repudiate that goal and therefore (despite being members of the ethnic nation) do not belong to a society defined by its adherence to it.

The role of nationalism as an ersatz religion has often been remarked on. What should be added is that few religions organize themselves internally as liberal democracies. It is not therefore surprising to find a similar tension between nationalism and liberal democracy. "Identification with and loyalty to the nation does not involve the voluntarism of a 'daily plebiscite,' rather it entails acceptance of the obligations of belonging and the mission of the nation as articulated by its guardians."[70] A

Bosnian Serb summed up the contradiction between ethnocultural nationality and liberal values when he lamented, "They want to make Serbs into citizens."[71] Nothing could more clearly bear out Renan's foreboding, expressed in "Qu'est-ce qu'une nation?" that increasingly what seemed to matter most was not to be an Italian or an English or a French citizen, but to be Italian, English or French.[72]

It is possible for a society to emerge from the worst excesses of ethnocultural nationalism, but the evidence suggests that it takes a long time. "History," said Stephen Dedalus, "is a nightmare from which I am trying to awake."[73] Leopold Bloom, too, denounced history at the climax of the Jew baiting in Barney Kiernan's pub from which the epigraph for this chapter is drawn. "But it's no use, says he. Force, hatred, history, all that. That's not life for men and women, insult and hatred."[74] Their creator, James Joyce, was an equally vehement opponent of "educating the people of Ireland in the old pap of racial hatred."[75] Joyce himself never set foot in Ireland again after 1912, and he was followed into exile in subsequent decades by thousands of men and women who found themselves stultified by the burden of history, in the form of the attempt to revive Gaelic, the subservience of state to church, and the official denigration of any culture except that of the peasantry. Only a half century after Irish independence in 1921 did the country begin to shake off the dead hand of Cathleen ni Houlihan.

A further objection to nationalism is its tendency to glorify war. To be fair, I should add that there is a strand running from Herder through Mazzini whose ideal was a world of nations living in perfect harmony in their distinct moral universes. But opposed to this pleasant notion is another, darker, vision. In this, warfare is welcomed as the sphere in which the supremacy of the nation reaches its apogee. It is not an accident that nationalists are belligerent or that national history consists largely of battles lost and won. A few days before he fell from office in 1992, Yitzhak Shamir made a speech in which he said: "We still need this truth today, the truth of the power of war, or at least we need to accept that war is inescapable, because without this the life of the individual has no purpose and the nation has no chance of survival."[76] It would be only too easy to find similar sentiments in the mouths of other political leaders in the region. Defenders of nationalism cannot, I believe, shrug off as an unfortunate idiosyncrasy this connection between nationalism and the idea that "without [war] the life of the individual has no purpose." Once the value of the collectivity is exalted above the value of the individuals making it up, some sort of fanaticism can scarcely fail to follow.

One line of argument in favor of national states is that the sense of solidarity and the shared values are conducive to the redistribution of income from the rich to the poor.[77] This is poor political sociology. It is a well-established fact that the nationalist card is typically played by parties of the right. Nationalist theorists like to invoke the analogy between a nation and a family, and indeed, an ethnic nation is a (mythical) extended family. But an appeal to the "interests of the family" against claims by individual members of it may very well be a cover for the pursuit of the interests and objectives of the one who decides the agenda. Similarly, elevating to a similar position the "interests of the nation" normally goes along with the suggestion that it is at best irrelevant and at worst disloyal to divide the nation by making demands on behalf of one socioeconomic group against another.[78] Redistribution has never come about in the way fantasized by Walzer and Miller, the general recognition that shared values require it. Rather, it has invariably required the creation of a political party that has deliberately sought to divide the electorate on socioeconomic lines.

A contemporary illustration of the malign effect of nationalism on the interests of the worst-off members of a society is provided by the way in which even the feeble and subservient Palestinian authority created by the Oslo accords has weakened working-class organization. Edward Said reports a labor activist as having

> chronicled the rise of Palestinian working-class sentiment during the intifada, and its decline since Oslo, as Fatah operatives took over and converted the unions into nationalist organizations. "This is our bane," he said with considerable animus, "the use of nationalist discourse to cover over social inequities, real injustices and the sorry state of our civil life generally."[79]

Despite all its drawbacks, I have conceded that in some circumstances an ethnically pure state may be better than the alternative, given the course that history has actually taken. This
would create a difficulty for cosmopolitanism if nation states
could legitimately resist demands for international redistribution and could claim immunity to international intervention
aimed at the enforcement of the basic essentials of cosmopolitan
morality. But there is, I wish to maintain, nothing to be said for
the anti-redistributivist and anti-interventionist conclusions
drawn by the theorists of nationalism that I set out in section III.

Let us take seriously for a moment the analogy that nationalists like to draw between a nation and a family. It is quite compatible with cosmopolitanism that members of families should
have obligations to one another that they do not have to others.
(I shall explain this in the next section.) But what if these obligations are not met? David Miller (as we saw in section III)
claims that nation-states' failure to meet their responsibilities
does not create a responsibility for others to act. But when children are neglected or abused by their parents, what virtually
everybody (including, I am sure, Miller) believes is that the state
should step in to protect them. Similarly, if political authorities
fail in their responsibilities, this should create an obligation to
intervene.

A parallel line of analysis applies to redistribution. Suppose
we agree that families should, in the first instance, have autonomy to dispose of their income according to some internal decision-making process. This does not entail that the internal distribution is closed to outside scrutiny: indeed, in Britain (and no
doubt elsewhere) a man can be jailed for willfully failing to support his family financially. Nor—as Miller would be among the
first to insist—does it entail that families must be left to survive
(or not) on whatever income the market provides them. But if
the case for (qualified) autonomy for families does not rule out
redistribution among families, nor does (qualified) autonomy
for nation states rule out redistribution among states.

Walzer, as we saw in section III, posits a "morally necessary"
assumption that there is a "fit" between community and state, to
be overthrown only by gross abuses such as slavery and genocide. A cosmopolitan should, I believe, argue for a reversal of

that assumption in the following sense. We are familiar with the line taken by a number of third-world governments in international gatherings such as the 1993 Vienna World Conference on Human Rights that demands for the observance of human rights are Western "cultural imperialism."[80] But are there really societies with a consensus on the virtues of detention without trial, routine torture of suspects, child labor, suppression of trade unions, and strict limits on education and employment for women? Or are these practices supported only by dominant groups in the society? The onus should, I suggest, be on those who maintain that there is a consensus to prove it. I very much doubt if it would prove possible to sustain the burden of proof.

What would be needed to establish the existence of a consensus supporting repressive and radically unequal institutions? To have any value, a consensus would have to have arisen in conditions in which everyone (especially including the victims of these institutions) had the capacity and opportunity to evaluate alternatives. It is, moreover, elementary that consent, if it is to be valid, must be unforced. This entails that opponents of the status quo can express dissent publicly without having any reason to fear adverse consequences, either from the state or from powerful private agents (for example, landlords and employers). If all these conditions were met, I should be very surprised if a consensus against basic human rights would emerge. Indeed, there are obvious logical limits to the possibility of establishing the conditions for valid consent. Women who are denied education cannot consent because they fail to meet the requirement of informed consent, and a regime that tortures and kills suspected "troublemakers" rules itself out of court right from the start.

I do not think a cosmopolitan is obliged to make any concessions to Walzerian cultural relativism, "a debilitating intellectual fashion indulged in by people who give the impression of never having been near a human rights violation."[81] There is much to be said for the robust position taken by Michael Freeman: "The doctrine of human rights does not entail intolerance of anything but injustice nor disrespect for any cultures except unjust cultures."[82] But even if we were to concede the theoretical possibility that a state might be able to plead for a waiver from an international court on the ground that some human right contradicted an important consensual value, I do not believe that it would make any practical difference, as long as the court was diligent in insisting on the presence of the conditions for valid consent.

VI. COSMOPOLITAN NATIONALISM?

Nationalism is Janus faced. Looking in one direction, it is an ideological construct in the sense of Marx and Engels: an obfuscatory idealization of a sordid reality. This is the form of nationalism I have been assessing until now. I must now add that it has a more benign face. In this form, it is essential to the successful operation of a liberal democratic polity. If the domestic aspect of cosmopolitanism is, as I maintain, liberal democracy, we may say that nationalism of this form is required by cosmopolitan morality. This would present a problem if it were inconsistent with the external aspect of cosmopolitanism. However, so far from being incompatible, its principles naturally support cosmopolitan redistribution and intervention.

Basic to liberalism is the idea of equal citizenship. This of course entails that legal rights should not be differentiated according to any ascriptive characteristics: there can be no castes or estates and no discrimination based on ethnicity or race or on sex. But equal citizenship calls for more than that. It is incompatible with a political division into first- and second-class citizens just as much as it is incompatible with a legal division. We can best understand what this means by recalling the kind of situation described in the previous section in which (even if there is universal suffrage) a majority community regards itself as the only legitimate source of inputs into the process of determining the future direction of the state. In complete contrast with this, equal political citizenship demands that all contributions to debate must be treated on their merits and not automatically discounted on the basis of the identity of the person making them.

This requires a politics of inclusion rather than the politics of exclusion characteristic of ethnic nationalism. The key is that loyalties to kith and kin and all other ascriptive groups must be subordinated to a wider loyalty; the primary loyalty of a citizen must be to fellow citizens. As Margaret Canovan has put it, liberal democracy can be sustained only if two conditions are met:

> the existence on the one hand of autonomous individuals who feel themselves to be free of ascriptive identities, and on the other of generalized trust among the members of the society, whatever their group membership. These are not conditions that can be taken for granted. In many parts of the world identity and solidarity are overwhelmingly ascriptive and communal.[83]

Michael Walzer has said, "Bring 'the people' into political life and they will arrive, marching in tribal ranks and orders, carrying with them their own languages, historical memories, customs, beliefs, and commitments."[84] If so, it has to be said that they are still at a prepolitical stage and are not fit to rule themselves. What I take from Liah Greenfeld's stimulating study *Nationalism* is a sense of the sheer amount of hammering that particularistic ethnic, religious, and cultural activities had to be subjected to in order to constitute a common English and French citizenship, a sense of allegiance to England and France overriding communal loyalties.[85] The historical contingency of this kind of state is scarcely surprising in the light of its strong preconditions.

But what are we to call this kind of state? Maurizio Viroli, in his book *For Love of Country*, proposes "patriotism," which he distinguishes from nationalism.[86] Of course, the most common contemporary usage of "patriotism" equates it with xenophobia. As intended by Viroli, it denotes a focus of loyalty to a state that must, as part of the definition, be committed to freedom and civic equality. Jürgen Habermas "proposes a 'patriotism of the Constitution' (*Verfassungspatriotismus*): that is, a patriotism [for Germans] based on loyalty to the universalistic political principles of liberty and democracy embodied in the constitution of the Federal Republic of Germany."[87] But there are strong historical grounds for calling it nationalism. Where we need to distinguish it from ethnocultural nationalism, we may call it civic nationalism.

In the nineteenth century, civic nationalism implicitly accepted the premises of cultural nationalism and concluded that equal citizenship required the assimilation of all citizens to the dominant (and, it was assumed, most "advanced") culture within the state boundaries. Nationalism was thus seen as a progressive force destined to pull "backward" peoples such as the Welsh or the Basques out of their cultural stagnation. Certain nations— and only those—were charged by history with this leading role. As Margaret Canovan has observed, there was a "strong element of historicism" in this theory.

> Given historicist assumptions, there is no more problem about discerning the gradually emerging boundaries of historic nations than there is in identifying the boundaries of Marxist classes. . . . Confidence in the march of history made it possible for Mazzini to envisage a fully nationalist Europe made up of only eleven genuine nations, and to dismiss the claims of the Irish (among others) to constitute a nation on the grounds that they possessed no national language and no special historic mission.[88]

Liah Greenfeld has picked up this similarity and argued that Marxism is historicist nationalism adapted so that classes instead of nations become the bearers of historical change. German nationalists contrasted the backward political and economic condition of Germany with its cultural superiority, and for Marx, "the view of the proletariat as the universal class, in distinction from all other classes, reflected the idea of Germany as the pan-human nation in distinction from all other nations."[89]

Faith in the redemptive power of nationalism has waned along with faith in the redemptive power of the proletariat. Contemporary civic nationalism must make its peace with cultural diversity. The trick is to find a focus of loyalty to fellow citizens and a basis for granting them equal respect that will transcend other identifications. Habermas's "patriotism of the constitution" is too thin: it does not provide a grounding for relations among German citizens as against citizens of other liberal democratic states. It is useless to imagine that particularistic loyalties can be attenuated unless there is some wider focus of loyalty that can be charged with some emotional force. We do need nation states. But this does not mean a state as the property of a preexisting ethnocultural nation. Rather, the nation must be constructed out of the materials lying to hand. This requires goodwill, intelligence, and imagination. Since these tend to be in short supply in politics, it is not surprising that nation states approximating the ideal are rare. Thus, contrary to the prescriptions of the ethnocultural nationalists, it would require the majority community in Quebec and Israel to reach out to the minority, to celebrate cultural diversity, and to incorporate its members into the national life, ensuring that they were well represented in every important decision-making body.

Unlike statism and ethnocultural nationalism, cosmopolitan nationalism has no principled position on boundaries. If the breakup of an existing state would make the maintenance of liberal institutions easier (or at least no less likely) and is desired by those in the area (without any division about its desirability between different groups within it), there is no reason for a cosmopolitan to oppose it. Thus, Scottish nationalism has always in the modern period been territorially based rather than ethnoculturally based. (Unlike Welsh nationalism, for example, it does not put the Gaelic language at the center of its conception of Scottish identity.) So if there were a majority in Scotland for independence, a cosmopolitan would wish it well. Illiberal secessionists, however, deserve no such sympathy. Ethnonationalists whose demands for a separate state "are likely to justify institutionalized patterns of exclusion and marginalization" must be opposed in the name of civic nationalism.[90]

I earlier introduced David Miller as one of those academic supporters of nationalism who claims an incompatibility between nationalism and cosmopolitanism. However, when he discusses the problems of creating a national identity within the boundaries of a state, what he says is very much to the point. I shall resolve this paradox by showing that civic nationalism of the kind explored in chapters 5 and 6 of his *On Nationality* does not have the anticosmopolitan implications presented in chapter 3 of the same book and discussed in section III.

According to Miller, a sense of common nationhood requires—as a precondition of a common, societywide self-understanding and a common arena of political discussion—that the overwhelming majority of the inhabitants must speak the same language, though not necessarily as their first language. Beyond that, it requires widespread adherence to certain rules of the game and to the principles underlying them. In the last chapter ("Conclusion"), Miller writes: "I have defended a civic education that presents to students the principles on which their society operates, and traces the historical process whereby those principles have come into play."[91] He goes on to say immediately: "Liberals and nationalists will find themselves somewhat at odds over issues such as these." But if this kind of thing is to count as "nationalism," I simply cannot see why it should be regarded as being in principled conflict with liberalism.

Liberals are presumably, first and foremost, people who want to see liberal institutions thrive. If, as seems plausible enough, Miller has correctly identified the conditions for their thriving, it would have to be a perverse liberal who would object to measures necessary for the fostering of those conditions. Indeed, it is notable that the avowedly liberal American political theorist, Amy Gutmann, in her work on what she calls "democratic education," advocates a form of civic education that incorporates everything proposed by Miller and, if anything, goes beyond it.[92] This no doubt reflects the American belief (which goes back well over a century) that the primary mission of the public school system is to turn a country of immigrants from a diversity of political cultures into a body of citizens capable of making liberal democratic institutions work. The only ingredient in Millerian "nationalism" that a liberal might be inclined to gag at is one that I have not so far referred to, the idea that the virtues necessary to the maintenance of a liberal democratic polity have to be supported by some common view of a shared collective purpose or perhaps even destiny. There is no question that this can (and usually does) take forms that are profoundly incompatible with liberal principles, as we saw in the previous section.

What does Miller have in mind? We get the best idea in his extended discussion in chapter 6 of the contested concept of British nationality. What is most important here are the alternatives that Miller rejects. He is explicit that a country containing English, Welsh, and Scots (he ducks Northern Ireland), with a sizable minority of immigrants or their descendants from the Caribbean and Indian subcontinent, cannot be defined in any terms that include nationality (in the sense that the English, Welsh, and Scots are nationalities), race or ethnicity, religion or culture. The British Empire might be thought to have provided a world-historical project between 1880 and (at the outside) 1960, but it has had no successor. Margaret Thatcher's vision of Britain p.l.c., a purely economic enterprise within which liberty of association and democratic accountability were to be sacrificed to the Moloch of economic growth, clearly failed to inspire anyone outside the small group who grew rich quick from her efforts to implement it. Is some more promising alternative waiting in the wings?

Miller is, I am bound to say, not a great deal of help here. Apart from hoping that we might rally round the (yet-to-be-written) constitution that he says Britain needs, he seems to suggest that the common project at the moment is to search for a common project. My own view is that there are a number of things that British people can legitimately take pride in, first among which is the country's remarkable contribution to the arts, the physical and biological sciences, and the social sciences—out of all proportion to its size and obscure location. If it is asked why somebody whose parents hail from Trinidad should feel any connection with these achievements, I would reply that they have as much reason as I have. As far as I can tell, my ancestors were small artisans and workmen in London, agricultural laborers in Devon, and peasants in Waterford. I very much doubt if any of them had any personal connection with great events (except, according to one speculation, being on the receiving end of the Revocation of the Edict of Nantes). Other candidates are our role (in which the Commonwealth shared) in the defeat of Hitler, our record of preserving the countryside, and the qualities of decency and diffuse kindliness celebrated by Orwell and still, perhaps surprisingly, surviving. (For example, I do not believe that there is any country in which passersby will come as quickly to the aid of somebody who falls down in the street or is involved in a car accident.)

Although such things might form the basis of a national identity unique to Britain, I would be the first to concede that they are scarcely the stuff out of which an all-embracing national purpose is going to be forged. But do we need one? Do we want one? For my own part, I regard the lack of one as among the most attractive features of contemporary Britain. And I do not see any reason for fearing that the absence of any such thing compromises the kind of national identity that is needed. On the contrary, I believe that there are reasons for thinking that the possibility of appealing to a supposed national purpose or destiny is always a danger to the integrity of a liberal democracy. For it offers the constant temptation to use it as a way of short-circuiting debate about the country's future and delegitimating the views of those who reject it.

Contrary to what Miller claims, civic nationalism is not inconsistent with cosmopolitanism. It is quite true that fellow nationals (that is to say, fellow citizens) have obligations to one another that they do not have to people in the rest of the world. But this in no way contradicts the universalistic tenets of cosmopolitanism. Morality is indeed universal in its nature— Miller's fundamental error lies in denying this cosmopolitan claim. But that universal morality consists largely in general prescriptions that, in the actual circumstances of everyday life, generate specific obligations: to keep promises, to reciprocate benefits, and to play our part in the social practices of our society. If I ask why I am obliged to contribute to the old-age pension of somebody I have never met and have no particular interest in who lives in Rotherham, but not to the pension of somebody equally distant to me who lives in Rennes, the answer is that I belong to the same scheme of social insurance as the first but not the second.

It may be said that this is to make too large a concession to particularism, since a contributory scheme of social insurance in a rich country provides benefits that people in poor countries can only dream of. But this does not impugn the idea that countries are the appropriate units for schemes of social insurance. For it is quite legitimate for priorities to differ according to collective preference. If the Germans want very high pensions and the French very generous child allowances, for example, that is up to them. What we have to add is the necessity of a redistribution of resources across state boundaries so that decisions about resource allocation face more similar overall resource constraints.

There is no reason for civic nationalism to be opposed to this redistribution. On the contrary, anyone who wishes to see the spread of civic nationalism must recognize that it has material preconditions. Transferring resources from rich countries to poor ones does nothing to injure civic nationalism in the rich ones (almost all of them were the same in that respect when they were half as rich) but offers at least the chance to the poor countries of creating civic nations of their own. As far as intervention is concerned, liberal democracies should welcome external adjudication to keep them up the mark. The European Court of Justice and the European Court of Human Rights are not threats to the liberal democratic states making up the European Union but valuable guarantees against backsliding.

Let me conclude by taking up one last argument against cosmopolitanism made by Miller. This is that cosmopolitanism cannot be right because its implications—for example, about the need for international redistribution—conflict with widely held convictions. The same would no doubt have been true two centuries ago if it had been suggested that slavery should be abolished worldwide. And a proto-Millerian only a century ago would have laughed to scorn the idea that women should have the same political and civil rights as men. Perhaps in another century, it will be a matter for amazement that transfers from rich countries to poor ones of 0.2 or 0.3 per cent of GNP were once thought adequate to meet the moral obligations of people in rich countries. Whether they do or not, to adduce as an argument against there being such an obligation that a lot of people currently do not believe that there is seems to me unutterably feeble. If we have convictions, let us have the courage of those convictions.

NOTES

1. James Joyce, *Ulysses*, ed. Hans Walter Gabler (Harmondsworth: Penguin Books, 1986), pp. 271–72.
2. The events chronicled in *Ulysses* occurred, as all Joyceans will be aware, on June 16, 1904.

3. Hans Morgenthau, *Politics among Nations* (New York: Knopf, 1948); Kenneth Waltz, *Man, the State, and War* (New York: Columbia University Press, 1959).

4. Thomas Hobbes, *Leviathan*, ed. Richard Tuck (Cambridge: Cambridge University Press, 1991), p. 109.

5. Ibid., p. 110.

6. Ibid., p. 244.

7. "And every Sovereign hath the same Right, in procuring the safety of his People, that any particular man can have, in procuring his own safety" (ibid.). The academic exponents of the morality of states, such as Hedley Bull and Terry Nardin, tend to play down the Hobbesian element, but I cannot see that they are in a position to make an appeal beyond the long-run interests of states. See Hedley Bull, *The Anarchical Society* (London: Macmillan, 1977); and Terry Nardin, *Law, Morality, and the Relations of States* (Princeton, N.J.: Princeton University Press, 1983).

8. Susan Strange, "Political Economy and International Relations," in Ken Booth and Steve Smith, eds., *International Relations Theory Today* (Cambridge: Polity Press, 1995), pp. 154–74, p. 170.

9. See David Gauthier, *Morals by Agreement* (Oxford: Clarendon Press, 1986). In *Justice as Impartiality* (Oxford: Clarendon Press, 1995), pp. 44–45, I argued that the morality of mutual advantage can count as a morality for this reason.

10. See Lea Brilmayer, "The Moral Significance of Nationalism," *Notre Dame Law Review* 71 (1995): 7–33, p. 20.

11. Elizabeth Kiss, "Five Theses on Nationalism," in Ian Shapiro and Russell Hardin, eds., *NOMOS XXXVIII: Political Order* (New York: New York University Press, 1996), pp. 288–332, p. 310.

12. Howard Adelman, "Quebec: The Morality of Secession," in Joseph H. Carens, ed., *Is Quebec Nationalism Just? Perspectives from Anglophone Canada* (Montreal and Kingston: McGill/Queen's University Press, 1995), pp. 160–92, p. 182.

13. Brilmayer, "The Moral Significance of Nationalism," p. 8.

14. Ibid., p. 20.

15. "Since the Romantic insight is that we need a language in the broadest sense in order to discover our humanity, and that this language is something we have access to through our community, it is natural that the community defined by national language should become one of the most important poles of identification for the civilization that is heir to the Romantics." Charles Taylor, *Reconciling the Solitudes: Essays on Canadian Federalism and Nationalism*, ed. Guy Laforest (Montreal and Kingston: McGill/Queen's University Press, 1993), pp. 46–47.

(Taylor explicitly acknowledges the influence on his thinking of Herder on p. 136.)

16. See, for example, Will Kymlicka, *Multicultural Citizenship: A Liberal Theory of Minority Rights* (Oxford: Clarendon Press, 1995).

17. See Charles Taylor, *Multiculturalism and "The Politics of Recognition,"* ed. Amy Gutmann (Princeton, N.J.: Princeton University Press, 1992).

18. Especially Michael Walzer, *Spheres of Justice* (New York: Basic Books, 1983), "The Moral Standing of States: A Response to Four Critics," *Philosophy and Public Affairs* 9 (1980): 209–25, and "Notes on the New Tribalism," in Chris Brown, ed., *Political Restructuring in Europe: Ethical Perspectives* (London: Routledge, 1994), pp. 187–200.

19. As'ad Ghanem, "State and Minority in Israel: The Case of the Ethnic State and the Predicament of Its Minority," *Ethnic and Racial Studies* 21 (1998): 428–48.

20. Michael Freeman, "Democracy and Dynamite: The Peoples' Right to Self-Determination," *Political Studies* 44 (1996): 746–61, p. 748, italics in original.

21. Robert M. Hayden, "Focus: Constitutionalism and Nationalism in the Balkans," *East European Constitutional Review* 4 (1995): 59–68, p. 64, quoting "Recognition of the Yugoslav Successor States," position paper of the German Foreign Ministry, Bonn, March 10, 1993.

22. See Robert H. Jackson, *Quasi-States: Sovereignty, International Relations, and the Third World* (Cambridge: Cambridge University Press, 1990).

23. Chris Brown, *International Relations Theory: New Normative Approaches* (Hemel Hempstead: Harvester-Wheatsheaf, 1992), p. 112.

24. "In recent years no normative principle has been more vigorously asserted by the less-developed countries than that of 'permanent sovereignty over natural resources,' a concept generally defined by its proponents as the 'inalienable' right of each state to the full exercise of authority over its natural wealth and the correlative right to dispose of its resources fully and freely." Oscar Schachter, *Sharing the World's Resources* (New York: Columbia University Press, 1977), p. 124; for relevant UN resolutions, see p. 159, n. 52.

25. Peter Jones, "International Human Rights: Philosophical or Political?" in Simon Caney, David George, and Peter Jones, eds., *National Rights, International Obligations* (Boulder, Colo.: Westview Press, 1996), pp. 203–4. Jones also cites article 2, which says much the same as article 25.

26. See Schachter, *Sharing the World's Resources*, pp. 87–105.

27. The international norm prohibits intervention but permits influence. This clearly leaves open a large area of uncertainty: when does influence turn into intervention? See Brown, *International Relations Theory*, p. 112. Withholding aid may seem noncoercive, but what about withdrawing it if a country has adapted its economy so as to rely on it?

28. "Response," in David Miller and Michael Walzer, eds., *Pluralism, Justice, and Equality* (Oxford: Clarendon Press, 1995), pp. 281–97.

29. Margaret Canovan, *Nationhood and Political Theory* (Cheltenham: Edward Elgar, 1996), p. 11.

30. Jean Bethke Elshtain, "International Politics and Political Theory," in Booth and Smith, eds., *International Relations Theory Today*, pp. 263–78, quotation from p. 270.

31. Ken Booth, "Dare Not to Know: International Relations Theory versus the Future," in Booth and Smith, eds., *International Relations Theory Today*, pp. 328–50, p. 335.

32. David Miller, *On Nationality* (Oxford: Clarendon Press, 1995).

33. Ibid., pp. 65–79.

34. For Angola and Rwanda, see ibid., p. 78, n. 31; for Somalia, see ibid., pp. 63–64.

35. Anthony Smith, *Theories of Nationalism* (London: Duckworth, 1971), p. 171.

36. See Walzer, "The Moral Standing of States," esp. pp. 210–12.

37. For these conventions, see Warwick McKean, *Equality and Discrimination under International Law* (Oxford: Clarendon Press, 1983), chap. 7. About the Genocide Convention, the International Court of Justice wrote that its object is "to confirm and endorse the most elementary principles of morality" (ibid., p. 105).

38. Kymlicka, *Multicultural Citizenship*, p. 167.

39. Ibid., p. 165.

40. Kymlicka claims that collective autonomy is a rival liberal value in ibid., pp. 167–68.

41. Ibid., p. 168.

42. All quotations in this paragraph are from ibid., p. 168.

43. Charles R. Beitz, *Political Theory and International Relations* (Princeton, N.J.: Princeton University Press, 1979), and "Cosmopolitan Nationalism and the States System," in Brown, ed., *Political Restructuring in Europe*, pp. 123–36; Thomas W. Pogge, *Realizing Rawls* (Ithaca, N.Y.: Cornell University Press, 1989), and "Cosmopolitanism and Sovereignty," pp. 89–122 in Brown, ed., *Political Restructuring in Europe*; Peter Singer, "Famine, Affluence, and Morality," *Philosophy and Public Affairs* 1 (1972): 229–43.

44. Brown, *International Relations Theory*, p. 24.

45. Avi Shlaim, "The Fighting Family," *London Review of Books*, May 9, 1996, pp. 16–18, p. 18, reviewing (*inter alia*) Benjamin Netanyahu, *Fighting Terrorism: How Democracies Can Defeat Domestic and International Terrorism* (New York: Farrar, Straus & Giroux, 1995).

46. Jonathan Glover, "State Terrorism," in R. G. Frey and Christopher W. Morris, eds., *Violence, Terrorism, and Justice* (Cambridge: Cambridge University Press, 1991), pp. 256–75, pp. 257, 273.

47. Beitz, "Cosmopolitan Liberalism," p. 129.

48. Ibid.

49. See Freeman, "Democracy and Dynamite," p. 752.

50. Maggie O'Kane, "The Wake of War," *The Guardian*, May 18, 1996, pp. 35–42, p. 35.

51. Ibid., p. 42.

52. Glover, "State Terrorism," p. 272.

53. Brilmayer, "The Moral Significance of Nationalism," p. 21.

54. Ibid., p. 17.

55. Hayden, "Focus," p. 64, italics added.

56. Hobbes, *Leviathan*, p. 107.

57. Martin Brusis, "Ethnic Rift in the Context of Post-Communist Transformation: The Case of the Slovak Republic," *International Journal on Minority and Group Rights* 5 (1997): 3–32.

58. See Joseph H. Carens, "Democracy and Respect for Difference: The Case of Fiji," *University of Michigan Journal of Law Reform* 25 (1992): 547–631.

59. Adelman, "Quebec," pp. 181–82.

60. Ibid., pp. 186–87.

61. I am grateful to Ofer Castro Cassif for this information. For a relevant discussion, see Y. Peled, "Ethnic Democracy and the Legal Construction of Citizenship: Arab Citizens and the Jewish State," *American Political Science Review* 86 (1992): 432–43.

62. The *locus classicus* is V. O. Key, *Southern Politics in State and Nation* (New York: Knopf, 1950).

63. Kiss, "Five Theses on Nationalism," p. 288.

64. A sampler of this research that I have found useful is John Hutchinson and Anthony D. Smith, eds., *Nationalism* (Oxford: Oxford University Press, 1994).

65. See Russell Hardin, *One for All* (Princeton, N.J.: Princeton University Press, 1995).

66. The only way of studying this with any hope of reaching definitive conclusions would be to randomly assign matched sets of dysfunctional families to one of two categories: those who divorce and those

who stay together. There would be obvious legal and ethical difficulties with a random controlled test of this kind.

67. Zygmunt Bauman, "Communitarianism, Freedom, and the Nation-State," *Critical Review* 9 (1995): 539–53, p. 551.

68. Taylor, *Reconciling the Solitudes*, pp. 165–66.

69. Ibid., pp. 175–76.

70. Julie Mostov, "The Use and Abuse of History in Eastern Europe: A Challenge for the 90s," *East European Constitutional Review* 4, no. 4 (1995): 69–73, p. 71.

71. Ibid., p. 72.

72. Ernest Renan, "What Is a Nation?" in his *The Poetry of the Celtic Races, and Other Studies* (Port Washington, N.Y.: Kennikat Press, 1970), p. 73. The expression in the next to last quotation, "daily plebiscite," refers to this essay.

73. Joyce, *Ulysses*, p. 28.

74. Ibid., p. 273.

75. "What I object to most in [Griffith's] paper ["Sinn Fein"] is that it is educating the people of Ireland on the old pap of racial hatred whereas anyone can see that if the Irish question exists it exists for the proletariat chiefly." Letter to Stanislaus Joyce, September 25, 1906, in Richard Ellman, ed., *Selected Letters of James Joyce* (New York: Viking, 1975), p. 111.

76. Shlaim, "The Fighting Family," p. 17.

77. Miller, *On Nationality*, pp. 92–96; and David Miller, "In What Sense Must Socialism Be Communitarian?" *Social Philosophy and Policy* 6 (1988/89): 51–73.

78. As Rosa Luxembourg put it, "The national idea of the organic existence of a people 'as a homogeneous social and political entity' is a 'misty veil' obscuring classes with antagonistic interests and rights." Joan Cocks, "From Politics to Paralysis: Critical Intellectuals Answer the National Question," *Political Theory* 24 (1996): 518–37, p. 522.

79. Edward Said, "Lost between War and Peace," *London Review of Books*, September 5, 1996, pp. 11–12.

80. See Kevin Boyle, "Stock-Taking on Human Rights: The World Conference on Human Rights, Vienna 1993," in David Beetham, ed., *Politics and Human Rights* (Oxford: Basil Blackwell, 1995), pp. 79–85, esp. p. 84.

81. Fred Halliday, "Relativism and Universalism in Human Rights: The Case of The Islamic Middle East," in Beetham, ed., *Politics and Human Rights*, pp. 152–67, p. 166.

82. Michael Freeman, "Nation-States and Minority Rights: A Cosmopolitan Perspective," in Moorhead Wright, ed., *Morality and Interna-*

tional Relations: Concepts and Issues (Aldershot: Avebury, 1996), pp. 37–51, p. 50.

83. Canovan, *Nationhood and Political Theory*, p. 40, paraphrasing A. B. Seligman, *The Idea of a Civil Society* (New York: Free Press, 1992). I have set out what seem to me to be the preconditions of a satisfactory liberal democratic regime in chapter 4 of my *Justice as Impartiality*.

84. Walzer, "Notes on the New Tribalism," p. 188.

85. Liah Greenfield, *Nationalism: Five Roads to Modernity* (Cambridge, Mass.: Harvard University Press, 1992).

86. Maurizio Viroli, *For Love of Country: An Essay on Patriotism and Nationalism* (Oxford: Clarendon Press, 1995).

87. Ibid., pp. 169–70.

88. Canovan, *Nationhood and Political Theory*, p. 8.

89. Liah Greenfield, "The Worth of Nations: Some Economic Implications of Nationalism," *Critical Review* 9 (1995): 555–84, p. 562. Marx and Engels continued to believe that "the right of historical evolution" belonged to nations as well as classes. "For example, Engels regarded Czech nationalism as 'ludicrous' and 'anti-historical,' and also defended the German claim to Schleswig as 'the right of civilization against barbarism.'" Canovan, *Nationhood and Political Theory*, p. 14, n. 14.

90. Kiss, "Five Theses on Nationalism," p. 312.

91. Miller, *On Nationality*, p. 194.

92. Amy Gutmann, *Democratic Education* (Princeton, N.J.: Princeton University Press, 1987), and "Civic Education and Cultural Diversity," *Ethics* 105 (1995): 557–79.

2

EQUALITY OF WHAT AMONG WHOM? THOUGHTS ON COSMOPOLITANISM, STATISM, AND NATIONALISM

DEBRA SATZ

At the end of Jean Renoir's film *The Grand Illusion*, two French prisoners of war are escaping from German troops over the Alps into Switzerland. They have become exhausted and can no longer outrun their pursuers. As the German soldiers raise their guns to deliver their final shots, one soldier suddenly notices that the Frenchmen have crossed into neutral Switzerland and thus cannot now be killed legitimately.

Which side of the state's territorial line the two prisoners in Renoir's film are on seems to me to be irrelevant to both the justification (or lack) we have for shooting them and the duties that we have to aid them. Humanity's claims are international. This is no mere theoretical point. I lost many family members during the Holocaust because of the side of the line on which they resided, whereas other relatives were saved because, living a few kilometers away, they were on Russian soil.[1]

I believe that neither nationality nor state boundaries, as such, have moral standing with respect to questions of justice. Call this the *cosmopolitan thesis* (CT). CT is a potentially powerful claim given that the level of material inequality between nations is substantially higher than the level of inequality within most nations. Even if all intranational inequality were eradicated, roughly 75 percent of world inequality would remain.[2] In a vastly unequal world with closed state borders, the international poor have been aptly compared with the serfs of medieval Europe: a closed caste to whom even minimal human requirements do not apply.[3] For example, the life expectancy in Sierra Leone (forty-two years) is approximately half that in Japan (seventy-nine years). That is, the birthright privileges of citizenship create both material and nonmaterial inequalities. A defender of CT will ask, why should a person be denied basic freedoms and resources because she happens to be born in Saudi Arabia rather than in France?

Many people, and most political philosophers, disagree with CT, believing that state and/or national boundaries are deep moral fault lines that track our obligations and commitments to one another in important ways. They also believe that states and/or nations have intrinsic moral value and set restrictions on justified actions. For instance, some international relations theorists argue that one nation or state cannot intervene in the actions of another. Others do not deny some concept of international human rights but contend that our obligations to conationals are greater than our obligations to outsiders. David Miller, for example, claims that "nations are ethical communities. In acknowledging a national identity, I am also acknowledging that I owe a special obligation to fellow members of my nation which I do not owe to other human beings."[4]

Statists and nationalists believe that we have special relationships with those with whom we share a state or nation, relationships that justify unequal international distribution and obligation. If Western living standards, measured in terms of energy and resource consumption, had to fall drastically to enable non-Western living standards to reach current Western levels, then most statists and nationalists would reject attempts at equalization.

In this chapter, I would like to challenge the arguments of both statists and nationalists. Instead, I defend CT, drawing on some contemporary cosmopolitan arguments, especially those of Thomas Pogge, Chuck Beitz, Martha Nussbaum, and Brian

Barry, even though I differ with them in the considerations that I regard as relevant to cosmopolitan conclusions.[5] I argue that Beitz and Pogge are insufficiently attentive to special features of the state-citizen relationship[6] and that in his conclusions, Barry gives too much weight to certain existing state-citizen relationships. In particular, I argue that despite the reasons to value our *relations* with our fellow citizens—reasons that have to do with shared vulnerabilities to coercion and domination—these reasons do not justify substantial inequalities in the well-being of people born into different territorial states. This is because there are features of the international order that also render one person vulnerable to coercion by another—even though they are strangers.

I. STATES AND NATIONS AS INTRINSICALLY VALUABLE

The two dominant approaches to international relations, as Barry notes in chapter 1 of this book, are nationalism and statism. Statists argue that states are the appropriate units of moral concern, and they endorse a principle of the legal equality of all states. Nationalists, by contrast, believe that it is those nations that are the bearers of moral value that deserve our allegiance. Nations, and not states, are what we have reason to value.

The contrast between state and nation can be made clearer by considering the former Yugoslavia, which included Serbia, Croatia, and Bosnia. To Serbian nationalists, a multicultural Bosnia is an arbitrary entity, and they desire and value a monoethnic Serbia. Serbian nationalists do not believe that they have a valuable relationship with members of the other ethnic groups with whom they have shared a state. Statists and nationalists disagree about the value of a unified Serbo-Croatian-Bosnian state.

Most states are composed of numerous nations; almost nowhere do we find a single national people uniquely associated with a state and a homeland. Populations are everywhere mixed up, mottled, and interspersed. Thus, whether we see states or nations as the bearers of value has important practical consequences for our actions.

Statists and nationalists come in many varieties. In his perceptive chapter in this book, Barry distinguishes between two types of nationalists: academic nationalists and real-world (practical) nationalists. Practical nationalists claim that "blood and soil" is the basis of a significant relationship, and they appeal to a common descent and a common (often mythical) homeland. Academic nationalists, however, argue that a significant relationship is founded on the shared distinctive culture and meanings of "a people."

Blood and soil nationalism is currently ascendant, drowning out claims of a common human identity. There are numerous problems, however, with this form of nationalism, particularly when it is used as a basis for political organization.[7] Given the mottling of populations, treating blood and soil as a principle of political order leads in practice to policies of ethnic cleansing, mass deportations, and second-class citizenship for minority nationalities living in the so-called homeland. To be secure, certain national relationships require trampling basic moral requirements, such as fundamental human rights to life and liberty. As recent history shows, practical nationalists do not tend to accord the same value to nations not their own. The case of the former Yugoslavia is instructive in this regard.

Academic nationalists, such as Michael Walzer, David Miller, and Charles Taylor, view nations as necessary cultural contexts in which people live their lives. These theorists emphasize shared culture and value rather than shared descent. Within nations, inhabitants use a common language that provides them with meaning and orientation. Such cultural contexts, they claim, need national states to protect them. Academic nationalists endorse (at least in theory) the value of every national people. But shared cultural understandings rarely, if ever, coincide with a state's legal boundaries. The necessary fit between a people and its government that the academic nationalists imagine simply does not exist. The academic nationalists' program—a state for every nation—almost everywhere requires the politics of the practical nationalists for its realization (see Barry, chapter 1 of this book).

Statists believe that states as such have intrinsic moral value. They hold that states generate special relationships among conationals[8] that they have (net) reason to value. Statists, like nationalists, come in many varieties, and some defend the existing system of states. The United Nations is an obvious example of this approach: with few exceptions, the United Nations has consistently sided with current states against secessionist movements. But existing states are arbitrary, ad hoc creations. Thus, contemporary movements for secession and self-determination challenge the legitimacy of existing states and their boundaries in ways to which statists have no principled reply. Even if states had intrinsic value, they could not acquire that value for us simply by means of their existence.

Other statists hold that states are necessary in order to transform individuals into citizens, participants in a common life. States, existing or possible, are bearers of order and organization: they make our social cooperation possible. They restrain our individual liberties in the interests of the liberties of all. As Anthony Appiah put it, "States matter morally intrinsically . . . because they regulate our lives through forms of coercion that will always require moral justification."[9] This form of statism emphasizes the need for territorially based coercive institutions that require legitimation for those they coerce. The fact of a shared coercive state, rather than a shared culture or descent, is used to justify special obligations: we have special responsibilities to those whose liberty we restrain. Later I address the question of whether and to what extent this form of statism can be accommodated by CT.[10]

II. COSMOPOLITANISM

Not surprisingly, most nationalists and statists are hostile toward, or reluctant to endorse, international intervention and redistribution. Each takes some existing ethnic/cultural tie or political boundary as defining a relationship that one has (net) reason to value over one's relationship to others. Cosmopolitanism, by contrast, takes the morally salient relationship between persons to be that of their common humanity: "it does not recognize any categories of people as having less or more weight; and it includes all human beings" (Barry, chapter 1).[11]

Like nationalism and statism, cosmopolitanism comes in many forms. Utilitarianism, for example, is a form of cosmopolitanism, its main principle asserting that everyone is to count as one, no more and no less. Other cosmopolitans give Rawlsian or Aristotelian justifications for their universalist perspective. For example, Beitz and Pogge suggest that nationality, like race and gender, is arbitrary from a moral point of view and thus equally irrelevant to a Rawlsian distributive scheme. Nussbaum argues that as "citizens of the world," each of us is entitled to the conditions required for the exercise of our basic and important capabilities.

Which form of cosmopolitanism is the most plausible? I believe (although I do not argue for this position here) that most utilitarian theories are flawed insofar as they tend to reduce all values to a single kind.[12] They are therefore unable to distinguish between different values and different types of valuable things; that is, most utilitarian theories are reductionist. I therefore assume that either Rawlsian or Aristotelian versions of CT are more plausible, but nothing turns on this assumption with respect to arguments against statism and nationalism.

In *Political Theory and International Relations*, Chuck Beitz argues for a global view of Rawls's original position. Rawls designed this position so as to nullify the effects of the morally arbitrary contingencies of race, class, gender, natural talents, religious beliefs, and individual values on the distribution of the advantages of social cooperation. Beitz contends that national origin is equally morally irrelevant and that we accordingly should design principles of justice on a global level. In particular, he recommends that Rawls's difference principle, which ties the justification of inequalities in primary goods to the position of the least well off person, be applied globally: "When, as now, national boundaries do not set off discrete, self-sufficient societies, we may not regard them as morally decisive features of the earth's social geography."[13] Thus, international economic cooperation, combined with the moral arbitrariness of national origin, gives rise to claims for international distributive justice.

Beitz's conclusion in favor of a global difference principle rests on the auxiliary argument that social cooperation across nations is similar to social cooperation within nations. Undermining this argument would provide an opening for statists to differentiate between citizens and noncitizens. They could claim that nonnationals do not engage in ongoing cooperation with one another in the relevant sense that triggers the claims of distributive justice. Beitz's argument hinges on the answer to the following question: Are the institutions of international trade and credit sufficiently similar to the institutions of the national state?

Some theorists sympathetic to cosmopolitanism answer this question in the negative. Brian Barry notes that no degree of mere trade and economic interaction can form the moral equivalent of the thick relational ties among citizens of a modern state.[14] Others point out that states coerce their citizens in a way that has no international analogue and that without such shared coercive institutions, claims of distributive equality do not arise.[15]

These criticisms, although I believe they ultimately fail, do implicitly appeal to an important consideration, as both rely on the idea that the "space" of equality—the relevant dimensions of well-being we want equally distributed—shifts across our different relationships.[16] That is, the kind of equality we have reason to care about depends on the nature of our relationships. For example, two persons who participate in a shared political structure have special reasons for wanting a substantial equality of resources (and substantially similar levels of human functioning).[17] Certain dimensions of equality are relevant only to people who relate to one another in institutional contexts—for example, a concern for equality of power arises in the workplace or in the family but not on the football field. By contrast, the absence of significant relationships between American citizens and certain groups of Pacific Islanders who live outside the world's economy does not generate a basis for a substantial equality of resources.[18] There is no relational context between a Pacific Island tribesman and a United States citizen that gives rise to the demand that we be equally politically empowered or even equally endowed with resources with respect to each other. When distributive inequality in resources does not lead to domination, marginalization, or status hierarchy, it is unclear that egalitarians should be concerned with it rather than ensuring the minimum threshold of resources needed by human beings (including Pacific Islanders) to function as humans. In my view, the answer to the question "equality of what?" depends on the question "equality between whom?"

As human beings, we have a powerful claim, wherever on earth we are, to certain threshold levels of human functioning and well-being. While some might dispute the existence of such a claim, it has been gaining ground in our century, at least in thought. It has been encoded in the idea of universal human rights that guarantees to all persons an adequate level of liberties, powers, and immunities,[19] as well as material provision. But even though these human rights generate an argument for equality in certain spaces (that is, equal standing and value for each individual life, equal basic liberties—including liberty of conscience and liberty of the person), the demand for more substantial kinds of equality among persons is generated for those who participate in shared institutions. Equality in political power, for example, arises only in the context of common political institutions.[20] Barring externalities, I have no reason for wanting an equal ability to influence the elections of legislative bodies of societies of which I am not a member. The demand for what Rawls termed "the fair value of political liberty"—the equal chance for equally talented and motivated people to influence political decisions and to achieve political office—comes from the moral imperative of avoiding domination.

Barry is correct that it is not trade per se that gives rise to claims for equality of resources or equality of liberty.[21] Certain claims of equality—that is, equality in the fair value of political liberty—obtain only among people who share a set of political institutions. The appropriate space of equality varies with the relationships among people. Nonetheless, I think that Barry's attempt to differentiate between international economic and national political relationships is mistaken. The web of relationships among most nations that engage in trade and among most people who, despite separate territorial locations, share economic positions in industry, is dense and significant and falls within the scope of justice. There are two reasons for this. First, consider whether a Detroit autoworker really shares a closer relationship with a Vermont cheesemaker than with a Korean autoworker. Even though the Detroiter and the Vermonter share a political state, she and her Korean counterpart are embedded in a web of relationships in which the actions of each can significantly and often directly affect the well-being of the other. Organizing by Korean autoworkers improves not only their own level of well-being but also that of their American counterparts. Furthermore, protectionist policies by one country can take away the jobs of autoworkers in the other country, as such policies can eliminate competing industries. Indeed, protectionist policies by one country can cause another country's state to topple. We live in a world in which markets often allow us to interact more closely with those in other countries than with some of our conationals. Therefore, the operations of the auto industry in the United States may end up regulating the life of the Korean autoworker to an extent rivaling that of his own state—by creating conditions that threaten his livelihood and his community. International markets, credit institutions, and protectionist tariffs have profound effects on the life chances of those around the globe. Citizens in different states and corporate entities can maintain relations of domination and unequal power even when the structures in which they cooperate are far apart.

It is important in this regard not to fetishize the political state. Whereas states can put their citizens in prison, a country's national economic policies can lead another country to chronic underdevelopment. Gross inequalities of power can have negative effects on humanity's claims even when there is formal equality of legal status. Even in the absence of a world political state, human rights can be violated; just entitlements can be denied; and undemocratic power can hold sway. In Thomas Pogge's words,

> In a world with large international inequalities, the domestic institutions of the poorer societies are vulnerable to being corrupted by powerful political and economic interests abroad. This is something we see all around us: manipulative and self-serving interferences by politicians and business people from rich nations with the internal political, judicial and economic processes of third world societies.[22]

The second reason that international trade and economic co-operation are part of the theory of distributive justice is that even if current state coercion differed in kind from the effects of contemporary economic policies, trade relations and states are not facts of nature like earthquakes and monsoons but are human institutions that need justification. Why should the current assignment of international political and economic power be the legitimate limit for claims for equality? Why should the current web of international relationships be placed above egal-itarian criticism? A key issue for distributive justice concerns the relationships among people within which goods are distributed, not just the distribution of the goods themselves.[23] To say that relationships matter to equality is not to regard current relation-ships as givens, without need of justification.

Barry suggests that we need territorial states to ensure the "successful operation of a liberal democratic polity" (chapter 1). According to him, states provide a necessary system of rules and institutions that allow individuals to coordinate their activities with one another.[24] National states are therefore the appropriate units for schemes of mutual advantage. Moreover, the existence of such schemes creates special obligations to fellow citizens: states make possible the good of political membership in a com-munity. Thus, although state borders are arbitrarily set, they have moral significance from the point of view of distributive justice. As Barry observed in chapter 1,

> If I ask why I am obliged to contribute to the old-age pension of somebody I have never met and have no particular interest in who lives in Rotherham, but not to the pension of somebody equally distant to me who lives in Rennes, the answer is that I be-long to the same scheme of social insurance as the first but not the second.

Barry calls this form of statism "civic nationalism" because it is founded on an allegiance to the democratic principles and norms that govern the state and so determine the relationships among its citizens. Civic nationalism is patriotism toward one's own democracy, and political institutions are endorsed insofar as they create democracy.

Is civic nationalism compatible with cosmopolitanism? And is a civic nationalism expressed through territorial states the optimal form of democratic association? Let us consider the latter question first. To argue for territorial (for example, the area from London to Rotherham) states as optimal coordination solutions, we need to compare them with other possible solutions, such as those provided by international cooperative schemes (Rennes to Calcutta), or smaller-scale schemes (the Upper West Side of Manhattan) below the level of the state. There are numerous worldwide problems whose solution requires global coordination, for example, problems of population, food supply, and environmental issues concerning the pollution of the earth's air and water. World pollution cannot be kept at a tolerable level without a systematic redistribution from the high to the low polluters. Nor can the affluent countries easily contain the costs of defending their borders against economic refugees without global redistribution that redresses the pressure to migrate. Or consider the problem of ensuring a stable world order: those states that are powerful enough to solve their domestic collective action problems may threaten their neighbors.

Other collective action problems may be best solved by towns, factories, or cities. This is particularly true of certain resource allocation problems, like those governing the use of local fields, parks, and rivers that may be most efficiently monitored close to home.[25] Nor are states necessarily the appropriate institutional frameworks to deal with other issues confronting modern societies. For example, what are the particular implications of state-based coordination solutions for contemporary debates about immigration, protectionism, environmentalism, and economic development assistance, as well as the values we should teach in our schools? Are we sure that state-based approaches to these issues are best?[26]

Some theorists worry that the only alternative to territorially based insurance schemes is an all-powerful world-state. But the contrast between a system of sovereign states and a centralized world-state is too crude. There are many other possibilities, including a state system restrained by international and intergovernmental institutions, a non–state-based economic system, a global separation-of-powers scheme, international federalism, and regional political-economic structures, such as those currently being developed in western Europe and the Americas (via NAFTA). Consider also institutions such as the World Court, the European Court of Justice, the European Court of Human Rights, the World Bank,[27] NATO, and various nongovernmental organizations such as Amnesty International and Human Rights Watch.[28] Many of these institutions have as their aim securing the conditions for people to relate to one another as equals in various institutional settings.[29] Some have also proposed making national sovereignty more flexible and permeable to international interventions in order to maintain human rights or even a sustainable environment.

At the moment, the international community does not appear to have the capacity to defend or secure even a minimal level of human functioning around the globe. Campaigns of ethnic cleansing (in Bosnia) and even genocide (in Cambodia and Burundi) have proceeded largely unchecked. Moreover, even when the world has been able to intervene, it has lacked the will. Rich nations give less than half a percentage of their GDP to poor nations. In such a context, it is not surprising that so many democratic theorists have taken the transformation of international relationships off the agenda.

Let me suppose, then, for the sake of argument, that territorial states are necessary and optimal forms of democratic social organization. We have reason to value our relations with conationals because these relations secure the conditions for our form of democratic order. Can a cosmopolitan committed to "universal civil and political rights and the redistribution of material resources for the benefit of those with the least, wherever on earth they may be living" (Barry, chapter 1) also embrace these special obligations to conationals? Are special obligations to conationals compatible with CT?

Sharing state institutions places us in a special relationship with our fellow citizens: each of us is participating in an ongoing democracy. To ensure the conditions of this democracy, we must equalize political power and restrict the scope of resource inequality. In this way, we are obligated to ensure fair access to the media, the regulation of campaign spending, and public investment in children's education to give everyone a chance to compete for jobs and offices. These dimensions of equality may reasonably be thought to apply only within the limits of a shared state, and so, contra Beitz, some dimensions of equality apply only to conationals, to people who stand in certain relationships to one another in their basic institutions.

Can a cosmopolitan accept the limitation of certain kinds of equality for citizens who share a state? Yes. First, cosmopolitans have no reason to fetishize equality because equality in a particular dimension becomes a relevant demand only in certain relational contexts. Notice, however, that this is a general point, not limited to specific national contexts. Second, saying that citizens of a state have these obligations to one another does not mean that they have the right to determine the conditions of entry and exit from their state. Nor does it yet tell us what the citizens of one state owe to those of another. Even if territorial state–bounded cooperation is needed, a cosmopolitan cannot accept without further argument that such states can determine the conditions for inclusion and exclusion in the common insurance scheme or, more broadly, in the democratic form of life.

This is one facet—an essential one in my view—of civic nationalism that Barry's discussion downplays. Civic nationalism is not merely a form of collective identification based on an allegiance to common democratic principle as Barry defines it. Rather, it can be, and has been simultaneously, a basis for exclusion—of immigrants and national minorities. The politics of "inclusion" that Barry celebrates is tied to a politics of "exclusion"—backed by border patrols with guns whose task is to keep out those whose only crime is that they were born outside its territorial edges.[30]

In other writings, Barry has criticized the idea of open borders, pointing out that its likely negative effects make it an unattractive ideal. These negative effects are taken to include the dramatic worsening of the standards of living in the rich countries, the increasing world population growth, disastrous effects on ozone levels, and the instability of democratic institutions. These are, of course, debatable claims that many (if not most) economists would probably dispute. Nevertheless, it should be apparent that if open borders have disastrous effects on global

human well-being, then egalitarian cosmopolitans should not
endorse them. What follows from this? I have already argued
that the actions of national states (and their agents) have third-
party costs that must be justified to those who bear these costs.
Even though noncitizens may not need equal political power in
states where they do not reside, their nation does require sufficient liberty and resources if it (and they) is not to be dominated
(coerced without justification) by other states. This level of resources and liberties is not constrained by the requirements for
equal citizenship, but it is constrained by the requirements of
opposing relationships of domination and hierarchy through
which some people (citizens of state X or state X itself) exercise
unaccountable power over others (citizens of state Y or state Y
itself). I believe that securing the conditions for nondomination
requires a substantial redistribution of international resources,
as well as the development of intranational economic and political institutions.

How much redistribution and along which dimensions? I believe that the minimal amount of redistribution required is far
greater than what would provide a subsistence level of functioning for all those around the globe, although obtaining even this
would be a great improvement over a status quo in which a billion people live in conditions of degrading poverty. I also believe that the distribution required by justice may be more substantial than that endorsed by Barry. Barry argues in chapter 1
that there must be sufficient international redistribution to allow
poor countries to establish functioning democracies of their
own:

> Transferring resources from rich countries to poor ones does
> nothing to injure civic nationalism in the rich ones (almost all of
> them were the same in that respect when they were half as rich)
> but offers at least the chance to the poor countries of creating
> civic nations of their own.

This principle can be interpreted in two ways. First, it may
imply only that each country requires a certain threshold of resources and liberties on which to establish its national democracy. This level is absolute, and once it has been reached, the obligations of richer countries to the poor cease. If this is what

Barry means, I disagree: a threshold equality of resources is insufficient to prevent domination in an interdependent world. Moreover, this principle—creating the threshold conditions for national democratic institutions—is quite different from the principle Barry himself endorsed earlier in his chapter—maximizing the conditions of the least well off people, no matter where on earth they may be living. I do not see how Barry can reconcile this inconsistency if he understands his principle in this way.[31]

Second, Barry's principle may imply that even though each country requires a certain threshold of resources, it also requires relative equality (along certain dimensions) with other nations if it is to remain democratic and not be dominated by the unaccountable actions of others. If this is what Barry means, I agree, but such civic nationalism requires that we pay attention to the inequality between nations and not merely ensure a minimum internally defined national threshold of democratic citizenship. So understood, Barry's principle differs from the global Rawlsianism that Pogge and Beitz endorse, since it does not require that Rawls's difference principle (maximizing the minimum position of the least advantaged) be applied without consideration of institutions and relationships. But it does not accept existing relationships and institutions as givens.

III. Conclusion

In defending the thesis that humanity's claims are international (CT), I have presented (in sketchy form) several arguments. (1) The kinds of equality we have reason to value depends on our relationships with one another. (2) Comembership in existing states and nations does not, merely as such, constitute an important relationship. (3) However, if territorial states are the best way of creating efficient cooperation and democratic citizenship, then the relationships that enable those states have value. These relationships also carry with them certain distributive obligations, including the fair opportunity for all citizens to shape public power. (4) But the existence of such distributive constraints says nothing about our obligations to citizens of other nations. (5) The facts of global interdependence mean that we must ensure the conditions for nondomination for all those who relate to one another in such institutions. This in turn requires strengthening international economic and political institutions and ensuring that the decisions made by some do not undemocratically affect the circumstances of others. I believe that cosmopolitans such as Beitz and Pogge have failed to recognize argument (1) and that Barry has given argument (5) insufficient weight in his conclusion.

Perhaps the greatest challenge to contemporary cosmopolitans is to imagine solutions that can attenuate the mismatch between the demands of global justice and the territorially based forms of democratic government. On the one hand, we need to restrain certain forms of global domination if democratic sovereignty within a polity is to be meaningful. But on the other hand, we must restrain some forms of democratic sovereignty if global justice is to be achieved. For example, a concern with international human rights requires us to oppose forms of closed border exclusion that make some people vulnerable to genocide or torture. This also leads cosmopolitans to reject the view that national democracy is a conclusory argument for the scope of distributive justice. What forms of institutions can facilitate global resource transfers without dislodging manageable forms of democratic governance?[32] How might such transfers be enforced? How might power be more equally distributed in a world system of states having vastly different levels of population? These are not easy questions, and solving them will require imagination, attention to institutional design, and political will. We must look toward regional, international, and nonstate institutional bodies to promote the ideals of our common humanity. We must think as far as practically possible beyond nationalism and statism as forms of political order.

NOTES

1. This does not mean that states or other sovereign institutions are irrelevant to punishment, because of the coordination problems with allowing everyone the right to punish everyone else, as Locke, among others, noted.

2. Income inequality between nations is pervasive and dwarfs intra-national inequality. Of a total world GNP in 1989 of approximately U.S. $18 trillion, the two richest countries—the United States and Japan—accounted for 45 percent. The forty-four least developed countries had a share of world income of less than 0.6 percent. The two largest countries—China and India, which contain 40 percent of the world's population—had a share of 3.8 percent. See Sudhir Anand, "Inequality between and within Nations," prepared for the Workshop on Economic Theories of Inequality, Stanford University, March 1993.

3. For a discussion of the analogy between feudalism and the current system of closed territorial borders, see Joe Carens, "Aliens and Citizens: The Case for Open Borders," *Review of Politics* 49, no. 2 (Spring 1987).

4. See David Miller, *On Nationality* (Oxford: Oxford University Press, 1995), p. 49.

5. See Thomas Pogge, *Realizing Rawls* (Ithaca, N.Y.: Cornell University Press, 1989); Charles Beitz, *Political Theory and International Justice* (Princeton, N.J.: Princeton University Press, 1979); Martha Nussbaum, "Patriotism and Cosmopolitanism," in Joshua Cohen, ed., *For Love of Country: Debating the Limits of Patriotism* (Boston: Beacon Press, 1996); Brian Barry, "Statism and Nationalism," chapter 1 of this volume.

6. I am indebted to discussions with Michael Blake for help in locating some problems with the Beitz/Pogge accounts.

7. See the fine discussion of this point in Elizabeth Kiss, "Five Theses on Nationalism," in Ian Shapiro and Russell Hardin, eds., *NOMOS XXXVIII: Political Order* (New York: New York University Press, 1996).

8. "Conational" refers here only to shared legal citizenship and not shared descent or culture.

9. Kwame Anthony Appiah, "Cosmopolitan Patriots," in Cohen, ed., *For Love of Country*, p. 28.

10. Barry does not explicitly consider this form of statism and does not refer to the need for legitimation. However, I believe that this form of statism that values shared citizenship as a source of obligation is analogous to what Barry terms "civic nationalism." See also Michael Blake, "Social Justice and State Borders" (Ph.D. diss., Stanford University, 1998).

11. I follow Barry in excluding, in this chapter, questions of the status of nonhuman animals, but I believe that such questions need to be addressed.

12. There are more sophisticated utilitarian theories, of course, such as those of John Stuart Mill and James Griffin.

13. Beitz, *Political Theory*, p. 176. Rawls's later writings seem to reject this idea, viewing societies as self-sufficient and self-contained.

14. Brian Barry, "The Quest for Consistency: A Skeptical View," in Brian Barry and Robert Goodin, eds., *Free Movement: Ethical Issues in the Transnational Migration of People and Money* (State College: Pennsylvania State University Press, 1992).

15. See Robert Goodin, "What Is So Special about Our Fellow Countrymen," *Ethics* 98 (1988): 663–86. See also Blake, "Social Justice."

16. See Debra Satz, "Status Inequality," unpublished manuscript, Stanford University, 1996. My thanks to Michael Blake for helping me see the international implications of the approach to equality that I develop in this chapter.

17. See Rawls's discussion of the fair value of political liberty in his *A Theory of Justice* (Cambridge, Mass.: Harvard University Press, 1971).

18. See also Beitz, *Political Theory*.

19. These can be taken to include immunities from torture, arbitrary arrest, and killing as well as rights such as equal protection under the law and equal citizenship.

20. Blake, "Social Justice." Blake's emphasis on the context-dependence of our obligations to one another has certain affinities to my own idea of relational equality. However, I believe that Blake errs in assuming that only coercion exercised through *legal* institutions requires justification.

21. On the one hand, there is a tension between Barry's view of international trade as an inadequate basis for justice and his support of civic nationalism and, on the other hand, his commitment to the Rawlsian idea that we should maximize the well-being of the least well-off, no matter where on earth they are living. I return to this tension later.

22. Thomas Pogge, "An Egalitarian Law of Peoples," *Philosophy and Public Affairs*, Summer 1994, p. 20.

23. See Satz, "Status Inequality."

24. For many purposes, such coordination solutions require coercion, and this coercion requires moral justification.

25. See Elinor Ostrom, *Governing the Commons* (Cambridge: Cambridge University Press, 1990).

26. On the value of a cosmopolitan, as opposed to a national, education, see Nussbaum, "Patriotism and Cosmopolitanism."

27. The World Bank recently announced that it will use its leverage to fight corruption in poorer countries. See *New York Times*, August 11, 1997, p. 4. The power of international capital over domestic decisions is well documented. See, for example, Maurice Pastor, "The Effects of

IMF Programs in the Third World: Debate and Evidence for Latin America," unpublished paper, Occidental College, 1985.

28. Also consider the record of transnational political entities such as the Ottoman and the Austro-Hungarian Empires, both of which tolerated cultural and ethnic divergence to a far greater extent than did many territorial states.

29. Of course, some of these institutions may be devices for one nation to maintain domination over others, as critics have charged in regard to NAFTA.

30. Indeed, Barry's neglect of this dimension is surprising given that in the countries that most closely resemble his civic nationalism—the Scandinavian countries—citizenship is granted mainly on the basis of birthplace rather than explicit consent to democratic principle.

31. One problem I have with Barry's chapter is that in contrast to its finely nuanced and often brilliant discussions of statism and nationalism, the discussion of cosmopolitanism is far too abstract.

32. See Pogge's suggestion of a global resource tax in "An Egalitarian Law of Peoples."

3

THE CONFLICT BETWEEN JUSTICE AND RESPONSIBILITY

SAMUEL SCHEFFLER

I. Introduction. Global Justice and Special Responsibilities

Claims of global justice encounter considerable resistance among the members of affluent societies, whose way of life and standard of living they appear to threaten. If the resistance to these claims were motivated by nothing but simple self-interest, it would pose no moral or philosophical puzzle, despite its obvious practical, political significance. In fact, however, such resistance is often couched in normative terms and defended by appeal to familiar moral ideas. It is argued, for example, that we have special responsibilities to the members of our own families, communities, and societies and that these responsibilities are both weightier and more extensive than our responsibilities to other people. Accordingly, the argument continues, it is not only permissible but obligatory for us to give the interests of our associates—the people with whom we have significant interpersonal ties—priority over the interests of nonassociates. We would be remiss if we failed to do this. It may be conceded, of course, that the required priority is not unlimited and that the interests of nonassociates cannot be completely disregarded. Within certain broad limits, however, we are duty bound to give priority to the interests of our associates when deciding how to allocate our time, energy, and resources.

To those who take the idea of global justice seriously, these claims of special responsibility can seem like transparently self-serving rationalizations whose primary function is to make the limited generosity of the wealthy look like a matter of high principle and to encourage complacency about the shocking disparities between rich and poor nations. Yet, at the same time, the idea that we have special responsibilities to our families, friends, and communities—to those with whom we have significant interpersonal ties—is taken for granted by most people, and not only in affluent societies. To be sure, there are significant disagreements both about the types of interpersonal bonds that give rise to special responsibilities and about how far such responsibilities extend. Notwithstanding these disagreements, however, the idea of special responsibilities counts for many people as one of their bedrock moral convictions, a rare fixed point in a world of rapid moral change. Not only do claims of special responsibility not strike most people as being, in general, objectionably self-serving, but on the contrary, such responsibilities may be viewed as a bulwark against the kind of sterile individualism that seems to characterize so much of modern life, particularly in affluent societies. Accordingly, the seriousness with which one takes one's special responsibilities may be seen as both a measure of one's moral virtue and a mark of one's success in avoiding the feelings of rootlessness and isolation that are so prevalent in highly individualistic societies. These considerations suggest that if the idea of global justice is to make headway among the affluent, the widespread resistance to that idea cannot be dismissed as just a manifestation of simple self-interest. Instead, if arguments for global justice are to be persuasive, they must engage with, and identify difficulties or limitations in, those notions of responsibility that appear to legitimate such resistance. The question is whether this can be done. In this chapter, I assess the force of one objection that might be offered, in the name of global justice, to claims of special responsibility.

II. The Distributive Objection

Suppose that none of three women, Alice, Beth, and Carla, has a special relationship with any of the others, and accordingly, none has special responsibilities to any of the others. The absence of such responsibilities, however, does not mean that none of the three women has any responsibilities whatsoever toward the others. On the contrary, each of them presumably has, for example, a responsibility not to harm or mistreat the others, and each may also have a responsibility to assist the others in certain types of situation. Let us call the responsibilities that the three women do have toward one another—despite the absence of any special relationships among them—their *general responsibilities*. For our purposes, the precise content of these general responsibilities is not very important. What is important is the fact that the distribution of these responsibilities is perfectly egalitarian in character; each woman has exactly the same responsibilities toward every other woman. Suppose, however, that, at some point, Alice and Beth become members of a group of which Carla is not a member and which we may call the In Group. Let us also suppose that Alice and Beth attach considerable importance to their membership in this group and that they experience their participation in the group as extremely rewarding. We can imagine, if we like, that over time, each of them comes to see membership in the In Group as an important aspect of her identity.

If, as a result of their membership in the In Group, Alice and Beth come to have special responsibilities to each other, then by hypothesis, each of them will in certain contexts be required to give the other's interests priority over the interests of people like Carla. The relevant contexts may be of two importantly different kinds. First, in the absence of their special responsibilities to each other, Alice and Beth might on occasion have done certain things for Carla despite their not having a duty to do so. Now, however, discharging their responsibilities to each other must take priority over providing any sort of optional assistance to Carla. Second, there may now be situations in which Alice and Beth may have to give their responsibilities to each other priority, not over the provision of optional assistance to Carla, but over their general responsibilities to her. For example, Alice may sometimes have to help Beth rather than help Carla, if she cannot do both, even though she would have been obligated to help Carla had Beth too not needed help. Thus, in short, the special responsibilities that Alice and Beth have to each other will at times take priority over any *inclination* they may have to help Carla and will at times take priority over any *responsibility* they may have to help her.

This means that if as a result of their membership in the In Group, Alice and Beth come to have special responsibilities to each other, the egalitarian distribution of responsibility that previously prevailed no longer obtains. Instead, Alice and Beth now have stronger claims on each other than Carla has on either of them. For each of them, correspondingly, Carla's claims have been demoted in relative importance. Thus Carla's claims on each of them are now weaker both than her claims on them were before they joined the In Group and than their claims on each other are now. Indeed, it would also appear that the claims that she now has on them are weaker than the claims that they now have on her. For we may suppose that Carla has no associates to whose interests she is required to give priority over the interests of Alice and Beth. Thus, their claims on her would appear not to have been weakened as a result of their joining the In Group, in the way that her claims on them have been. All things considered, then, it would seem that if Alice and Beth do indeed acquire special responsibilities to each other by virtue of their membership in the In Group, the overall distribution of responsibility that obtains once they have joined the group is both inegalitarian in character and notably unfavorable to Carla.

Now it may seem that such a redistribution of responsibility would be unfair to Carla. For why should the fact that Alice and Beth have joined the In Group alter the distribution of responsibility in a manner that is so unfavorable to her? After all, it may be argued, since both Alice and Beth find their participation in the group to be very rewarding, they have already benefited from their membership independently of any redistribution of responsibility: they have already acquired an advantage that

Carla lacks. The effect of the proposed redistribution of responsibility is to build a second advantage on top of this first one. In
other words, if Alice and Beth have special responsibilities to
each other, then in addition to enjoying the rewards of group
membership, which Carla lacks, Alice and Beth also get the benefit of having stronger claims on each other's services than Carla
has. Why should this be? Why should the fact that Alice and
Beth are in a position to enjoy the first sort of advantage give
rise to a moral requirement that they should also get the second
and that Carla, who already lacks the first advantage, should
now lose out with respect to the second?

It would be natural for anyone advancing this objection to
qualify it in one way and to generalize it in another. The natural
qualification is that the objection is waived if Carla herself had
an opportunity to join the In Group and chose not to do so. The
natural generalization is that the objection applies whenever
Alice and Beth have significantly greater resources than Carla
does, independent of any redistribution of responsibility,
whether or not the greater resources that they have are actually
a consequence of their membership. Thus, for example, if Alice
and Beth are much wealthier than Carla—either because this
has always been so or because their membership in the In Group
has made them wealthy—the idea that morality requires them
also to receive the advantage of having increased claims to each
other's services may be seen as objectionable. And this may remain the case even if Carla and other people of modest means
join together to establish a responsibility-generating group of
their own. Proponents of the objection may still feel that by requiring those who are wealthier to give one another's interests
priority over the interests of those who are poorer, the putative
redistribution of responsibility unjustifiably reinforces the prior
inequality in resources.

If we abstract from this example, we can see that the objection
as generalized may be offered as a systematic objection to special responsibilities. It may be understood to hold that such responsibilities confer additional advantages on people who have
already benefited from participating in rewarding groups and
relationships and that this is unjustifiable whenever the provi-

sion of these additional advantages works to the detriment of those who are needier, whether they are needier because they are not themselves participants in rewarding groups and relationships or because they have significantly fewer resources of other kinds. I will call this the *distributive objection*.[1]

Insofar as claims of special responsibility are invoked as a way of justifying resistance to the idea of global justice, the distributive objection may be presented by defenders of global justice as a challenge to that justification. The distributive objection challenges the idea that the members of affluent societies have special responsibilities to their associates that they do not have to other people. Such responsibilities, it asserts, provide an unjustifiable mandate for the members of wealthy societies to lavish resources on one another while largely ignoring the suffering and deprivation of people in much poorer societies. It may be said that there are important differences of character and motivation between those who take such responsibilities seriously and those who act out of crudely self-interested motives. Nevertheless, special responsibilities serve to validate a natural tendency toward partiality or favoritism within groups, and the effect of this form of validation is to confer unfair advantages on the members of wealthy groups while placing other people at an unfair disadvantage. In effect, such responsibilities provide the wealthy with the moral equivalent of a tax shelter. They provide those who are better off with a moral justification for channeling their time, energy, and other resources into rewarding relations and associations and away from people who are needier. For simply by entering into such relations and associations, one acquires special responsibilities to one's associates, and within limits, these responsibilities then take priority over, and thus serve to shield one from, the claims of others for assistance. Furthermore, fulfillment of these responsibilities normally contributes to the flourishing of the rewarding relations themselves. Thus, simply by entering into rewarding relations and associations, those who are better off can shelter their resources from potentially burdensome demands made in the name of global justice and invest those resources in enterprises that they find more satisfying.[2]

III. RESPONSES TO THE DISTRIBUTIVE OBJECTION

What is the force of the distributive objection? To what extent, if any, does it cast doubt on the legitimacy of claims of special responsibility? Is it successful in undermining the normative basis of resistance to the idea of global justice? Before trying to answer these questions, let us consider some possible responses to the objection.

First, it might be argued that the distributive objection rests on a misunderstanding inasmuch as it assumes that one's special responsibilities to one's associates serve to weaken one's general responsibilities to other people. In reality, it might be said, the acquisition of special responsibilities to some people leaves unchanged both the content and the strength of one's general responsibilities to other people. Special responsibilities do not compete with general responsibilities; they simply are additional responsibilities. Thus their effect is not to weaken one's obligations to nonassociates but, rather, to increase one's total share of responsibility.

If this argument were correct, the distributive objection as stated would indeed fail. Yet the argument would also undermine any attempt to use the idea of special responsibilities as a way of legitimating resistance to claims of global justice. The point of the argument is that the extent of our responsibilities to nonassociates is fixed independently of our special responsibilities to our associates. Thus, if the argument were correct, we could not cite our special responsibilities to the latter by way of justifying our resistance to claims offered on behalf of the former. This means that if the argument were correct, it would indeed rebut the distributive objection but that in the process of doing so, it would concede the illegitimacy of the very conception of responsibility that the objection seeks to undermine. In rebutting the objection, in other words, it would nevertheless grant the conclusion that the objection seeks to establish.

In fact, however, although the argument is not altogether without merit, it is ultimately untenable. We may grant that special responsibilities serve in part to increase one's total share of responsibility. Yet at the same time, part of what it is to have such responsibilities to one's associates is to be required, within limits, to give their interests priority over the interests of nonassociates, in cases in which the two conflict. This is the observation from which our discussion began, and it represents common ground between supporters and critics of special responsibilities. It is, of course, this feature of special responsibilities that leads them to be invoked in opposition to claims of global justice. And by the same token, it is this feature that exposes them to the distributive objection.[3]

Although the first response to the distributive objection is not persuasive, the recognition that special responsibilities serve in part to increase a person's total share of responsibility paves the way for a second response to the objection. This response complains that the distributive objection focuses exclusively on the benefits that special responsibilities confer on the participants in interpersonal relations while ignoring the burdens that such responsibilities also impose on them. For example, once Alice and Beth have joined the In Group, Alice may indeed benefit from Beth's newly acquired special responsibilities toward her. At the same time, however, Alice has also acquired special responsibilities toward Beth, which means that Alice's total share of responsibility has increased. And it may be argued that since Alice's overall moral burden has thus grown heavier, the claim that special responsibilities give her unfair advantages loses its force. More generally, the benefits that such responsibilities confer on the participants in interpersonal relationships are always offset by the burdens they impose. Special responsibilities confer no net advantage on participants and, *a fortiori*, no unfair net advantage.

There is an obvious complement to this argument. The complementary argument is that in addition to overlooking the disadvantages of special responsibilities for the participants in interpersonal relationships, the distributive objection overlooks the *advantages* of such responsibilities for *nonparticipants*. This argument begins by challenging something that our initial formulation of the distributive objection suggested, namely, that the acquisition by the participants in interpersonal relationships of special responsibilities to one another leaves undiminished their claims on nonparticipants. This argument maintains that on the contrary, when Alice and Beth join the In Group, the strengthening of their claims on each other is accompanied by a simultaneous weakening of their claims on Carla, even if Carla herself has no comparable special responsibilities to others. For the fact that Alice and Beth can now call on each other for assistance is reason for Carla to give their interests less weight than she would previously have done.

Suppose, for instance, that Carla is in a position to help either Beth, who is a member of the In Group, or Denise, who is not. Suppose also that Beth and Denise are in equal need of assistance and that before Beth joined the In Group, their claims on Carla, which derive exclusively from Carla's responsibilities to other people in general, would have been equally strong. If, however, Beth now has special claims on Alice and the other members of the In Group, she has independent resources on which she can call and that Denise lacks. This, it may be argued, is reason for Carla to assign less weight to Beth's interests than she does to Denise's. This will obviously work to Denise's advantage, and presumably, Carla will receive a symmetrical advantage in the form of an increased priority assigned to her interests—relative to those of In Group members—by Denise and other nonmembers. Furthermore, the same consideration that gives Carla a reason to assign less weight to Beth's interests than she does to Denise's may in other circumstances make it appropriate for her to assign less weight to helping Beth than she does to pursuing her own projects and activities. Since Beth can turn to other In Group members for assistance, Carla may legitimately feel that there is less need for her to take time out from her own pursuits to help Beth. It is not unreasonable to expect Beth to look first to her fellow members for the assistance she needs. This means that the special responsibilities of In Group members work to Carla's advantage in two different ways. Not only do they strengthen her claims on Denise and other nonmembers, but they also reduce her total moral burden by allowing her to assign less weight to the interests of In Group members in deciding how to allocate her time and resources. Correlatively, it may be argued, those same special responsibilities can now be seen to work to the disadvantage of Alice and Beth in two different ways. In addition to increasing the total moral burden on each of them, they also weaken the claims of each on

Carla, Denise, and other nonmembers. The upshot is that the advantages that special responsibilities confer on the participants in interpersonal relationships are fully offset by the disadvantages, and the disadvantages they confer on nonparticipants are fully offset by the advantages. Special responsibilities represent neither a net improvement for participants nor a net loss for nonparticipants, relative to a baseline situation in which everyone has only those responsibilities that arise independently of any special relationships. Thus there is no unfairness of the kind alleged by the distributive objection.

This argument makes it clear that the effects of special responsibilities on the overall distribution of responsibility are more complex than originally suggested. Yet the argument claims too much when it asserts that such responsibilities represent neither a net gain for the participants in interpersonal relationships nor a net loss for the nonparticipants. Consider first the case of the nonparticipants. The special responsibilities of In Group members are said to work to Carla's advantage by both strengthening her claims on Denise and other nonmembers and allowing her to assign less weight to the interests of In Group members in deciding how much of her time and resources to devote to her own projects and pursuits. These points seem correct as far as they go, but they do not suffice to establish that the advantages mentioned fully offset the disadvantages for Carla of her reduced claims on In Group members. To see this, we only have to imagine that Carla is an inhabitant of a poor third-world country and that the In Group is our own society. Or, what amounts to the same thing, we have only to suppose—for the sake of argument at least—that Americans have a responsibility to give higher priority to one another's interests than they do to the interests of impoverished third-world residents. We may then ask ourselves whether the disadvantages of this fact for poor non-Americans are fully offset by their having stronger claims on one another or by its being permissible for them to pursue their own projects and plans without giving as much weight to the interests of the affluent. If, without underestimating the benefits of communal self-reliance, it seems clear that the answer to these questions is negative, that is presumably because the value of one's claims to other people's assistance depends in part on the extent of their resources and because the value of being permitted to pursue one's own projects and plans depends in part on the extent of one's own resources. Thus if the inhabitants of Chad or Bangladesh are told that the citizens of affluent Western societies have little responsibility to assist them, they are unlikely to take much comfort from the assurance that they may rely all the more heavily on one another or from the reflection that they may pursue their own projects unburdened by excessive concern for the welfare of affluent Westerners.

Consider next the case of the participants in interpersonal relationships. Obviously, the considerations just mentioned have some tendency to undermine the argument that the advantages of special responsibilities for them are fully offset by the disadvantages. For the participants, it seems, the advantages of having stronger claims on one another outweigh the disadvantages of having weaker claims on other people, at least in cases in which they already have greater resources than others do. Thus, for Americans, the advantages of having stronger claims on one another outweigh the disadvantages of having weaker claims on the citizens of Chad and Bangladesh. However, the original argument cited two putatively offsetting disadvantages for the participants, of which the weakening of their claims on nonparticipants was only the first. The other supposed disadvantage was that special responsibilities increase one's total moral burden and thereby place additional constraints on one's ability to advance legitimately one's projects and pursuits. If, as has now been suggested, the value of that ability is partly dependent on the extent of one's resources, it may seem to follow that the more affluent one is, the greater this disadvantage will be. But to one degree or another, it may appear to constitute a genuinely offsetting disadvantage for all participants.

However, this overlooks one of the legitimate insights of the distributive objection. The insight is that when one's participation in an interpersonal group or relationship is rewarding—quite apart from the responsibilities to which it gives rise—and when the fulfillment of those responsibilities in turn contributes to the flourishing of that very group or relationship, then although the responsibilities serve in part to increase one's total share of responsibility, it is misleading to conceive of that extra measure of responsibility solely as a burden for the person who bears it. Although special responsibilities are sometimes experienced as burdensome and although fulfilling them can undoubtedly involve various kinds of costs, it is misleading to describe such responsibilities as placing constraints on one's ability to advance legitimately one's own projects and pursuits. The reason is that those responsibilities may enhance relationships and associations that must themselves be numbered among one's projects and pursuits broadly construed. Indeed, as we will soon see, it may even be argued that accepting special responsibilities not only enhances interpersonal relationships but is a necessary condition for their stable existence. The more valuable a relationship is and the more important the role is of one's special responsibilities in establishing and sustaining that relationship, the more misleading it will be to classify those responsibilities as burdens.

Where does this leave us? The argument we have been discussing purports to establish that special responsibilities represent neither a net improvement for the participants in interpersonal relationships nor a net loss for nonparticipants, relative to a baseline situation in which everyone has only those responsibilities that arise independently of any special relationships. However, we have found reason to doubt this claim. When nonparticipants have fewer resources than do participants, the disadvantages for them of such a redistribution of responsibility outweigh the advantages constituted by an increase in the strength of their claims on one another and a decrease in the strength of the participants' claims on them. In such circumstances, similarly, the advantages for the participants of having stronger claims on one another outweigh the disadvantages of having weaker claims on the nonparticipants. And in general, it is a mistake to suppose that the benefits for the participants in rewarding relationships of having stronger claims on one another are offset by the burdens of having greater responsibilities to one another. For the idea that such responsibilities constitute burdens for those who bear them is misleading. In short, then, the core of the distributive objection remains intact. It still maintains that special responsibilities confer additional advantages on people who have already benefited from participating in rewarding groups and relationships and that those additional advantages are unjustifiable whenever they work to the detriment of people who are needier.

Admittedly, it has not been shown that *only* those interpersonal relationships that are rewarding for the participants give rise to special responsibilities. If this is not so, then the extent to which special responsibilities are advantageous for those who bear them may vary considerably from case to case, depending on the value of the relationships that generate them. Furthermore, it may be argued that it is wrong to assess the advantages and disadvantages of special responsibilities solely in terms of the strength or weakness of the claims they confer on people. A strong claim that is never exercised may benefit a person less than a weak claim that is exercised. And correspondingly, a more extensive responsibility to assist one's associate may prove less onerous than a more limited responsibility to assist a stranger, if it turns out that one's associate never needs the assistance to which he is entitled. Thus, it may be argued, a more accurate measure of the impact of special responsibilities on participants and nonparticipants alike would take into account not only the strength and weakness of the various claims conferred but also the extent to which those claims are actually exercised. And since this is a contingent matter that will vary from case to case, so too the advantages and disadvantages of special responsibilities—whether for participants or nonparticipants—will also be contingent and variable. Although those advantages and disadvantages may tend to conform to the patterns that have been identified, these will be only tendencies and not exceptionless regularities.

Yet these points require no significant modification of the distributive objection. Even if we suppose that some participants in unrewarding relationships also acquire special responsibilities, this does not undermine the claim that the participants in rewarding relationships receive additional advantages from the responsibilities to which their relationships give rise. And even if these additional advantages only *tend* to work to the detriment of those who are needier, that does not undermine the claim that they are unfair when they do.

Although the line of argument we have been pursuing does not, in the end, succeed in rebutting the distributive objection, it may provide a springboard for a third response to that objection. If the distributive objection claims only that special responsibilities arising out of certain kinds of relationships tend to work to the detriment of those who are needier and that they are unfair when they do, it may be said that the real target of the objection has been misidentified. The distributive objection is not an objection to special responsibilities per se. Rather, it is a response to the effects that such responsibilities tend to have in otherwise unjust situations. When there is already an unjust distribution of resources, special responsibilities may compound the injustice. But if the underlying injustice were eliminated, there would be no remaining objection to those responsibilities. Although they may reinforce existing injustices, they are not unjust in themselves, and they cannot by themselves transform just situations into unjust ones. Thus the real target of the distributive objection is the unjust distribution of resources and not special responsibilities. Admittedly, if such responsibilities do indeed reinforce or compound existing injustices, there is a way in which the relationships that give rise to those responsibilities are compromised. Those of us fortunate enough to participate in networks of rewarding interpersonal relationships in a world replete with injustice conduct our relationships under a kind of moral shadow. This is unfortunate, if not terribly surprising, but it does not constitute an objection to special responsibilities per se. Since they are not unjust in themselves, they remain genuine responsibilities and continue to possess normative authority even when they arise in the context of distributive injustice.

Although it aims to defend special responsibilities against the distributive objection, this argument implies that appeals to such responsibilities can at most justify only limited resistance to claims of global justice. For the argument provides no reason to doubt the legitimacy of those claims; it concedes that special responsibilities may serve to compound distributive injustice; and accordingly, it allows that interpersonal relations may be compromised by such injustice. It insists only that special responsibilities should be seen as genuine, or as possessing normative authority, even when they do compound injustice. If the argu-

ment were persuasive in other respects, this conclusion, limited
though it is, would still require additional defense. It is not obvious why the normative authority of special responsibilities
should not be called into question on those occasions when they
do indeed compound injustice. But the argument is flawed in a
more fundamental respect: the distributive objection does not
limit itself to asserting that special responsibilities are unfair
when they compound injustice. It asserts instead that such responsibilities are unfair whenever they work to the detriment of
those who are already needier. This means that the alleged unfairness depends on the existence of prior inequalities, but as
far as the distributive objection is concerned, those inequalities
need not be unjust. In general, an unequal distribution that is
not unjust may be transformed into an even more unequal distribution that is unjust, through the provision of additional benefits to those who were better off under the original distribution.
And the distributive objection may be construed as holding that
even if an initial inequality is not unjust, the effect of special responsibilities may be to introduce injustice where there was
none before. It might be claimed, for example, that there is no
injustice in the fact that Alice and Beth enjoy the personal rewards of membership in the In Group while Carla does not but
that it is unjust if, in consequence, Alice and Beth also acquire
special responsibilities to each other and those responsibilities
then work to Carla's disadvantage. Or it might be said that it
need not be unjust if one society is richer in natural resources
than another but that it is unjust if the members of the wealthier
society are then required to give one another's interests priority
over the interests of people in the poorer society. The central
point is that according to the distributive objection, it is unfair if
special responsibilities work to the detriment of people who already have less, whether or not their already having less is also
unfair.

This formulation highlights the way in which the distributive
objection seems to treat the advantages conferred by special responsibilities as entirely separable from the other advantages
that the participants in interpersonal relationships may enjoy,
including the other rewards deriving from participation in those
very relationships. In so doing, this formulation invites a fourth

and final response to the distributive objection. This response challenges the idea that the other benefits of participation in an interpersonal relationship are secured independently of special responsibilities and that it is then an open question how, if at all, the relationship affects the distribution of responsibility. In fact, this response argues, the processes by which otherwise rewarding relationships are established and the processes by which special responsibilities are generated are inseparable. A commitment by the participants to give priority to one another's interests in suitable contexts is a precondition for the stable existence of a rewarding relationship, and it is these commitments that give rise to special responsibilities. Thus, one cannot secure the other benefits of participation in interpersonal relationships without acquiring special responsibilities in the process. Inasmuch as the distributive objection treats such responsibilities as conferring advantages that arise independently of the other benefits of rewarding relationships and that, accordingly, need not accompany them, the objection fails.

This response raises a variety of interesting questions. For example, there is the question of whether commitments of the kind it refers to are genuinely required for the stable existence of rewarding interpersonal groups and relationships of all kinds. In addition, there is the question of how exactly such commitments, assuming they are required, are supposed to give rise to special responsibilities. In other words, assuming that people must commit themselves to give priority to one another's interests if they are to establish a rewarding relationship, how exactly do those commitments succeed in generating moral requirements making obligatory the assignment of such priority? There is also the important question of whether all special responsibilities can plausibly be construed as having the voluntaristic origins suggested by the word *commitment*. For our purposes, however, the fundamental point is this: By emphasizing the role of putatively responsibility-generating commitments in making rewarding relationships possible, the response just sketched implies that there is an important respect in which the acquisition of special responsibilities serves the interests of prospective participants in such relationships. But this is not something that the distributive objection denies. On the contrary, one of that objection's central aspirations is precisely to call attention to the ways in which special responsibilities work to the advantage of the participants in interpersonal groups and relationships. Its correlative observation, of course, is that such responsibilities may also work to the significant disadvantage of nonparticipants. And the response just sketched does not dispute this observation. So if, as that response maintains, people cannot obtain the benefits of participating in rewarding personal relations without acquiring special responsibilities in the process, the distributive objection will conclude that there must be constraints on the legitimacy of securing such benefits. More precisely, it will argue that the effects of special responsibilities on third parties serve to constrain (1) the capacity of commitments to generate such responsibilities, (2) the legitimacy of making those commitments that do generate responsibilities, and (3) the content of the responsibilities that are in fact generated.

IV. CONCLUSION: THE FORCE OF THE DISTRIBUTIVE OBJECTION

Once the conclusions of the distributive objection are framed in this way, it is clear that the objection does not delegitimate all claims of special responsibility or even show that such claims can never take precedence over considerations of global justice. The objection's ambition, it now seems, is merely to constrain those claims in various ways. On the other hand, it seems equally clear that none of the four responses we have considered provides a good reason for dismissing the objection or the concerns that underlie it. Instead, we are left with two ideas—the idea of special responsibilities and the idea of global justice—which are evidently in tension with each other, and each of which purports to limit the authority of the other. This kind of tension and mutual constraint is exactly what we should expect if, as I believe, each of these ideas is rooted in values that occupy a central place in the moral outlooks of many people. But this simple observation about the provenance of the two ideas, which should seem obvious, has lately been obscured by the widespread reliance in moral and political philosophy on a cluster of stylized and exaggerated contrasts: between universalism and particularism, between liberalism and communitarianism, between thin and thick ethical concepts, between Kantian ethics and an ethics of virtue, between Enlightenment morality and the morality of patriotism and loyalty. Each of these contrasts encourages the belief that the values of justice and equality, on the one hand, and the values of personal friendship and communal solidarity, on the other hand, derive from mutually exclusive and fundamentally opposed systems of ethical thought. I doubt whether this is correct as a matter of intellectual history. I am quite sure that it is false as a characterization of the experience of many people, including many who have come to rely more or less uncritically on dichotomies like those mentioned. I am quite sure that many people take seriously both sets of values, without any sense that they represent alien or mutually exclusive commitments. This does not mean, of course, that these values are never experienced as being in tension with each other. The point is, rather, that for many, to experience such a tension is not to register a clash between rival theories or philosophies but to feel torn by considerations internal to one's own moral outlook. If these tensions are sometimes experienced as uncomfortable or even painful, it is not because the sound of theories in collision can be deafening but because the failure to be true to one's own values can be devastating.

Let us say that two values are in tension with each other if the following two things are true: First, the values are *mutually constraining*, in the sense that each, if accepted, will limit the ways in which the other may legitimately be realized or advanced. Second, the values are *practically competitive*, in the sense that institutions and policies that serve to recognize or foster one of them sometimes undermine or erode the realization of the other.[4] I do not believe that tensions of this kind among our values can ever be eliminated, but such tensions may be more or less problematic. The tension between two values will be problematic to the extent that we are committed to both of them but have been unable to identify any way of accommodating one without slighting or doing violence to the other. We resolve such problems, to our own satisfaction at least, when we fix on a course of action, or design a policy or institution, or identify a set of principles, that will enable us to claim, in good faith, to have found a way of doing justice to both.

The real thrust of the distributive objection, and its contribution to arguments for global justice, is to suggest that the tension between our special responsibilities as we have interpreted them, on the one hand, and our commitment to the equal worth of persons, on the other hand, is more problematic than we normally suppose. It is to suggest, in other words, that in the name of those responsibilities, we have been prepared to acquiesce in policies and institutional arrangements that cannot be reconciled with any serious commitment to the proposition that all people are of equal worth. There is, in principle, nothing surprising about the idea that the tensions among certain of our values may be more problematic than we realize. In general, we have powerful incentives to overlook such problems. Moreover, a principle, policy, or institutional arrangement that represents a reasonable way of accommodating diverse values in one set of circumstances may cease to do so once conditions change. Thus, changing circumstances can transform an unproblematic tension into a problematic one without our noticing. In the end, however, the force of the distributive objection in particular must rest on its success in evoking in us an uneasiness about the relations between the specific values with which it is concerned. To the extent that the objection does have force, its tendency, as I have said, is not to support the repudiation of special responsibilities. Indeed, the idea that the particular interpersonal relationships in which one participates help shape the normative landscape of one's life is so fundamental that I cannot imagine any argument powerful enough to overturn it. And although there are moral theories—such as utilitarianism—that do not treat it as fundamental, they invariably take care to accommodate it at some putatively derivative level, as indeed they must if they are to be taken seriously. Rather than supporting the repudiation of special responsibilities, the tendency of the distributive objection is to challenge us to find a better way of integrating our values if we can.

To meet this challenge, what would be required would be a way of defining the relations of mutual constraint between special responsibilities and the equal worth of persons that we were stably disposed to perceive as doing justice to both. If the ubiquity of the stylized and exaggerated contrasts mentioned earlier is an obstacle at the level of theory to our meeting or even recognizing this challenge, the situation at the level of political practice is even more complex. The broad movement in recent years toward greater global integration has increased interest in the problem of global justice. Yet far from producing a solution to the problem, that movement seems instead to be transforming it. The "traditional" problem of global justice, if it can be called that, is a problem concerning the relations between poor nations and wealthy nations. Inasmuch as appeals to special responsibility may be offered by the citizens of wealthy nations as a way of justifying their resistance to the idea of global justice, the bearing of special responsibilities on the traditional problem is relatively straightforward. But without solving this problem, the movement toward global integration has given rise to another problem as well. The new problem concerns the relations between an affluent, technologically sophisticated global elite and the large numbers of poor and undereducated people worldwide. The role of special responsibilities in relation to this new problem of global justice is less straightforward. Individual members of the cosmopolitan elite may, of course, seek to justify their resistance to proposed solutions of the problem by appealing, in the familiar way, to special responsibilities arising out of their own interpersonal relations. But unlike the citizenry of an affluent country, this elite is not itself united under any political authority, nor is it bound together by a sense of group loyalty or, indeed, by any shared ethos of responsibility. Certainly, individual members of the elite do not normally see themselves as having special responsibilities to their fellow members as such. Instead, appeals to special responsibility are more likely to be made, in this context, as part of the identity politics with which the movement toward global integration finds itself increasingly in conflict. And the function of such claims may be not to justify resistance to the idea of global justice but, rather, to call attention to the interests of those whom the movement toward global integration has left behind. To this extent at least, such claims may serve to express considerations of justice rather than to oppose them.

The traditional problem of global justice and the new problem coexist and cut across each other in ways that make the task of integrating justice and responsibility even more complex than it initially may have appeared. The challenge of reducing the tensions among our values and overcoming the oppositions within our thought is thus a formidable one, and there is no guarantee that it can be met, at the level of either theory or practice. But the stakes could hardly be higher, and we are almost certain to fail unless we try.

NOTES

1. My development of the distributive objection in this chapter draws on, but also modifies, my discussions of that objection in two earlier essays: "Families, Nations, and Strangers" (the Lindley Lecture) (Lawrence: University of Kansas, 1995), and "Liberalism, Nationalism, and Egalitarianism," in Robert McKim and Jeff McMahan, eds., *The Morality of Nationalism* (New York: Oxford University Press, 1997). All three essays are part of a larger investigation of the sources and limits of special responsibilities. As the two earlier essays emphasize, the distributive objection may be used to challenge special responsibilities, whether or not those responsibilities are thought to arise solely from the voluntary choices of the individuals to whom they are ascribed. The objection is compatible with but does not presuppose a voluntaristic understanding of special responsibilities.

2. For a related discussion, see Thomas Pogge, "Loopholes in Moralities," *Journal of Philosophy* 89 (1992): 79–98.

3. However, Pogge appears to overlook the point when he writes, for example, "I have no quarrel with the idea that persons, by becoming members of a social arrangement, may *increase* what they owe the other members and may thus come to owe them more than they owe all outsiders. What I find problematic is the idea that persons, by so increasing what they owe certain others, may *reduce* what they minimally owe everyone else" (ibid., pp. 86–87, italics in original).

4. I borrow this formulation from my discussion in "Liberalism, Nationalism, and Egalitarianism."

4

WHO IS MY NEIGHBOR? A RESPONSE TO SCHEFFLER

JOHN KANE

The paternal and filial duties discipline the heart and prepare it for the love of all mankind. The intensity of private attachments encourages, not prevents, universal benevolence. The nearer we approach to the sun, the more intense his heat: yet what corner of the system does he not cheer and vivify?

Coleridge

Professor Scheffler's paper leaves me with curiously mixed feelings. Though in broad sympathy and agreement with some of its conclusions, I am in doubt about, and rather bemused by, its way of reaching them. Let me begin by expressing my agreements.

First, Scheffler is surely right to reject the absurdly dichotomizing tendency of much recent ethical theory that encourages the idea that justice and equality, on the one hand, and personal friendship and communal solidarity, on the other, are mutually exclusive and fundamentally opposed values. If we were to accept such a view, our only choice would be between the "kinship is all" view of morality, characteristic of societies besieged by enemies and rivals, and the sort of inhuman, "telescopic philanthropy" parodied by Dickens in the figure of Mrs. Jellyby, who could identify objects of charitable concern only at a very great distance.[1] But most of us are happy to accept that we have both the kin and communitarian responsibilities that Scheffler terms *special responsibilities* and what he calls *general responsibilities* to others beyond our own community (however narrow or broadly "community" is conceived). In fact, we accept this combination as ethically superior to one confined to either branch of the supposed dichotomy.

Nor (a second point of agreement) are we too surprised—though we may often be dismayed—when one set of responsibilities conflicts with the other and forces on us difficult and painful choices. It is worth noting here that we are, after all, used to encountering such conflicts even in the realm of our special responsibilities. Isn't it common for business people, for example, to regret that their work responsibilities too often cause them to fail in their responsibilities to their immediate families—spouses, sons, and daughters—who are at the supposed center of their interpersonal lives? Just as we are not tempted to think that the pressing duties of work, because they conflict with family duties, require the repudiation of one or the other, we do not imagine that the frequent necessity of choice between special or general responsibilities requires the repudiation of either. Rather, as Scheffler argues, it offers the challenge of finding better ways of integrating all our values.

Third, and finally, Scheffler draws appropriate attention to the way in which the forces of economic globalization shift the focus of the special- versus general-interest debate from relations between rich and poor nations to relations between a global elite and the poor of the world. His brief closing remarks on this subject hint at a broader analysis which, if pursued, might reap rich dividends of understanding for the problems of justice and responsibility confronting us all at the close of the century.

Let me turn, then, to my difficulties with the method of argument that Scheffler uses to approach his conclusions. He notes, first, that notions of special responsibility (when they are not merely rationalizations for the selfishness of the rich) appear to legitimate resistance to claims of global justice. Rather than offering stronger arguments for the latter claims, Scheffler chooses to try to weaken this resistance by identifying certain "limitations" in the notion of special responsibilities (see Scheffler, chapter 3, "The Conflict between Justice and Responsibility"). His strategy is to offer a thought experiment that generates an outcome whose apparent blatant unfairness gives rise to a generalized objection to special responsibilities (the *distributive objection*). Scheffler then considers a number of objections to this objection that might be offered by defenders of special responsibilities and argues that the distributive objection survives them all, thus arguably proving that it has some validity in at least constraining those demands of special responsibility that may conflict with demands of global justice.

This seems to me a roundabout way of tackling the issue, and it has several worrying features that may rob it of the force it desires to exert on behalf of global justice. First is the problem of what we should make of the initial thought experiment. This, to reiterate, involves three women with no special relationships to one another, and therefore no special responsibilities. Each has, of course, the usual complement of "general responsibilities" that people have to strangers. The distribution of responsibilities is, Scheffler stresses, "perfectly egalitarian in character; each woman has exactly the same responsibilities toward every other woman" (Scheffler, chapter 3). He then analyzes what happens to this pattern of responsibility when two of the three form a special and personally rewarding relationship in a so-called In Group. Scheffler's argument is that this upsets the egalitarian distribution of responsibility, because now the members of the In Group have special responsibilities toward one another that will, in certain contexts, take priority over their general responsibilities to the other woman. Worse, if this other woman has herself formed no special relationships, her responsibilities toward the other two will remain undiminished, so that the In Group members will win both ways.

The evident unfairness of this outcome is what gives rise to the generalized, systematic objection to special responsibilities that Scheffler calls the *distributive objection* (see chapter 3). This asserts that special responsibilities are unfair when they confer on already advantaged people additional advantages that work to the detriment of those who are needier.

I find this strategy puzzling for a number of reasons. Suppose, for instance (as Scheffler does not), that the In Group is an organization dedicated to, and effective at, providing some sort of aid or care to the poor of other countries. Obviously this will not be objectionable, since it benefits the needy, although equally with associations that may disbenefit them, it will have generated special responsibilities to one's associates and to the association itself and also perhaps proved enriching and rewarding to the participants. But how is the generality of the argument about the inequitable effects of special associations affected if, on some occasions, they clearly do not have them? I think it leaves the initial schema looking overly abstract and underspecified. Apart from containing implicit assumptions about the goals of the associations formed, the thought experiment insufficiently distinguishes between interpersonal responsibilities and organizational responsibilities.

The thought experiment also appears (at least initially) to regard general responsibilities as in some way fundamental or prior, and special responsibilities as subsequent and unfortunate disruptions of the egalitarian norm. Furthermore, it seems to portray special responsibilities as excessively voluntaristic products of chosen, rewarding associations. (It is true that Scheffler, at one point in his discussion of commitment in chapter 3, pp. 91, 104–105, briefly questions the voluntaristic origins of special responsibilities, but this only makes his schema even more puzzling.) Such impressions seem in contradistinction to most people's perceptions of the matter, namely, that we are born into special responsibilities and that we do not choose many of those we subsequently acquire. We are usually made acutely aware of our special responsibilities from the start and are only later instructed (if we ever are) about our more general responsibilities to others. It is true that Scheffler argues only that his three women initially have no special relationship with one another, not that they have none at all. But as surely must be the case, if they already have special responsibilities to someone, isn't the initial pattern of distribution of special and general responsibilities more muddy and confused than can safely be extrapolated in this way?

I believe that Scheffler's rather voluntaristic characterization will probably seem to most opponents of global justice to miss the main point. Their underlying argument is usually based on analogies of blood relationships, of kith and kin. It is the implicit appeal to family ties that provides the strong emotive element that Scheffler fails to address. Blood is thicker than water; help your own first; charity begins at home; and so forth. Note, too, that Scheffler's model of special responsibility is between two equally advantaged partners gaining further advantages by means of their beneficial association. But isn't the argument of his opponents at least sometimes couched in terms of an inequality between partners in a special association: to wit, why should we give to the poor in India when we have our own poor at our doorsteps? Isn't our first obligation to the latter?

It is true that Scheffler's initial picture of the redistribution of responsibilities caused by the formation of special associations becomes significantly modified and more complicated as he proceeds to deal with four possible objections to the distributive objection. Indeed, I am tempted to think that the need for this complexification may be a reflection of its inadequacy as an heuristic device. At any rate, it becomes clear (as of course we knew from the start, and especially from the moment that Scheffler generalized and qualified the distributive objection by making Alice and Beth much wealthier than Carla) that the real objection is not to special responsibilities per se, but only to those between relatively rich people that might conflict with their general responsibilities toward relatively poor people. (I presume this may apply within a country as much as between countries.) No one will object to poor people's forming special relationships among themselves to try to improve their lot, though this will be of limited benefit if their access to the resources of the rich are cut off (see chapter 3).

Scheffler's final position, then, is a qualified acceptance of special responsibilities as unavoidable and, to that extent, legitimate because they are generated by, and essential to, the establishment of rewarding personal relationships (though I suspect this may appear to be a rather bloodless concession to those whose arguments revolve around loyalties to kith and kin). The legitimacy of benefits conferred by special responsibilities is constrained, however, by their potential effects on third parties. The distributive objection, Scheffler concludes, "does not serve to delegitimate all claims of special responsibility or even to show that such claims can never take priority over considerations of global justice. The objection's ambition, it now seems, is merely to constrain those claims in various ways" (p. 102).

There seem to be echoes of John Rawls in all this. In fact, the distributive objection can easily be reframed as a type of Rawlsian principle: namely, special responsibilities generated by interpersonal commitments are legitimate only insofar as they do not work to the detriment of needier third parties. However, such a principle may prove to be a considerable constraint, since it would be difficult, I think, to show, for any particular special responsibility, that it did not work to the detriment of a third party somewhere. For example, we all discharge our special responsibilities to our children according to our means, and those with larger means typically spend larger—sometimes much larger—amounts of money than those with smaller means. Not only would this principle throw into doubt the legitimacy of all such differentials, but it might even delegitimize spending on children at low levels. How are we to determine the level above which spending on one's own children becomes illegitimate because it reduces the amount that we would otherwise have available to discharge our alleged general responsibilities toward needier people?

At the end of his chapter, Scheffler speaks rather vaguely of the tensions and mutual constraints between our ideas of special responsibilities and global justice and of having to find a proper balance between them, but his own argument does not appear to me to provide adequate tools for achieving such a balance. In fact, in trying to defend the idea of global justice by attacking the idea of special responsibilities, he perhaps comes dangerously close to defending a position that might allow unlimited claims on people for the sake of global justice. This is the reverse of his intention, which is, I think, to show that the claims of special responsibilities cannot be limitless but must leave room for the claims of general responsibilities to the world at large.

Bubbling beneath the surface of Scheffler's complicated procedure is, I think, a more direct argument concerning this "leaving of room." If it is not special responsibilities per se that is the problem, but only those that may conflict with our duties to others less well off than ourselves, then the task is surely to show that the general claims of the latter on us are not weakened by the associations (existing or future) that have made us well off or may make us even better off but are, in fact, strengthened by them. The central question is the differential in resources between ourselves and others. Our relative wealth may give us greater capacity (and maybe duty) to help our own, but it also surely gives us greater capacity to help those other than our own.

The global justice problem seems to revolve around the question put to Jesus after he commanded his listeners to "love thy neighbor." "Who is my neighbor?" someone asked, and Jesus responded with the parable of the good Samaritan. From the Samaritan's point of view, what made a neighbor of the robbed and injured Judean, who had already been ignored by two of his own eminent fellow countrymen, was simply a combination of opportunity and capacity to help.[2] The fact that the victim was outside his own group and, in fact, a traditional enemy was considered by Jesus to be irrelevant. The point of his parable seems to be a corollary of the traditional moral-philosophical maxim that *ought* implies *can,* to the effect that *can,* at least in some circumstances, implies *ought.*

If we accept our general responsibilities as genuine, we can hardly regard additions to our capacity to fulfill those responsibilities (such as might accrue from the sort of special associations among the already advantaged that Scheffler is talking about) as excuses for not fulfilling them. More is generally required of those to whom more is given. Scheffler addresses the question of additional responsibilities crowding out general responsibilities at times when the two conflict (see chapter 3) but takes this as showing that an increase in special responsibilities results in a weakening of one's general responsibilities. (His disagreement with Pogge in note 3 seems to confirm this.) I think this is a mistake. Pressing special responsibilities may occasionally weaken the likelihood that general responsibilities will be fulfilled, but they will not weaken the responsibilities themselves. In the earlier example of business people whose work duties conflict with family responsibilities, the crucial and painful point is precisely that obligations are not weakened because they are inadequately fulfilled.

This may seem like a distinction with no difference, at least in practical terms, but I believe it has some importance. If one's special associations result in an increase in one's disposable resources (and this is, to repeat, at the heart of Scheffler's distributive objection), then we may assume a *prima facie* case for an increased capacity for fulfilling one's general (as well as special) responsibilities. Conducting the argument at an abstract level of unspecified responsibilities in competition on unspecified occasions obscures the fact that it is resources and capacities that are centrally at question, and the moral opportunities and responsibilities that flow from their possession. If the claims that our special responsibilities may make on us are limited, the limits are more likely to be discovered in demonstrably strong claims of general responsibility than in some distributive flaw in the notion of special responsibility as such.

To conclude, I agree with Scheffler's closing comment that the theoretical and practical challenges of harmonizing our values and responsibilities in this age of change are formidable but that we need to try, nevertheless. Yet I would argue that a more positive case on behalf of our general responsibilities—one that points to our real capacities to fulfill them—might serve the purpose better than a negative and perhaps overelaborate strategy that tries to find chinks in the notion of special responsibilities per se.

NOTES

1. Charles Dickens, *Bleak House* (London: Bradbury and Evans, 1853). Mrs. Jellyby's eyes "had a curious habit of looking a long way off. As if they could see nothing nearer than Africa" (p. 26). When Mr. Jarndyce asks Esther's opinion of Mrs. Jellyby, she replies, "We thought that, perhaps, it is right to begin with the obligations of home, sir; and that, perhaps, while those are overlooked and neglected, no other duties can possibly be substituted for them?" (p. 45).

2. A further, legal answer was given to this question in the famous English case of *Donoghue vs. Stevenson* (1932) which founded the tort of negligence in British common law. Lord Atkinson argued there that the ratio of the case was based on the commandment "Love thy neighbor" and that this translated legally into a duty of care toward "anyone

who may be adversely affected by my actions or omissions." It is possible that some combination of the ideas of capacity, opportunity, and causal connectedness could be used to make the general case for general responsibilities, but such a task is beyond the scope of this critique.

5

COMMENT ON SCHEFFLER'S "THE CONFLICT BETWEEN JUSTICE AND RESPONSIBILITY"

LIAM B. MURPHY

I.

Samuel Scheffler rejects any suggestion that the claims of global justice and the claims of special responsibility arise from fundamentally incompatible normative outlooks. Instead, both kinds of claim, and thus the conflict between them, are present in the ethical outlooks of most of us. Accordingly, philosophical investigation of this conflict should not aim to achieve total victory for one value over the other but, rather, to "fix on a course of action, or design a policy or institution, or identify a set of principles, that will enable us to claim, in good faith, to have found a way of doing justice to both" values.

Scheffler's claim for what he calls the *distributive objection* is therefore not that it refutes the claims of special responsibility but that it brings out an aspect of the conflict between these claims and claims of global justice that has not been adequately acknowledged. Before being introduced to the distributive objection, we would think that we could do no better than reflect on our beliefs about the relative strength of claims of global justice and of claims of special responsibility in a range of particular cases, and try to develop from this process a general account of the scope of special responsibilities that seems more plausible than the alternatives. With the distributive objection, a higher-level normative thought is introduced into our reflections, and this new thought has the potential to substantially weaken the claims of special responsibility.

Even without the distributive objection, however, it seems to me doubtful that the claims of special responsibility would justify current levels of first-world indifference to claims of global justice.[1] Here it is important to distinguish different kinds of special responsibility. Scheffler writes about special responsibility to our "associates—the people with whom we have significant interpersonal ties." But his examples of groups to which a person may have special responsibility include our communities and societies.[2] And indeed, it seems that it is only if we believe in special responsibility to such groups that the claims of special responsibility have a chance of justifying current practice with respect to global justice. For although it is true that many moderately well off first-worlders can legitimately claim that they have no resources remaining after meeting the basic needs of their children and parents, it also is abundantly clear that many very rich people could meet all the plausible claims of family and friends and still have a good deal of income and wealth left over. It is not plausible for a rich parent in the United States to assert that the needs of sick children in the third world are morally outweighed by her responsibility to satisfy her teenage child's desire to own a new sports car, for example.[3]

There also are many very poor Americans, however, and if we believe in special obligations to members of a person's own society, it is not implausible to think that all the surplus money of rich Americans should be directed to the benefit of the very poor members of their own society.[4] If Americans give priority to other Americans up to the point that all Americans have access to decent health care and education, then it will be a long time before the claims of global justice are addressed.

The extent of the threat posed to claims of global justice by obligations of special responsibility thus depends crucially on the scope of such obligations. If the scope is narrow, not extending beyond a person's immediate family, the threat to claims of global justice may be weak. If, on the other hand, the

scope is wide, extending to entire political communities, the
threat is very strong. But it is also true that the more compelling claims of special responsibility are those of narrow
scope. The wider the scope is, the more plausible it is simply to
reject the claimed responsibility. Although he does not focus on
the issue, Scheffler himself seems to regard special responsibilities to friends and family as more firmly established than the
more extensive claims of responsibility to society or nation. And
much of what he says about special responsibilities generally
seems to apply only to those of narrow scope. For example, as
he says in chapter 3,

> the idea that the particular interpersonal relationships in which
> one participates help shape the normative landscape of one's life
> is so fundamental that I cannot imagine any argument powerful
> enough to overturn it. And although there are moral theories—
> such as utilitarianism—that do not treat it as fundamental, they
> invariably take care to accommodate it at some putatively deriva-
> tive level, as indeed they must if they are to be taken seriously.
> (P. 104)

These remarks are plausible only if we have in mind close interpersonal relations; they not plausible if we have in mind merely
political bonds, such that of cocitizenship. Certainly it is not the
case that utilitarians bend over backward to find a derivative justification of special responsibilities among conationals.

It is evident that the difference between special responsibilities of narrow and wide scope is not merely one of degree. The
reason that special responsibilities to friends and family seem so
uncontroversial is that they reflect our strongest emotional
needs. Political allegiance need not be, and preferably is not,
grounded primarily in emotional attachment. Indeed, it is clear
that special responsibilities generated by political and other social ties would have to have a source fundamentally different
from those generated by close personal ties. It is therefore
somewhat misleading, I think, to discuss both kinds of special
responsibility as a single topic.

So Scheffler has perhaps exaggerated the seriousness of the
conflict he is investigating. Not all claims of special responsibility appear to be irresistible at first sight. Those involving our

closest associates do, but these claims do not pose a drastic threat to claims of global justice.

II.

If I am right that Scheffler's conflict is not as stark as he suggests, the new normative reflection that is the distributive objection is less urgently needed, but not less interesting for that. Even those claims of special responsibility that are based on close personal ties pose some threat to claims of global justice. Furthermore, though claims of special responsibility of wider scope are controversial, they are clearly not entirely implausible; indeed, many people take them for granted. We can say therefore that the distributive objection casts doubt on the apparently irresistible force of narrow-scope claims of special responsibility and also has the potential to undermine whatever initial plausibility might attach to wide-scope claims.

The distributive objection has it that recognition of special responsibilities introduces a kind of higher-order unfairness into our world, unfairness that should matter to us because it is incompatible with the basic idea that all people are of equal worth (see Scheffler, chapter 3, p. 88). The unfairness is "higher order" because the distributive objection is supposed to point to a source of unfairness that is not already taken account of in the idea of global justice. That is, even if our commitment to global justice is itself based on a sense of the unfairness of a grossly unequal distribution of well-being or resources in the world, Scheffler's claim is that an additional and neglected kind of unfairness is introduced when special responsibilities alter the distribution of responsibility generally. This must be so, or else the distributive objection would just be one way of restating the claims of global justice, and no new normative thought would be available to assist our reflections. The distributive objection tells us that claims of special responsibility are unfair in themselves (see chapter 3, p. 88).

In what follows, I simply raise questions about what this special kind of intrinsic unfairness is supposed to consist in.[5] It is clear that the distributive objection is not concerned with some kind of abstract equality in the distribution of responsibility, in the distribution of the claims that people can make on one another. It would be hard to see why that distribution should matter in itself. Instead, the concern is with a distribution of responsibility that is inegalitarian in that it has unequal effects on people's well-being. More exactly, the distributive objection is that special responsibilities unfairly disadvantage people who are already needier, relative to a baseline situation in which there are no special responsibilities but only general responsibilities (see chapter 3, p. 91).

It seems undeniable that strong special responsibilities, especially those of wide scope, do disadvantage people who are already needier, relative to a baseline situation in which there are only general responsibilities. But I am not sure that I fully understand the sense in which Scheffler thinks that this is unfair.

My first question concerns the focus of the distributive objection. Why is the redistribution of responsibility occasioned by the introduction of special responsibilities unfair only insofar as it disadvantages those who are already worse off? If this is unfair, it is not clear to me why a redistribution of responsibility that introduces inequalities into a previously equal distribution of well-being would not also be unfair. In other words, it seems to me that the "natural generalization" of the distributive objection that Scheffler introduces does not go far enough: if there is an objection to what happens to Carla, who is worse off than Alice and Beth only because they have the benefits of a responsibility-generating relationship and she does not, there should also be, Scheffler says, an objection to any redistribution of responsibility that works to the detriment of people already worse off (see chapter 3, p. 90). Why not take the next step and object to any redistribution of responsibility that leaves some people relatively worse off? The focus of the distributive objection seems to be arbitrarily narrow.[6]

But we can leave to one side the issue of the focus of the distributive objection, since my more important questions do not depend on it.

The central idea of the distributive objection, as I have understood it, is that the distribution of the effects of compliance with special responsibilities on people's welfare is unfair in a sense that is distinct from any unfairness that we might see directly in the resulting distribution of well-being. The unfairness of special responsibilities does not arise just from the fact that they can lead to a distribution of well-being which is such that, however that distribution had been caused, we would think it unjust. The distributive objection points to a kind of unfairness that is not already acknowledged in ordinary ideas of justice. A moral principle that works to the detriment of people who are already worse off is in itself unfair.

It is not clear to me how plausible this claim is. If the distributive objection is meant to have general application, it has striking implications. The obligation of very poor people not to steal works to their detriment and also works to the benefit of the better off. In a more important example, if I can save ten badly off people by killing one well-off person but am prohibited from killing the one, the moral prohibition on killing works to the relative detriment of people who are already worse off. Are familiar elements of "commonsense morality" such as the prohibition on killing also subject to the complaint that they have unfair effects on others? If the distributive objection is meant to have general application, its evaluation would require extensive discussion of these and other areas of morality. And at first glance, it seems unlikely that the result would be favorable for the plausibility of the objection. If, on the other hand, the objection applies only to claims of special responsibility, we need to know why we should be concerned with the fairness of the distribution of the effects of compliance with some kinds of moral principle but not others.

My other main concern with Scheffler's argument is that I find it difficult to assess independently the claim of unfairness that is being leveled against special responsibilities. Is it really unfair if the effects of claims of special responsibility work to the disadvantage of people who are already worse off? To have a view on this question, we would need to have some idea about what fairness might require in this domain. Scheffler invokes the overriding norm of the "equal worth of persons." But both the idea of fairness and the idea of equal worth can be understood in a variety of ways. At the most formal level, fairness requires that people be treated alike unless there is good reason for treating them differently. But of course, there are good reasons for the detrimental effects of special responsibilities: the case in favor of special responsibilities is not in dispute. So if special responsibilities are unfair because of their effects on nonparticipants, we apparently need to appeal to a more substantive notion of fairness. And indeed, the distributive objection does just that—it claims that fairness requires that people's fulfillment of their special responsibilities should not work to the disadvantage of worse-off people.

But to repeat the question, is this substantive idea of fairness plausible as an abstract and independent idea? It would help if we could rule out the possibility that whatever appeal the idea has stems from our ordinary concern with the distribution of well-being that underlies the claims of global justice. One way to test this is to focus on a case in which the impact of special responsibilities on nonparticipants would not be significant enough to raise a claim of justice if it were due to other causes. Perhaps Scheffler's first example is such a case.[7] If we imagine that Alice, Beth, and Carla all are very well off, though Carla is somewhat worse off than the other two, I am not struck by the evident unfairness of the fact that Carla, though remaining very well off, is somewhat further disadvantaged because Alice and Beth acquire special responsibilities to each other. But if the three characters are America, Britain, and Chad, with Chad already very much worse off and then further disadvantaged enormously because America and Britain have special responsibilities to each other, then the injustice of the situation does seem rather glaring. But in this second case, the additional inequality in the world would seem unjust whatever its cause.

This pair of examples may incline one to think that the distributive objection does not in fact introduce new material into our normative reflections but indeed just restates the claims of global justice. This has not yet been established, however. It may be that the intuitive force of the distributive objection makes itself felt only when the stakes are high for the nonparticipants. It certainly remains possible, then, that the unfairness highlighted by the distributive objection is independent of our ordinary ideas of justice. But further evaluation of the plausibility of the distributive objection as an independent normative thought would seem to require further elucidation of the underlying idea of fairness on which it depends. The interesting claim that it is unfair that special responsibilities work to the detriment of those who are already worse off is also a rather specific claim, and it would help if we knew more about why, as a general matter, we should be concerned about the way in which the allocation of certain kinds of responsibility can have detrimental effects on worse-off persons.

NOTES

1. Scheffler does not explicitly claim that they would, but he does say that "if arguments for global justice are to be persuasive, they must engage with, and identify difficulties or limitations in, those notions of responsibility that appear to legitimate . . . resistance [to the idea of global justice]" (chapter 3 of this book, "The Conflict between Justice and Responsibility," p. 87).

2. See p. 87. In a later example, Scheffler uses a society as the relevant group (p. 95). In the same passage, his words make it clear that he is not convinced "that Americans have a responsibility to give higher priority to one another's interests than they do to the interests of impoverished third-world residents."

3. My point here is not that it would be wrong for the parent to favor her child but that it is not plausible to say that she is morally obliged to favor her child.

For a demanding view of the priority that people may legitimately assign to the less important interests of their family and friends, see Peter Unger, *Living High and Letting Die* (New York: Oxford University Press, 1996), pp. 149–50.

4. The United States presents the clearest case, but the same point holds for many other first-world countries.

5. My questions echo to some extent my own discussion of the related issue of the distribution of the effects of compliance with moral theories, in *Moral Demands in Nonideal Theory* (New York: Oxford University Press, forthcoming), a discussion that was, in turn, influenced by Samuel Scheffler, *Human Morality* (New York: Oxford University Press, 1992), pp. 98–99.

6. If I were a hermit in a baseline situation in which there are only general responsibilities but people are fulfilling those general responsibilities to my advantage, the introduction of special responsibilities would disadvantage me. Is this unfair? The distributive objection holds

that it would be unfair only if I am already worse off in the baseline situation. So if in the baseline situation, the only people who know about me and help me have but few resources—and thus I am much worse off in the baseline situation than are most other people—the loss of those people's help that follows the introduction of special responsibilities would be unfair. But if in the baseline situation, the people who know about me have sufficient resources to ensure that I am about as well off as anyone else is, the loss of these people's help that follows the introduction of special responsibilities would not be unfair according to the distribution objection.

7. Pp. 88–90. The point that I am investigating here is not the same as that in the "third response" to the distributive objection (see Scheffler, chapter 3, pp. 99–102).

6

PATRIOTISM, MORALITY, AND GLOBAL JUSTICE

CHARLES JONES

I. INTRODUCTION

The defense of universalist or cosmopolitan conceptions of distributive justice is a many-sided task.[1] It requires setting out some positive arguments in favor of, say, assigning specific rights to all human beings.[2] This is controversial terrain, but it is only part of the story that needs to be told by the cosmopolitan. This chapter addresses the equally important task of assessing (one version of) the case for denying universality of scope to ethical arguments, a task that calls for investigating various challenges to the universalist ambitions of liberal theories of justice in particular. In general terms, we can understand the antiuniversalist case as one concerned with several sorts of *limitation arguments*, that is, arguments designed to show that contrary to the conclusions of defenders of universal human rights, there are good reasons for limiting the scope of the obligations of justice to some subset of humanity. A limitation argument is designed to prove that the pretensions of cosmopolitans are illusory, incoherent, overridden by some morally more important considerations, or otherwise wrongheaded. We can identify at least four types of limitation argument: constitutivist, relativist, nationalist, and patriotic. So-called constitutive theorists maintain that while there are perhaps good grounds for recognizing the claims of human beings qua human beings, cosmopolitans fail to take proper account of the value of what we might call certain *intraspecies collectivities*, the most important of which are sovereign states. Since sovereignty is a value and since cosmopolitan arguments appear to ride roughshod over the sovereignty of states, it follows that the sort of moral universalism embodied in the basic human rights approach (that is, my favored version of cosmopolitanism) overlooks a value of great significance—at least in contemporary circumstances and for the foreseeable future—and is consequently mistaken in its conclusions.[3] Relativists hold that justice, and morality in general, is subject to community-relative standards that make cross-cultural comparisons impossible. Hence, universal claims to justice make no sense.[4] Defenders of nationality attempt to base substantive conclusions on the ethical value of the "nation" and to claim that distributive justice can be discussed properly only in the context of a given national community. According to this view, justice can gain no footing in the absence of some group whose members experience various sentiments toward one another on the basis of their shared history, language, and territory. In other words, there is no such thing as cosmopolitan justice; there is only what we might call *national justice*.[5]

In this chapter, I assess the views of patriots, who emphasize devotion to one's country as a primary moral virtue and conclude that in practice, such devotion entails favoritism for compatriots and, therefore at least potentially, the denial of some of the claims of noncompatriots. If such a view requires the denial of the full force of human rights claims, then patriotism conflicts with cosmopolitanism.

In the main, I deny the claims of constitutivists, relativists, nationalists, and patriots in their strong forms. Yet we will see that introducing some distinctions might make it possible to hold on to some forms of each view. Some forms of patriotism, nationalism, and constitutive theory might be ethically defensible, yet they do not in any way permit violations of the rights of foreigners, nonnationals, or noncitizens of one's state. And a version of relativism might even be plausible, but it is not sufficiently strong to rule out the sort of moral universalism that

I defend. In this chapter, then, I begin my investigation of limitation arguments by analyzing the merits and demerits of patriotism.

II. EXCLUSIONARY PATRIOTISM, COMPATRIOT FAVORITISM, AND MORALITY

Two important questions for our purposes are (1) Is there an ethically defensible form of patriotism? And if there is, (2) what does patriotic loyalty imply about duties of justice to noncompatriots?

I first assess competing conceptions of patriotism, arguing that patriotism need not be an overtly immoral doctrine—it can be consistent with a defensible account of morality. However, I find no airtight arguments in favor of a blanket version of what I call *compatriot favoritism*. Supposing, for the sake of argument, that patriotism can be ethically justified, I then look at the status of international justice in light of the legitimate patriotic commitments that persons may accept.

Patriotism is love of one's country and one's compatriots, and patriotic loyalty is the species of loyalty that requires devotion to one's country and a willingness to sacrifice one's own interests to some degree for one's fellow countrymen or countrywomen. Hence the patriot is someone who believes that he is justified in extending greater concern to some persons—compatriots—than to others—noncompatriots or "foreigners."[6] Beyond this basic characterization of patriotism, opinions diverge, and it is the inclusion or exclusion of additional features that generates competing conceptions of patriotism.

Patriotic special duties are a species of what are known as *associative or communal obligations*, special duties connected with membership in groups of various kinds (families, neighborhoods, political communities), duties that appear to be recognized without having been chosen by members. For Ronald Dworkin, people who have associative obligations must see those obligations as forms of special, personal concern for particular others, and this concern must be expressed equally for all members of the group in question.[7] Although Dworkin has defended associative obligations, A. John Simmons has pointed out that such localized duties are binding for Dworkin only when they meet standards of justice that apply to both insiders and outsiders alike. In that case, we want to know why the local group should be ethically prior when "other, foreign associations . . . may be better (more just) or more in need of support."[8] There is, therefore, a basic difficulty with defending patriotism in the face of global injustice. We shall return to this problem later, but in the meantime we should keep in mind that it seems plausible to assert that patriotic special concern must not ignore the condition of those in the wider world.

The wider world is ignored, however, in the following case. I have said that beyond the special concern itself, additional features produce specific versions of patriotism. The first extra characteristic that some writers include as constitutive of patriotism is the view that one should concern oneself only with the well-being of one's own compatriots. To say that patriots "extend greater concern" to compatriots is to say, on this reading, that noncompatriots fall outside the sphere of ethical concern altogether. This implies that "foreigners" count for nothing, morally speaking, so we can label this view *exclusionary patriotism*. This exclusion of outsiders from consideration is no doubt an element in the set of commitments of some real-life (so-called) patriots, but I think it is uncontroversial to conclude that such a form of patriotic concern is not ethically defensible, for the simple reason that it could legitimate any action or policy carried out in the name of one's country without taking any account of noncompatriots. One need not be a moral cosmopolitan—that is, a defender of impartialist, egalitarian individualism—to reject the idea that citizenship is the sole criterion of moral considerability. One odd consequence of accepting exclusionary patriotism is that it seems to commit one to the belief that gaining membership in a country would somehow have the effect of turning one into a subject of ethical concern (from the perspective of those who are already members). This would lead, in turn, to our attaching monumental significance to immigration procedures![9] But this bizarre implication is not the real reason that we should reject this view. For, more simply put, according to this conception of patriotism, patriots are people who believe that they are justified in pursuing policies that, from their own perspective, advance the interests of their country, even though they do so only by enslaving or killing persons in other countries, because these exterior effects count for nothing in the moral assessment of the legitimacy of such policies. If this is patriotism, then it should be rejected outright.[10] Even if we conclude that a country is, in general, a proper object of its citizens' loyalty, there are limits to the sorts of actions and policies that it is legitimate to pursue in its name, and part of the rationale of those limits is that noncompatriots should count to some extent.

Some versions of "realism" in international relations theory and practice are indefensible, in part for the reason that they exemplify the exclusionary approach to intercountry interactions. If individual egoism is unacceptable because persons are required to recognize the interests of other persons, then using similar reasoning, state egoism or national selfishness is not credible, since states—which are made up of individuals, each of whom has obligations to consider others to some extent—must recognize that other states have interests similar to their own. A wholesale renunciation of duties to other states is therefore not plausible. Brian Barry asked some questions that reveal the weakness in exclusionary patriotism: "Is there anything magical, after all, about one particular grouping—a nation-state—that can dissolve all wider moral considerations? Why should this one level of association be exempted from moral constraints that apply to all others?"[11] The realist might maintain that a state's concern for other states in an anarchic world is tantamount to irrationally leaving oneself open to exploitation by other states not naive enough to act in such an altruistic fashion.[12] But this claim is surely exaggerated, since concern for states other than one's own is compatible with the continued existence of one's state. Moreover, while we can debate just how much concern for other states is warranted, the realist claim (unless it is based on a wholesale moral skepticism) does in fact accept that noncompatriots count for something. The argument, as I understand it, is that the best way for every state to protect its own interests is to eschew concern for other states. But this line of reasoning is meant to apply to the leaders of all states, and it is unclear why one would offer such an argument if one thought those in other states were unworthy of any consideration.

Fortunately, a better conception of patriotism is available. According to this alternative view, patriots express their love of their country by showing greater care and concern for their country and compatriots than they do for other countries and noncompatriots, though the latter also count for something. "Greater care and concern" here means that some concern should be shown to noncompatriots, but the level of concern will be less than that accorded to compatriots. The patriot, then, believes that ethically speaking, "compatriots take priority."[13] I call this view *compatriot favoritism* (or CF, for short). Now our question is whether there is a sense in which this sort of favoritism is ethically defensible.

One reason that we might think it is not is that on the face of it at least, compatriot priority flies in the face of certain pervasive features of commonsense morality. For instance, it is commonly thought that adopting a moral perspective involves looking at a particular conflict of interests from a neutral position and thereby exempting oneself from viewing matters from the particular perspective of any one of the parties to the conflict. The reason that this abstraction from any one viewpoint is considered to be justified is that it enables one to judge the dispute without favoring one party's interests over those of any other. In short, morality seems often to require impartial concern and the consequent nonaccordance of priority to any particular individual or group. Consider, on the other hand, the vice known as *bigotry*, "the groundless downgrading of some selected subset of humanity."[14] Priority for one's compatriots can seem like the flip side of this coin: compatriot favoritists appear to upgrade groundlessly some selected subset of humanity. How can this be justified?

The challenge to cosmopolitanism that compatriot favoritism represents is to show not that morality can apply beyond nation-state boundaries but, rather, that these boundaries do not constitute a legitimate point at which the pull that generates a person's moral obligations decreases somewhat. The cosmopolitan must, that is, give some account of the special ethical relationships that compatriots are alleged to share. In doing so, he must try to resolve the difficulty represented by the claim that some persons, those identified as compatriots, are due greater concern than others are, a claim that on the face of it seems to contradict a root idea of cosmopolitanism and of much moral philosophy and commonsense moral thinking as well, namely, the idea that all persons are due equal moral consideration. Of course, the idea that compatriots take priority also has good commonsense credentials, so we cannot simply appeal to common sense to settle this dispute; we need to dig deeper.[15]

Let us make certain what is at issue here. There is a contradiction, superficially at least, between (1) a dominant moral tradition according to which each person is the moral equal of every other person and so merits equal consideration and (2) the demands of patriotic commitment, which say that compatriots legitimately count for more than do noncompatriots.

This conflict needs to be resolved, and several alternative resolutions are possible. First, one could deny that morality requires impartial concern for each person. This is not a realistic option. Impartiality is an important moral value, since it requires us not to make an exception of ourselves when deliberating about what it is right to do. We should retain the idea that morality forbids deliberative processes that take account of only the subject of deliberation or that make that subject "special" in such a way that general rules governing judgments about the acceptability of human behavior do not apply to him. Moreover, when interests conflict, a stable resolution is not likely unless it is possible to abstract from one's own particular perspective and see the potential legitimacy of the interests of all sides to the dispute, but it is just this sort of abstraction that impartiality requires.[16] A second resolution would be to deny that compatriot favoritism is ethically acceptable. This is a real option, although it would mean rejecting a widely held belief. Third, one could attempt a reconciliation of (1) and (2), thereby holding out the possibility of retaining them both in some form. Defenders of this third option might effect this move by distinguishing different levels at which morality applies to our lives: at one level, preferential treatment can be justified, whereas at a second level we must take up a perspective of impartial consideration of competing interests. The trick is to show that one of these

levels has moral primacy and that, from that level, taking up
the supposedly conflicting attitude can be defended (though
only at its proper level).[17] This resolution of the apparent conflict allows impartial concern to coexist with special ties to compatriots within the limits imposed on the actions those ties may
legitimately generate. The most important such limits are that
basic rights-violations are not permitted in the name of acts
performed in support of one's compatriots. It should be emphasized, however, that this reconciliation of compatriot favoritism with impartial concern shows only that the two are *compatible*, not that there are any independent reasons to be a compatriot favoritist in the first place. The third option, if successful, would show only that compatriot favoritism is consistent
with the impartial concern required of conscientious moral
agents, but this is not to say that compatriot favoritism is independently plausible.

We can put the problem in the form of a set of claims, one of
which must be rejected if the others are to be maintained.

1. The version of patriotism known as *compatriot favoritism*
   (CF) permits and often even requires persons to accord
   a higher priority in their ethical deliberations and actions to the interests and needs of compatriots than to
   the similar interests and needs of noncompatriots.
2. Adopting a moral perspective involves abstracting from
   a particular individual's (or group's) interests, thereby
   viewing matters from an impartial standpoint.
3. From the impartial standpoint of morality, it is imper-
   missible for the interests and needs of any one person
   or group to be accorded any ground-level priority; each
   party is thereby shown equal consideration.

From these three claims, it follows that CF permits or requires
deliberation and action ruled out from the viewpoint of morality. The priority claim pressed in (1) is disallowed by (3), which
elaborates on (2). Hence it looks as though we must give up either (1) or (3). We can call the present objection the *purported immorality of compatriot favoritism*. But is it an accurate portrayal of
the options to say that we must choose between priority for com-

patriots, on the one hand, and commitment to morality, on the other?

One thing seems certain: there is no across-the-board conflict between morality and special obligations. Some reason for admitting special ethical relationships into one's picture of an acceptable account of morality can be seen if we consider an objection one sort of impartialist might make to compatriot favoritism. This objection is a generalized version of the criticism we have been considering, since it questions compatriot favoritism by rejecting special duties as an entire class. This is the *special relationships objection*. The argument is that since impartial moral concern requires equal consideration of everyone affected by an action or policy, special relationships that require unequal consideration—in regard to special concern for some people rather than others—are incompatible with morality.

With special reference to patriotism, the argument says that patriotism is immoral because, first, it consists essentially of a form of special concern for some circumscribed group of people and, second, this special concern for some others is inconsistent with a proper moral consideration of each person equally. This line of reasoning is ultimately unacceptable because its second premise,—although it is both relevant to and (along with the first premise) sufficient to generate the desired conclusion—is, as stated, too strong and is therefore implausible. To accept the second premise, we must believe that no form of special concern for some particular person or group of people is ever morally justified. This would require us to believe that the desires and actions constitutive of parent-child relationships, for instance, are in fact lacking any sound moral justification. While I will not explain here why such desires and actions are morally legitimate and indeed morally required, I can safely say that any theory that mandates their abolition is deeply flawed in some way. Compatriot favoritism might not be, in the end, an acceptable view, but the fact that it is an instance of the view that special consideration for some others is morally legitimate is not sufficient to show that it is a morally unacceptable view. In fact, the reality is quite the opposite. We tend to think that the special duties parents owe to their children, for instance, are morally required, not merely permitted.[18] Nonetheless, the patriotic version of special ties is not necessarily defensible simply by virtue of the plausibility of its familial analogue.

To see this last point more clearly, I will mention briefly one type of argument for the special concern for compatriots that works by appealing to the meaning of the relation in question. Compatriot favoritism might be taken to be reasonable because the relationship of cocitizens to one another necessarily involves special duties. I think this is an unsatisfactory way to defend special duties to compatriots, but it is important to see how the argument might proceed and where it goes wrong. Some special relationships are necessarily associated with particular obligations. As Samuel Gorovitz points out, "To be a friend is to have certain obligations in regard to the object of one's friendship; to reject such obligations is to reject participation in that form of association known as friendship."[19] To be a friend is to assume certain duties toward one's friend, and the rejection of such duties means that the relationship itself does not hold: these obligations define the friendship relation. It would be incorrect to say that A is a friend of B, even though A would not "put himself out" for B any more than A would for anyone else. Unfortunately for compatriot favoritism, the obligations of citizenship are importantly different from the obligations of friendship. The whole question of what is required of compatriots is debatable, and it has changed over the past few hundred years—for instance, paying taxes for the funding of a substantial, national welfare state is now usually thought to be acceptable when once it was not—to such an extent that we are unlikely to find any uncontroversial duties that define the special relationship that compatriots share. And even if there were widespread agreement in some contemporary state about the content of those duties, it would legitimize those duties only if we accepted the doubtful claim that people have obligations simply because they believe themselves to have them. Consequently, it seems that compatriot favoritism cannot be defended by referring to an appeal to what the compatriot relation definitionally requires.

In response to this last argument, we can say that what is required of friends and family members has likewise changed over time, although this does not show that friendship and family relationships are not necessarily forms of group favoritism. We can admit that there are different conceptions of citizenship, friendship, and families while consistently maintaining that any such conception is a form of favoritism. This response is important, but it fails to show that compatriot favoritism is a morally justified version of special concern. This result is not surprising, for we should not have expected the patriot's justificatory task to be performed successfully by simply appealing to a definition.

We ought to consider some of the other arguments relevant to the acceptability of patriotism, but we should first consider the claim that compatriot favoritism will be fatally flawed if it cannot respond to the problem I have called the *purported immorality of compatriot favoritism*. In the next section I discuss a solution to this problem.

III. IS PATRIOTISM CONSISTENT WITH IMPARTIAL CONCERN?

Patriotic loyalty demands that persons deliberate in a partial manner, according moral priority to compatriots. But a dominant strand of commonsense moral concern demands that no one should specially privilege their own interests or those of people with whom they have special ties. We have seen that the rejection of special relationships as a class cannot be successful, but we have also noted that this does not necessarily help compatriot favoritism. If we take seriously both the particularist understanding of community comember relationships and the universalist claim that everyone is morally entitled to treatment as an equal of anyone else, we are led to a contradiction. On the one hand, people are permitted, and sometimes required, to show special concern for their compatriots, but on the other hand, people are obligated to show equal concern for any person, regardless of citizenship. If this contradiction cannot be overcome, we will have to give up one of these claims, both of which have evident appeal. Fortunately, we can make a distinction that dissolves the supposed conflict and allows us to retain, in a suitably qualified form, both compatriot priority and impartial concern for all persons.

The resolution of the conflict is achieved in a manner described by Alasdair MacIntyre (though MacIntyre does not himself think the resolution is successful). MacIntyre says that

> patriotism and all other such particular loyalties can be restricted in their scope so that their exercise is always within the confines imposed by morality. Patriotism need be regarded as nothing more than a perfectly proper devotion to one's own nation which must never be allowed to violate the constraints set by the impersonal moral standpoint.[20]

The idea is that patriotic deliberation is often permissible or required; we can legitimately reason that we want to pay an extra tax to benefit our compatriots or support a particular cause, even a war, against another country, but we must also be prepared to acknowledge that deliberation and action of this type is defensible for citizens of other countries in circumstances similar to our own. That is, from an impartial or impersonal second-order perspective, I must see that first-order thoughts such as "This is my country!" can figure in the legitimate ethical thinking of any person. Defensible partiality, then, is partiality that anyone can admit is justifiable for anyone else to act on. If it is all right for me to act for the reason that it is my country whose interests are at stake, I must also believe that it is all right for noncompatriots to act for that very same reason with reference to their country when the circumstances are similar.

Distinguishing levels of moral deliberation, beginning with first-order thinking and adding the crucial perspective of second-order thinking about the reasoning that goes on at the first-order level, dissolves the supposed incompatibility between patriotic special concern on the one hand and impartial consideration of the interests of all persons on the other.

One response to this argument is to deny that its acceptance of impartiality goes far enough: Why not be a first-order impartialist? The short answer to this question is that first-order impartialism is a version of fanaticism, for it embodies a misunderstanding of the role that impartial considerations should play in ethical deliberation and action.[21] In this context, it might be helpful to consider a classical discussion of this issue. I also include here my own contribution to this debate, namely, an example designed to show that compatriot favoritism is a clearly distinguishable species of the genus "special ethical concern" and that its appeal cannot ride on the back of more intimate relationships between persons.

The classic case I have in mind is the *Godwinian fire dilemma*. William Godwin describes a scenario in which someone is confronted with the choice of saving only one of two people who are trapped in a burning building. One of these unfortunate individuals is an archbishop, and the other is the archbishop's valet, who is perhaps "a brother, father, or benefactor" of the person who must save one of the two people.[22] Godwin, the impartialist fanatic, opts for saving the person who is likely to produce more benefit for humankind; in this case, it is presumed to be the archbishop. Hence, according to Godwin, one should not save one's own father if one can produce more overall expected benefit by saving someone else. This is a version of first-order impartiality.

Godwin's position exemplifies a confusion about the role of impartiality in moral thinking. He correctly recognizes that the ultimate justification of moral principles must be carried out from a perspective that regards each person equally. Moral justification of basic principles must not allow a person's particular likes and dislikes any fundamental importance. However, Godwin mistakenly assumes that impartiality—understood as the lack of special concern for any identifiable individual—is the way of life required of persons endeavoring to be morally upstanding. In short, the proper response to Godwin is to say that impartiality as a necessary condition of legitimate reasoning about basic moral principles should be distinguished from impartiality as a way of life and that the latter sense of impartiality is unlikely to be defensible from the impartial deliberative point of view.[23]

Bernard Williams discusses another version of Godwin's problem, in which the choice is between saving one's wife and saving a stranger, both of whom will drown if nothing is done.[24] Abstracting from Godwin's utilitarianism, it seems clear that first-order impartialism would require that one cannot appeal to any ground-level reason for favoring one person over another. Williams believes that not only is the impartialist conclusion incorrect but also the whole idea that there is a need for a general, reasoned justification for saving one's wife is mistaken. My view is that both Godwin and Williams reason incorrectly.[25] Godwin is wrong because although he rightly acknowledges the value of impartial concern, he applies his particular brand of utilitarian reasoning to each individual's particular context of action,[26] and he conflates two distinct senses in which impartiality is an option for us. As we have seen, partiality in such contexts is consistent with an overall commitment to impartial consideration of the equal claims of all persons. Williams, on the other hand, is wrong because he thinks there is no scope for reason giving in contexts like the fire dilemma and the drowning-spouse predicament. I think he is correct to say that it is obvious that a man should save his wife rather than a stranger—even an important stranger whose utility-producing potential is judged to be quite high (and much higher than his wife's potential in this regard). However, I also believe, contrary to Williams, that it is necessary to understand that "in situations of this kind it is permissible to save one's wife."[27] The fact that one does not offer such a justification before acting does not mean that it does not make sense to think that there are good reasons for so acting. After all, if we could give no reason at all, even in a cool hour sometime after the fact, wouldn't we have grounds for suspicion about the ethical status of the act?[28]

We can, of course, offer some very good reasons that "partner saving"—that is, wife saving, husband saving, long-term cohabitator saving—is justified in fire-dilemma cases. Sincere and committed participation in these sorts of close relationships fosters other virtues in a person, such as honesty and concern for another person's general well-being. This sort of concern may even be a necessary condition for having the capacity to sympathize with the suffering of people in faraway places. If these are the relations through which we become moral beings, we can hardly deny the moral obligations they involve. Intimacy is important to the living of a meaningful life, and it generates a need—as a means to ensuring that intimacy retains its authenticity—for dispositions to act in certain ways in particular contexts: the fire-dilemma case is one such context. In fact, we can now see that if we take seriously the importance of intimate relationships, there is no dilemma after all. One should regret that both persons cannot be saved, but this does not mean that there is not a correct answer to the question of which one should be saved.

There is an interesting point to be made about compatriot favoritism in connection with the Godwinian fire dilemma. Imagine a similar case with a burning building and two helpless individuals, only one of whom you can save. But now imagine that one is a compatriot and the other is a noncompatriot. Whom should you save? I think that one thing that becomes obvious as soon as one thinks about this sort of example is that any conclusion one might reach is much less obvious than in the standard Godwin-Williams example, in which one of the potential rescuees is a father, mother, or wife. At least with respect to the conclusions reached in the traditional case, Godwin is obviously incorrect and Williams is just as obviously correct (although he gives an unsatisfying account of the reasons for his choice). In the compatriot-dilemma case, on the other hand, one could perhaps think of reasons for saving one's compatriot before saving the noncitizen, but those reasons would not come anywhere near securing widespread agreement for their proposed recommendation for action. The simple yet vital point is that the traditional case and the compatriot case would not appeal to similar reasons, since the most important grounds for preferential treatment for one's partner are the intimacy of this relationship and the importance of intimacy in living a meaningful life. But of course, intimacy and its justificatory power cannot be wielded on behalf of compatriot saving, for most compatriots are strangers to us, just as most foreigners are. The fact that compatriots are slightly less "strange" strangers hardly counts as a powerful reason, certainly not in the way that intimacy counted in the traditional case. If intimacy is indeed part of the best supporting argument for partiality toward loved ones, then compatriot favoritism must appeal to reasons different from those appealed to in the cases of friends and family: intimacy can ground obligations only toward intimates, not toward people one has never even met.

There are two upshots of this discussion. The first, general, one is that first-order impartiality is not a reasonable view. The second is that compatriot priority cannot be justified in the same straightforward way that we justify priority for intimates. The latter conclusion in turn suggests that we look for other reasons for adhering to compatriot favoritism.

IV. Compatriot Favoritism: Further Clarification

I have just said that compatriot favoritism (CF) cannot be defended in precisely the same way that we justify favoritism for, say, our children or parents. But the defense of compatriot priority can be structurally the same as the defense of familial priority because, as we have seen, both are forms of ethical particularism and there is no general reason for eschewing ethical particularism. That is, there is no general objection to ethical particularism—understood as special ethical commitment to some person(s) rather than others—because some forms of particularism can be universalized. It is perfectly acceptable to show special concern for one's own children, but one must admit that others are justified in showing such concern for their children and that they need not show the same interest in your children as you do. Notwithstanding the structural similarity among different species of particularism, we still need to discover some more positive considerations in support of compatriot favoritism, along with the main objections to which it is subject. Sections IV and V of this chapter set out on this path of discovery. First, though, we should say something more about the form taken by compatriot favoritism, my label for the form of patriotism that might turn out to be defensible.

As we have seen, CF says that people are justified in showing greater concern for compatriots than they do for noncompatriots, although noncompatriots must also be subjects of moral consideration. And we have shown that such a view can be consistent with a defensible overall account of morality. One feature of any plausible account of CF is especially important to mention: defenders of CF agree that no person should be accorded any ground-level priority over any other or others (see section II, the third of my mutually incompatible points). That is, CF does not accord ground-level priority to any person or group of persons. Rather, it accepts that each person is ultimately on a moral par with every other. But it urges us to take account of the implications for our ethical obligations of the existence of certain public institutions in which we participate with a limited number of others (that is, our compatriots). Some compatriot favoritists might point out that ground-level moral equality does not rule out superstructural special concern grounded in the conduct of some but not others. This point is akin to the general claim that *what people do* affects how they should be treated.

It is crucial to note, however, that the CF version of the "conduct affects proper treatment" claim does not justify special treatment for compatriots. One argument in defense of CF might say that the fact of sharing a commitment to a set of mutually beneficial institutions can make legitimate a special concern for other, similarly committed persons. But this argument has several problems. First, it looks as though its defender would respond to an "outsider's" claim to "our" resources or "our" concern by pointing out that it is only insiders (that is, fellow citizens) who have contributed to the institutions in question and to the production of benefits that those institutions have spawned. This may or may not be true empirically, and if it turns out to be false—say, when a country's GNP has been substantially enhanced by the contribution of foreign labor—then compatriot favoritism lacks a defense. Moreover, even if we accept that it is only the citizens of a specific country who share the wealth they create by contributing to a public framework for generating cocitizen benefits, some of those citizens will not have contributed to the production of those benefits. Most interesting, this is true of the severely disabled citizens who nonetheless are usually thought to have a legitimate claim to help from compatriots. Yet the compatriot priority thesis itself would seem to provide no grounds for excluding noncontributors and explicit reason for including them. After all, handicapped compatriots are still compatriots. What we can call the *contribution requirement*—the demand that only those who have contributed to the production of general benefits have a claim on those benefits—is therefore not the key to understanding who does and who does not merit help from a set of public institutions. The second difficulty with this argument is the general oddity of its strategy for grounding special duties. If persons A and B enter into some group and gain the benefits of comembership, but C lacks these benefits because he was not included in that group, why should A and B get not only the advantages of membership but also the additional benefit of having stronger claims on one another's services than C has on the services of either one of them?[29] One might think that if people derive advantages from belonging to some collectivity, their obligations to those excluded from membership without their consent would be greater than their obligations to comembers, since exclusion can lead to increased vulnerability. Insofar as the argument for compatriot favoritism depends on something like the contribution requirement, it provides no justification for special obligations.

Another important feature of compatriot favoritism is its conditionality on the characteristics of the state in question.[30] It can never be true that someone rightly has special obligations to his compatriots simply because both he and they share a common citizenship. Consider the implications of denying this claim. Someone who held that shared citizenship alone is sufficient to generate ethical priority for another person would have to accept that German citizens during the Nazi era had a moral duty to look out for the interests of, say, high-ranking Nazis—that is, fellow citizens of Germany—before considering the plight of the non-German victims of Nazi oppression. I assume, on the contrary, that the opposite is in fact the case: a morally upstanding German citizen would have had a duty to concern himself with the safety and rights of the victims, even when those victims were noncompatriots.

To summarize, we have noted the following features of compatriot favoritism:

1. *Special Concern*: CF supports special concern for compatriots as against noncompatriots.
2. *Consistency with Impartiality*: This special concern need not violate the impartialist demands of morality.
3. *Ground-Level Equality and Superstructural Inequality*: CF accepts the claim that each person is due equal moral consideration, regardless of citizenship. It urges, however, that this ground-level ethical equality does not rule out the differential treatment of persons, treatment

perhaps based on the actions people perform as members of collectivities (the most important of which is the state of which they are citizens).

4. *Conditionality*: The acceptability of CF is conditional on the characteristics of the state in question. There is no such thing as a compatriot favoritist attitude that is justified independently of any information about the ethical character of the state concerned.

Apart from noting these elements of CF, we have also rejected an argument in its favor. Our criticism of that argument brought out the problems for CF generated by the third point just mentioned. That is, on the one hand, both compatriots and noncompatriots contribute to the well-being of the citizens of, say, the United States, so when contribution counts, there is no argument for limiting obligations to compatriots. On the other hand, some compatriots do not contribute to the well-being of their fellows, yet we think it is right to show concern for them, regardless of their inaction.[31]

Having thus clarified the main features of CF, we now pursue further the arguments on both sides.

V. COMPATRIOT FAVORITISM: FOR AND AGAINST

We have seen that compatriot favoritism can take some account of the interests of those outside one's borders and that although there is no general impartialist reason against special relations, this does not show that all special relations are justified. More needs to be said about arguments for and against compatriot favoritism. That is the purpose of this section.

One point merits repeating here. Patriotism is not a general duty of persons, since patriotic loyalty should not be directed toward one's country unless there are certain characteristics present in an accurate description of that country that give rise to legitimate loyalty. "My-ness" is a necessary but not a sufficient condition for a justified patriotism. (It is a necessary condition because it is impossible for someone to have a patriotic attitude toward some country that is not her own.) Commitment to a nonaggressive foreign policy or protection of the natural environment might be relevant loyalty-generating characteristics. There is no definite set of features whose presence guarantees that patriotic loyalty will be legitimate. Rather, some qualities will count toward considering a country as a proper object of loyalty, and other qualities will count against doing so, but many features will simply call for particular actions (on the part of patriots) aimed at either reinforcing those features or ending one's country's commitment to them. Hence the particularity of patriotic loyalty is conditioned by the need for any virtuous patriotism to include the citation of some admirable characteristics that add credibility to the (always elliptical) claim that "I should be loyal because it is my country."

There is one central reason, then, that compatriot favoritism might be desirable from an ethical point of view: One's country could have admirable characteristics that attract support from its members. If loyalty to one's country is, in part, dependent on appreciating those features of the country that make it worthy of one's devotion, then the need for individuals to support valuable collectivities will help justify the love of one's own country over others. Note again, however, that patriotic loyalty is, on this view, conditional on one's country possessing features that themselves either permit or require persons to become loyal supporters. Conditionality does not merely weaken the potential grip of patriotism, it also threatens to support antipatriotism. If a citizen of country A should show special concern for country A because it exemplifies certain virtues in its everyday practices, then a citizen of country B—a country more vicious than virtuous, or a country whose virtues pale in comparison with those of country A—should not be a compatriot favoritist. On the contrary, citizens of country B should show special concern for country A and therefore ought to be noncompatriot favoritists! Consequently, what appeared to be a strong reason for adhering to CF turns out on examination to provide a reason for pledging allegiance only to the country (or countries) that pass a more objective ethical test, so there can be no general defense of CF grounded on this argument.

Good reasons for acknowledging the ethical importance of close bonds with one's community are not hard to find, however, and they could provide a defense of compatriot favoritism in a specific instance. Individuals gain a sense of themselves only in the context of their particular communities. Each of us probably needs to feel that we belong somewhere and to participate to some degree in a culture. Being "at home" in a culture and a society provides us with some of the elements necessary for living a meaningful human life, and it seems inevitable that persons who develop cognitively, socially, and emotionally in a certain social and cultural context will come to regard the distinctive aspects of that context—of their country—with special affection. To the extent that one's culture is enabled to thrive by means of state support, one would have good reason to show special concern for one's state.

Further insight into the grounds for compatriot favoritism can be gained by attempting to answer the following question: Why should we care more for some people than we do for others? One plausible answer is that some people are especially vulnerable to us and our actions. It is this vulnerability that explains why special duties are properly assigned by an adequate moral theory in one way rather than another.[32] The problem for compatriot priority, as it relates to this argument, is that many foreigners are highly vulnerable to our actions, perhaps more vulnerable than our compatriots are. In that case, of course, the vulnerability argument recommends favoring noncompatriots over compatriots. This sort of argument is different from one in which comembership itself justifies special obligations. Here, rather, it is the supposed correlation between citizenship and some other, morally relevant characteristic (that is, vulnerability) that justifies compatriot priority. If that correlation fails—as, it is claimed, it does when noncitizens are more vulnerable to our actions than citizens are—the argument's conclusion is that (as long as the vulnerability relation remains as it is) noncompatriots take priority. Therefore, even if we accept the vulnerability model of special obligations, it does not provide a general rationale for compatriot favoritism. When there is a high correlation between vulnerability and cocitizenship, this model would support CF, but we would still have no reason for supposing that CF is, in general, an accurate account of our ethical responsibilities in this regard. All that would follow would be the wisdom of discovering degrees of vulnerability. Even when we find the aforementioned correlation, it is the vulnerability and not the shared citizenship that is doing the moral work of generating duties. Compatriot favoritism would be an alternative way to describe what we should call, more accurately, special concern for the vulnerable. And shared citizenship would be a decidedly secondary part of any satisfactory moral explanation, that is, an explanation of why persons have the moral obligations they are properly said to have.

This discussion about vulnerability leads to an interesting and important point about the proper focus of a citizen's concern: if one's own state can, by its actions, significantly affect the well-being of noncompatriots, then as a citizen who accepts the vulnerability criterion, one should take the most effective means to ensure that those persons are not made to suffer. In democratic states, it follows that citizens should especially concern themselves with the policies of their own government whenever those policies impinge on foreigners, since one's goal (to protect those vulnerable to one) is best promoted by focusing one's energies in those places where they are likely to have the most significant effect. But this special concern for the policies of one's own country is not to be confused with partiality in favor of the individuals who are one's compatriots. Again, the ethical work here is being done by the vulnerability of persons to the actions of one's government, and if one accepts the moral importance of the vulnerability relation, uncontroversial considerations of rationality dictate that one should concern oneself with the policies of one's own state. This concern is, however, only a means to protecting the vulnerable.

Let us now turn to some other considerations relevant to judging the acceptability of compatriot favoritism. Foremost among these considerations is the claim that individuals maintain various degrees of allegiance and loyalty to numerous, often rival communities.[33] This simple point is potentially devastating to compatriot favoritism because it might turn out on examination that some community or communities other than one's country take ethical precedence in many important contexts, thereby relegating compatriot favoritism to a secondary status. People are loyal to fellow members of religions, races, and ethnic groups, for instance, and nothing has yet been said to support compatriot priority in cases where it conflicts with allegiances to any of these groups. Why should moral significance be accorded to the borders of nation-states when doing so would override loyalties to one or more of these collectivities? We know why coreligionists feel attachments to one another: they share beliefs about fundamentally important aspects of human existence such as the origin and meaning of life. Consequently, they naturally feel a bond with others who share such deep commitments (regardless of the truth of their shared beliefs or the ultimate rationality of those commitments). Since compatriots do not necessarily share beliefs and commitments in this way, it is unclear why anyone should favor compatriots over coreligionists when it is necessary to choose between one group and the other.

We can call this the *problem of conflicting loyalties*. It is the problem of determining the ethical implications of the fact that people have deep attachments to more than one group—for instance, someone could consider herself both a Jew and a Canadian. We can imagine circumstances in which loyalty to one of these groups would require action that violated a requirement recognized by that same person in her capacity as a loyal member of the other group. The dilemma, then, concerns deciding which way to turn. This sort of problem shows—what many would take to be evident in any case—that nation-states are not obviously the supreme objects of loyalty in the modern world. The implications of this point for international justice are as follows. The restriction of duties of justice most often recommended in current discussions is a restriction of concern to compatriots, that is, fellow members of one's state. But if state membership lacks sufficient ethical pull in many contexts to override attachments to a religious group or intrastate national community, it is unclear why citizenship should be the proper feature for determining the obligations of justice. Even if there are grounds for limiting concern to some group, why should that group be the citizens of one's state? Since there are various individuals and groups to which we can show legitimate devotion, putting one's country first becomes an unrealistic demand, especially in cases of conflicts of loyalty.

In the context of severe global deprivation and poverty, we need to understand what could provide a reason for thinking that one's compatriots are the group to which one should recognize the strongest moral obligations. We have seen that family ties and the bonds of friendship—both of which are constituted by legitimate special responsibilities—are grounded in the importance of intimacy or depth of participation in close-knit relationships. Are compatriot relations analogous to these? Another potential foundation for heightened concern for compatriots is the presence of communitywide attachment to a set of values or principles. Sharing with one's compatriots a commitment to principles might constitute a reason for caring more for other adherents to these principles than one does for nonadherents.[34]

These two possible grounds advanced for moral priority are, first, intimacy and deep personal involvement and, second, agreement about basic principles or values. The first sort of ground may be priority generating, as in the case in which we say that spouses can justifiably show deeper ethical concern for one another than they do for those with whom they are not acquainted. But as we have seen, this is not likely to provide much support for compatriot priority, since people are not, nor could they be, intimate with all their fellow countrymen and countrywomen. Even if intimacy and depth of involvement generate special obligations, this is no help to the compatriot favoritist.

The second kind of reason for priority, that is, comembership in a "community of principle," is similarly unlikely to correlate with comembership in a nation-state. The reason for this is—as is all too clear—that compatriots are often deeply divided on questions of devotion to basic principles, values, and goals. This is, of course, one reason that liberals recommend that peaceful and stable political arrangements should not require that everyone be committed to the same basic values or "conceptions of the good." Public order itself perhaps demands that proposed solutions to disputes over such large issues should not be made matters of government policy. But not only is there disagreement among compatriots about moral and political principles, there is also the attachment to fundamental principles that people share with foreigners but not with compatriots. Nation-states are certainly not, in general, communities of principle in any sense that would exclude outsiders from the special duties owed to coadherents to a given set of principles. It might be objected that everyone in a liberal society must share a commitment to the society's principles of justice, if not to some unified account of the good life for human beings. The answer to this charge is that citizens need only act in conformity with those principles; they need not believe them to be true.

VI. PATRIOTISM AND GLOBAL JUSTICE

We have failed to find any cogent arguments in support of compatriot favoritism. CF is not necessarily an immoral doctrine, for its particularism does not itself render it guilty of any violation of morality. However, CF is just as clearly lacking any general, defensible rationale. We should be open to other arguments, of course, but so far we are right to reject it. Having said this, I now want to suppose for the sake of argument that compatriot favoritism is justified. On this basis, we can assess the relationship between patriotism thus conceived and the conclusions about global distributive justice that would be advanced by cosmopolitans. Even if we are correct to remain skeptical about the strength of claims for patriotic loyalty, here I suppose that patriotism can be a virtue and assess the implications of accepting this claim for the questions of international distributive justice. This strategy has the additional virtue of permitting us to evaluate the arguments of some prominent compatriot favoritists, so we can continue to look for reasons to accept that widely held but weakly defended doctrine.

The main claim I want to emphasize is that no defensible form of patriotism justifies denying the basic human rights of persons. It can be morally permissible, even required, that one be patriotic and loyal to one's country, but such permissions and requirements can never override the demands of impartial justice. I propose in this section to assess attempts on the part of some compatriot favoritists to show that justice is not the sort of virtue that can properly extend beyond one's compatriots. These attempts, by Alasdair MacIntyre, George P. Fletcher, Daniel Bell, and Richard Rorty, constitute explicit denials of the central positive claims I have made.

*Alasdair MacIntyre and Intercommunity Conflict over
Scarce Resources*

Alasdair MacIntyre argues against the possibility of maintaining
both (1) a commitment to one's country and (2) a commitment
to principles of impartiality.

This is a radical criticism insofar as it says that even a limited
compatriot favoritism is not possible so long as one acknowledges the impartial perspective. MacIntyre claims that so-called
patriots who at the same time accept "liberal impersonal morality" would show their lack of true patriotism when faced with
certain kinds of difficult choices. Interestingly for our purposes,
MacIntyre gives an example of a dispute between two communities over the use of scarce and vital natural resources.

Imagine two communities, both requiring the same essential
resources for their survival or prosperity as a community. According to MacIntyre, each community should strive to further
its own interests in this matter, and in fact, "patriotism entails a
willingness to go to war on one's community's behalf."[35] But
someone who acknowledges the claims of impartial morality
cannot simply opt for his own community when faced with this
sort of conflict. In violation of patriotic loyalty, he will choose
"an allocation of goods such that each individual person counts
for one and no more than one."[36] We can see, then, that MacIntyre's patriotism denies the basic moral idea that each person
counts equally from a moral point of view. But it is implausible
to hold, as MacIntyre does, that no account needs to be taken of
the interests of persons in the community whose interests conflict with one's own. We have distinguished between compatriot
favoritism and exclusionary patriotism, but MacIntyre's patriot
seems to be of the exclusionary variety. Moreover, even if one
adopts the compatriot favoritist standpoint, why should it follow
that one's community is not required to settle this sort of dispute
through an impartial negotiating process? MacIntyre seems to
see no merit in arriving at a settlement that satisfies both communities, but he gives us no reason to agree with him on this
point. This is especially troubling since compatriot favoritism, if
it is at all defensible, permits special concern for compatriots
only with respect to some of their interests; it does not necessi-

tate a total denial of the basic human rights claims of outsiders. Cosmopolitan arguments can be adduced in support of the importance of basic human rights, but MacIntyre's account offers no grounds for overturning those arguments, apart from his claim that patriots literally cannot take up the impersonal perspective of morality. This last claim, however, is patently false.

MacIntyre commits the notorious fallacy of incomplete disjunction. He offers us only two alternatives, but he ignores a third option that is not only available but is in fact correct. He assumes that persons devoted to their country, that is, committed patriots, cannot take up a detached perspective from which the claims of conflicting parties can be adjudicated.[37] Hence MacIntyre's scenario presents us with a stark choice: either we can support our country in its struggle with another country over the control of resources, or we can detach ourselves from the perspective of a patriot, thereby exposing our true lack of commitment to our country. It follows, according to MacIntyre, that someone who opts for the second alternative—the alternative favored by anyone who acknowledges the claims of both compatriots and noncompatriots—is not a true patriot. But there is a third alternative: patriots can be especially concerned with their fellow countrymen and countrywomen while at the same time recognizing that other communities have the very same need for the particular scarce resources in question. MacIntyre might object that his patriot can do this; it is simply that he attaches no moral weight to the needs of others. But nothing in MacIntyre's argument shows that recognizing the legitimacy of the claims of noncompatriots is impossible or that it is unjustified. Of course, this does not settle the difficult question of what to do when any distribution of resources will leave some people with their basic needs unsatisfied. But MacIntyre's position precludes our asking this hard question, since the dilemma it proposes does not arise for his patriots. An even greater worry here is that the general tenor of MacIntyre's position seems explicitly to deny that patriotic loyalty can itself be wrong in cases in which one's country is committed to evidently immoral ends.

The conclusion of this brief discussion is to reemphasize what we have seen earlier. First, exclusionary patriotism is indefensible. Second, it is possible for patriots to assume an impartial perspective, especially when faced with conflicts of interest. If this were not possible, such conflicts would be settled by force alone.[38] But there is no need to equate concern for one's compatriots with support for muscle flexing. Indeed, one benefit of compatriot favoritism (as identified by the third alternative and assuming it can be defended on other grounds) is that it holds out the hope of resolving conflicts through a discussion in which all interlocutors show consideration for one another.

George Fletcher, Patriotic Loyalty, and Justice

Is cosmopolitan justice in the end a credible doctrine? One good reason for trying to understand the pros and cons of compatriot favoritism is that some of its defenders have offered arguments to show that cosmopolitans are fundamentally mistaken in various ways. George P. Fletcher, for instance, cautions that "it might be an ideal to extend our loyalty to everyone on the planet, but nourishing utopian visions about faraway places sometimes makes people indifferent to the real suffering next door."[39] Cosmopolitans can make two responses to these claims. The first has to do with the possible objects of loyalty implicit in them. The second concerns the assertion about the neglect of local suffering that it is claimed will follow (sometimes) from the adoption of a more expansive view.

First the point about loyalty itself. Perhaps loyalty is the sort of commitment that loses its proper sense when faced with very large numbers of people.[40] So it might indeed be utopian to recommend that each of us should feel a sense of loyalty to everyone else, including those in "faraway places." But the cosmopolitan is not claiming that we should be loyal to the group of all human beings. He is, rather, committed to acknowledging the equal claims of all persons on everyone else, even though we experience a sense of loyalty to less inclusive groups. The point the cosmopolitan is trying to emphasize here is that even though the demands of loyalty cannot and should not be denied with respect to many of the claims we make on one another, there are some claims—most notably, claims to the protection of one's vital interests—whose content renders them immune to the (partly countervailing) ethical pull created by group loyalty.

What we might call *basic interest immunity* protects persons in other countries from the otherwise justifiable claims of patriotic loyalty that compatriots make on one another. The basic interests of badly off individuals in country A cannot be subject to dismissal by an argument from a relatively well off citizen of country B that appeals only to the value of compatriot relations.

Fletcher suggests that we should think of the patriot-versus-impartialist dispute as one of conflicting loyalties, in which we must choose between the undeniable attachments of the "historical self" to his compatriots, on the one hand, and the utopian ideal of "loyalty to everyone on the planet," on the other hand. In response to Fletcher, my point is that the issue is not one of deciding which of these two potential objects of loyalty has the more compelling ethical credentials. Instead, the cosmopolitan impartialist should grant that loyalty is a virtue, when it is so, only for circumscribed groups but refuse to conclude on that basis that the vital interests of some persons should count for less simply because they do not belong to the favored group.

My second response is as follows: As a reason against extending ethical commitment to all persons, regardless of citizenship, Fletcher says that doing so "sometimes makes people indifferent to the real suffering next door." Is Fletcher claiming that my concern for the plight of people in East Timor and Lebanon somehow could lead to my failing to care about those forced to sleep on the streets of London (that is, those close to home)? I suspect that whether this claim is true depends on what the grounds are for my caring about how people's lives are going. If those grounds turn out to be a concern for the protection of persons' vital interests, then I ought to care about deprivation and suffering wherever it exists. And if some people, in their zeal for the struggle against faraway injustice, lose sight of the importance of nearby suffering, it should be clear that a plausible theory of human justice provides no grounds for doing so.[41]

Fletcher's attack on cosmopolitan justice also includes a claim about the connection between justice and loyalty. "Loyalty is a critical element in a theory of justice; for we invariably need some basis for group cohesion, for caring about others, for seeing them not as strangers who threaten our security but as partners in a common venture."[42]

This seems to me to set up a false dichotomy between (1) thinking of others as "partners" or fellow group members and (2) thinking of these others as "strangers who threaten our security."

According to this view, other people are either part of my group, and hence the proper objects of my concern and devotion, or they are potential threats to the satisfaction of my interests as a "private self-seeking" member of a "consumer society."[43] Reality, however, is more complicated than Fletcher makes it out to be. My compatriots are, after all, mostly strangers to me, but I can regard them as partners in a common project nonetheless. Hence, in fact, most of my national "partners" are strangers, in which case we have a third alternative not identified in (1) or (2), namely (3), thinking of others as strangers with whom I am embarked on a joint venture insofar as we all register our allegiance to a set of institutions embodying reasonable principles of distributive justice.

Moreover, many other strangers are not participants in the common venture I share with my compatriots, and yet this other set of strangers can hardly be said to threaten my security, especially if "me" in this context refers to a citizen of a relatively rich country. If anything, it is I—or at least my government—who constitute a threat to the security of deprived persons in the poor nations. It is therefore incorrect to claim that "when we take people as they are," we need patriotic loyalty if we are to avoid being engulfed by self-centeredness and mistrust. There is another alternative: we can combine a concern for our own country with a commitment to helping those in need, regardless of citizenship.

But Fletcher continues to pursue his anticosmopolitan point: "There is no easy response to the idealist who insists that all five billion people constitute one community, with one cause. The answer must begin with an understanding of how we as human beings are constituted and what our natural limits of sympathy may be."[44] Three points in reply to Fletcher are suggested here. First, Fletcher sets up a straw man when he says that his opponents see all human beings as pursuing one cause. Second, once this first point is recognized, it is clear that we need not choose between (1) commitment to one cause for all persons and (2) acceptance of patriotic loyalty, with its consequently weakened moral ties to foreigners. Third, if the implication of Fletcher's remarks about the natural limitations of our capacity to feel sympathy for others is supposed to be relevant to a theory of international justice, the proper reply is that as human beings, we cannot (nor should we) feel the same sort of sympathy for every other person that we feel for those with special ties to us. If we did, we could scarcely go through life without constantly experiencing depression due to our awareness of the massive suffering our fellow human beings constantly endure. But the limits of human sympathy are not as Fletcher describes them, nor is the capacity for sympathy as straightforwardly relevant to global justice as might be thought. Many of us are capable of showing sympathetic concern for the suffering of other human beings, say, when they lack adequate food and water and physical security. We have a natural capacity to recognize that if things had been different in various ways, we might have been the ones who suffered, and the fact that none of us can feel sympathy in precisely the same way for every person whose plight could generate sympathy is beside the point. What matters is only whether or not we can recognize that deprivation exists and that we can understand arguments aimed at showing us that such deprivation calls for action designed to eradicate it.

Let me go over in more detail the three points mentioned in the last paragraph. First, it is indeed idealistic to maintain that the entire human population of the planet constitutes "one community, with one cause." It is an idealistic belief, but at any rate, there is nothing immediately mistaken about being idealistic. Some theorists would take the idealism of this view to be a point in its favor. More important, however, it is also clearly false. In any case, cosmopolitans need not believe that there is one cause that all human beings pursue in common.

Does anyone seriously maintain that all persons constitute one community, with one cause? Certainly, liberals do not need to subscribe to this, for one of the most prominent problems motivating research in liberal political theory is the realization that people pursue different and conflicting causes, and a popular solution to this plurality of causes is to construct governments so that such pursuits can remain live options for every-

one, within the constraints of an institutional structure that protects against rights violations. Perhaps some people believe that
all of us are pursuing "one cause," but this is not part of the
commitment of those who believe that every person's basic interests are sufficiently important to merit protection. The cosmopolitan can consistently say that everyone should be able to
pursue a variety of conceptions of the good life, within the limits
of justice.[45]

As I mentioned earlier, the fact that Fletcher has set up a
straw man here implies that our options are larger than he suggests, for we do not need to be compatriot favoritists simply because there is no single cause to which the entire human race is
committed. This is my second point: we can admit that people
pursue various and conflicting causes while at the same time
denying that as a consequence, we are justified in saying that
people should favor compatriots over others.

My third point is that the limits of human sympathy are relevant to the acceptability of impartialist accounts of international
moral obligations, but not in the way Fletcher thinks they are.
Fletcher suggests that loyalty is necessary because it provides the
basis "for caring about others" and that "our natural limits of
sympathy" are such that we are incapable of showing concern
for "all five billion people" in the world. If Fletcher's claim is
that we cannot in our daily lives show equal concern for everyone else, there is a sense in which this is true and a sense in
which it is false. It is true that we cannot, as individuals (nor
should we), show the same concern for strangers' children that
we show toward our own. But it is false to assert that we cannot
both realize that each person is equally a proper object of concern and respect and undertake to support institutions whose
purpose is to ensure that all people have their vital interests
protected. Consider a domestic analogue of this point: redistributive welfare states do not require each citizen to have an identical attitude of sympathy toward each and every compatriot. The
fact that we cannot extend similar sympathy to each person in a
country populated by hundreds of millions of people does not
mean that principles of justice cannot include this entire population in their scope.

More generally, I think that Fletcher's argument overlooks that fact that serious ethical thinking contains a complicated "interaction of sentiment and principle." Henry Shue suggests,

> with apologies to Kant, that sentiments unconstrained by principles lack authority, principles unsupported by sentiments lack effect. Sentiments, both in others and in ourselves, can be judged critically. The expression in action of some sentiments is to be welcomed, the expression of others is to be discouraged. For assessing sentiments one needs principles.[46]

The point, in brief, is that we no doubt need sympathetic identification with others to support our conclusions about moral obligations, but criticism of our sentiments is necessary to judge whether such identification meets the criteria suggested by moral principles. Applying this type of move to the present point, we might ask whether someone's claim that he cannot sympathize with the suffering of the distant poor is based on (1) some fundamental feature of human nature (from which it might follow that he cannot extend his sympathy so far) or (2) a convenient refusal to consider that the ethical principles he actually accepts might require that he extend his sympathy further. In the second case, if he can show equal concern for all other persons, then his stubborn refusal to do so amounts to nothing more than stubborn refusal. If there is some principled reason for limiting one's sympathy to compatriots, it can be introduced at this point in the argument, but Fletcher does not offer any such principled reason. In any case, if we recognize both that other people are due a certain respect as persons and that we are constitutionally incapable of uniform sympathy for everyone, there is a rationale for developing the impartial perspective in order to make up for our incapacity in this regard.[47]

Another point that some compatriot favoritists are apt to make is that we must accept a trade-off between commitment to our country, on the one hand, and our adherence to independent critical thinking about the requirements of justice, on the other. Again, Fletcher puts the point succinctly: "The moral challenge for every devotee of a cause is to find the proper balance of loyalty and independent moral judgment."[48] This suggests that we must strike a balance between two competing ethical values, loyalty on the one hand and independence of judgment on the other. On the contrary, however, I think there is no head-to-head conflict of the sort Fletcher hints at here, for the "independent moral judgment" to which he refers should always, I submit, take precedence when possible. If appeals to such judgment fail to support the loyalist, then loyalty is not in that case justified, but if loyalty is shown, by independent judgment, to be justified, then the two standpoints coincide. In the latter sort of case, it is incorrect to say that a balance has been struck between loyalty and independent moral judgment, since both lead to the same conclusion, and Fletcher gives us no persuasive examples in which one should remain loyal to some country while eschewing critical assessment of the reasons one can muster for such a commitment. Fletcher's problem of striking a balance between loyalty and independent moral judgment arises most clearly in cases in which one has a sense that the object of one's loyalty (for example, one's country) might not be worthy of one's devotion, but it is in precisely those cases that "independent moral judgment" is required. Moreover, the outcome of critical evaluation of one's country could well be that one is justified in explicitly denying the claim that one's country is a proper object of loyalty.

Analysis of Fletcher's views has led to the following conclusions: First, loyalty is indeed a special attachment to some person or group, so that it is implausible in normal contexts to maintain that one should be loyal to all human beings. But this point does not refute the cosmopolitan assertion that some human interests are sufficiently important to generate protections that no appeal to the value of loyalty can override. Second, care and concern for faraway suffering need not result in blindness to deprivation close to home. Third, we should be wary of attempts to portray compatriots on an analogy with comembers of more closely knit groups. Most of my compatriots are strangers to me, so it is inaccurate to say that we must choose between compatriots whose closeness generates mutual trust and others who threaten our well-being. The reality is that increased physical distance does not necessarily coincide with increased threats to our security. Fourth, cosmopolitans are not wedded to the view that all human beings are pursuing one cause; they need only believe that no human being's interests should be excluded from equal consideration. Finally, there is no unbridgeable conflict between loyalty to compatriots and critical moral judgment, for this sort of loyalty (and any other) is not without criteria; accordingly, there is always room to evaluate any object of loyalty.

Bell, Rorty, Communitarianism, and Bounded Justice

Daniel Bell's book *Communitarianism and Its Critics* is in the form of a dialogue between a liberal, Philip Schwartzberg, and a communitarian (and compatriot favoritist), Anne de la Patrie.[49] Judging from the book's introduction, Bell himself sympathizes with the communitarians, especially on the question of the scope (national versus global) of distributive justice. At one point, Bell has Anne say the following:

> Any effective scheme of distributive justice, as I see it, presupposes a bounded world of people deeply committed to each other's fate—most of us will not agree to enshrine generous actions in law, and to live by those laws, if we can't identify in some way with recipients of those generous actions—and it just so happens that the nation-state has emerged, for whatever concatenation of historical reasons, as the unit within which our sense of solidarity is strongest.[50]

Anne is mistaken. Three features of these claims call for comment. The first has to do with an apparent confusion between the descriptive and the normative; the second concerns Anne's point about solidarity, which I believe is correct but does not prove her larger point about "bounded" justice; and the third concerns the notion of generosity and its relation to the virtue of justice.

First, the claim that the nation-state is the de facto center of solidarity can help explain why the nation-state is generally thought to be the proper site of distributive justice. However, no claim about the way things are is conclusive in the context of an argument whose concern is with the way things ought to be. The presumption that allegiances do not currently extend beyond national boundaries does not make it reasonable to deny appeals for the extension of those allegiances to all human beings.

The second, related point is that Anne proposes the reasonable idea that identification with the recipients of welfare assistance is necessary if people are to agree to give up some of their own wealth and resources. But if one can present plausible arguments for the view that each person should, at some level, identify with every other person, the ground is laid for implementing a global redistributive regime. The burden of the argument for basic human rights is to show that there are indeed reasons for identification across the entire class of persons. In this context, it is important to remember the history of arguments for patriotic loyalty itself. Because justifications of patriotic loyalty have (historically) attempted to show the arbitrariness of devotion to local groups, those arguments have themselves made it possible to argue, in turn, that loyalty to one's country and loyalty to more local groupings are arbitrary in much the same way. If there was good reason to give up parochial attachments to clan and town in favor of nation-state allegiance, it might be reasonable to give up patriotism in favor of global moral concern. What we might call the *expansionary momentum* of these arguments from moral arbitrariness could very well make it reasonable to believe that nation-state allegiance lacks a credible defense of its restricted special regard for one subset of persons.[51]

Finally, Bell's use of the word *generous* in this context suggests, misleadingly, that the actions required by the demands of distributive justice exhibit a special sort of kindness or a commitment to sharing that goes beyond what might normally be required. But generosity comes into play only after the claims of justice have been met, and the meeting of rights claims can be demanded without requiring "generosity" on the part of duty bearers. People are generous when they give more than they are strictly obligated to give, but justice focuses on more strict obligations. Therefore, to be generous is to exemplify an attitude quite separate from any required for the demands of justice to be met.

Bell not only sympathizes with Anne's claim about the restricted character of distributive justice, he also cites Richard

Rorty on "the point that identification with 'fellow human beings' seldom provides the motivational force for generous actions."[52] Rorty offers an interesting piece of evidence against the possibility of global solidarity in the name of justice.

> Consider . . . the attitude of contemporary American liberals to the unending hopelessness and misery of the lives of the young blacks in American cities. Do we say that these people must be helped because they are fellow human beings? We may, but it is much more persuasive, morally as well as politically, to describe them as fellow *Americans*—to insist that it is outrageous that an *American* should live without hope. . . . [Our] sense of solidarity is strongest when those with whom solidarity is expressed are thought of as "one of us," where "us" means something smaller and more local than the human race. That is why "because she is a human being" is a weak, unconvincing explanation of a generous action.[53]

Daniel Bell continues in the same vein:

> That our sense of solidarity is strongest where "us" means something smaller and more local than the human race provides a strong argument against the feasibility of a world-wide system of distributive justice (regulated by law), but of course it doesn't follow that the range of "us" can't be extended in the direction of greater human solidarity for more narrow purposes, e.g. making people more sensitive to instances of cruelty in faraway lands (Rorty thinks that novels, with their detailed descriptions of particular varieties of pain and humiliation, are particularly suited for this purpose).[54]

By responding to several of the points made in these passages, we can better grasp the commitments of cosmopolitans on the question of international distributive justice.

On the last point—that novels are well suited to the purpose of increasing global sensitivity to suffering—this is no doubt true, but it is also important to take note of the reports of Americas Watch, Africa Watch, Amnesty International, and similar human rights organizations, since these are vital organs of information about torture and suffering around the world. Simple awareness of the facts of suffering is likely to generate widespread concern, even without literary devices of sentiment building.

More important, why can the extension of solidarity to all human beings embrace only sensitivity to cruelty? If we can sympathize with the plight of persons who are victims of torture in faraway lands, why can we not also sympathize with those far-off persons who lack access to basic nutritional requirements, adequate housing, education, and health care? That is, there is nothing in this argument that explains why expressions of concern should be limited to "instances of cruelty." But if no "limitation argument" can be given, then a "world-wide system of distributive justice" seems a plausible option.

Rorty's central claim—that it is best to point out that those who suffer are part of our community—seems to me to be a point about strategy rather than a point of any substance on the question of why it is that the destitute should be helped. If it is the case that this strategic move is properly recommended, this could signal at least two things.[55] First, it could signify moral shortcomings in the addressees of these calls for help, that is, the (relatively) wealthy and powerful Americans, who, according to Rorty, lack the moral vision to see that human suffering calls for ameliorative measures.[56] Second, and somewhat less plausibly, Americans could be appealing to their sense, as Americans, that they should not neglect coparticipants in their great national project. I believe that this option is less plausible because if we take a serious look at American history, it is evident that blacks in the United States were not considered to be coparticipants in that project. Consider a small sample of evidence from the history of the treatment of blacks in the United States. John Locke's *Fundamental Constitutions of Carolina* (1669), for instance, state that "every freeman of Carolina shall have absolute power and authority over his negro slaves,"[57] and in 1850 the morally indefensible Fugitive Slave Act was passed by Congress, signed by the president, and approved by the U.S. Supreme Court.[58] In many ways, the hopes of black Americans for equal treatment remain unrealized, and it is no wonder that the black U.S. Supreme Court Justice Thurgood Marshall, speaking at the Bicentennial of the Constitution in 1987, observed: "Some may . . . quietly commemorate the suffering, struggle, and sacrifice that has triumphed over much of what was wrong with the original document, and observe the anniversary with hopes not realized and promises not fulfilled."[59]

These elementary features of the American black experience threaten the credibility of Rorty's claims. Of course, black Americans once excluded are now, if only rhetorically, included in many contemporary conceptions of the American community. But as Marshall's words make clear and as the experiences of countless millions of black Americans bear witness, there are good grounds for suspicion of any appeal to a common project in which all Americans participate by virtue of their shared citizenship. There is, therefore, no moral argument we have yet seen that supports the restriction of arguments about justice for compatriots.

This discussion of Bell and Rorty has generated at least four positive conclusions. First, the fact that the prevailing view is that the nation-state is the proper focus of justice-related solidarity does nothing to show that this is the way things ought to be. Argument on this score is needed if the claim is to be maintained in the face of widespread global deprivation and suffering. Second, if solidaristic identification with others is a necessary condition for dependable commitment to a scheme of justice, cosmopolitan justice is precluded only if it can be shown that such identification is not possible with noncompatriots. That impossibility claim is deeply implausible. Third, once we admit that it is both possible and desirable to show concern for the victims of cruelty in faraway countries, there is no obvious reason for limiting our concern and opposition to acts of cruelty. It then becomes possible to recommend a worldwide scheme for the protection of basic human rights. Finally, despite claims to the contrary, it is not true that an argument from justice cannot appeal to the fact that it is wrong for a human being to suffer needlessly. If we phrase our arguments in terms of compatriots, as in the American appeal to the wrongness of "American" suffering, this can only be for strategic reasons that themselves suggest something about the moral corruption of contemporary ethical and political debate.

In closing, I want to return to another prominent discussion of one of the main issues on which I have been focusing. Richard

Rorty has addressed what he takes to be the question most in need of answering by "moral educators": "Why should I care about a stranger, a person who is no kin to me, a person whose habits I find disgusting?"[60] The following answer Rorty finds unconvincing: "Because kinship and custom are morally irrelevant, irrelevant to the obligations imposed by the recognition of membership in the same species." The problem with this answer, according to Rorty, is that it is "question begging"; it assumes that "mere species membership is . . . a sufficient surrogate for closer kinship."[61] If this is meant as an attack on a certain mode of cosmopolitan argument, it fails, for it misrepresents the role played in that argument by appealing to the fact of membership in the class of persons. The ties that we, as persons, have to other persons do not function as "surrogates" for the kinship ties we recognize (and value) toward those close to us. Rather, we neither can nor should renounce the close, deep relationships—and corresponding duties—we share with immediate family and trusted friends. But we do not have to choose between only two alternatives: (1) retaining kinship and friendship ties and (2) giving up those ties in favor of assuming obligations to all persons equally.

Rorty's accusation of circularity works only if impartial justice demands that we renounce kinship ties, but we have seen that impartiality, properly understood, requires just the opposite.

VII. Conclusion

This chapter has assessed the case for special duties to compatriots and the related question of the link between patriotism and obligations of global justice. I argued that compatriot favoritism is potentially compatible with a commitment to acting morally but that there is no sound, general rationale for being a compatriot favoritist. When considering patriotism and global justice, I defended cosmopolitanism against the central claims of MacIntyre, Fletcher, Bell, and Rorty on the ethical acceptability of favoring cocitizens over foreigners.

In conclusion, I should stress that my argument is not that no forms of partiality are justified. Am I saying that one is never justified in favoring one's own child over other children? Certainly not, but it is important to remember that even this legiti-mate version of favoritism itself is limited in its extent, because the reasons that justify such favoritism themselves suggest that impartial concern for others is a precondition for partiality. The problem of partiality is perhaps most evident when we consider global poverty: the absence of impartial justice may make valu-able forms of partiality impossible by denying some persons the material resources necessary for such partial conduct. Hence a proper concern for partiality requires that we focus on impartial justice. If impartial justice is not implemented globally, the par-tiality that is properly valued by many people—theorist and nontheorist alike—will lack the resource base necessary to make it meaningful, since preferential treatment does not (in many cases) adequately answer to the needs of many of the vulnera-ble.[62]

In any case, it is vital to recognize that the type of partiality with which we have been concerned is patriotism, and our ques-tion has been to evaluate the case for preferring compatriots to noncompatriots when determining the appropriate distribu-tions of benefits and burdens. While partiality is justified in the interactions of individuals with one another (though only when it is also consistent with impartiality), the concerns of justice are not addressed to this interactional level. Rather, appropriate principles of international justice aim to provide the theoretical underpinning for an institutional framework that can be de-fended to each person affected by that framework. My claim is that there are no good grounds for setting up a distributive scheme in such a way that the strength of a person's legitimate claims depends on that person's citizenship.[63]

NOTES

1. By "cosmopolitanism" I mean an egalitarian, universalist individ-ualism that requires moral argument to proceed by reference to impar-tial principles. The fundamental idea is that each person affected by an institutional arrangement should be given equal consideration. Indi-viduals are the basic units of moral concern, and the interests of indi-viduals should be taken into account by adopting an impartial stand-

point for evaluation. For related suggestions, see Charles Beitz, "Cosmopolitan Liberalism and the States System," in Chris Brown, ed., *Political Restructuring in Europe: Ethical Perspectives* (London: Routledge, 1994), pp. 123–27.

2. I set out the case for basic human rights to subsistence in Charles Jones, *Global Justice: Defending Cosmopolitanism* (Oxford: Oxford University Press, 1999), chap. 3.

3. A good example of constitutive theory may be found in Mervyn Frost, *Toward a Normative Theory of International Relations* (Cambridge: Cambridge University Press, 1986).

4. According to one interpretation, Michael Walzer defends a version of relativism in this sense in his *Spheres of Justice: A Defense of Pluralism and Equality* (Oxford: Basil Blackwell, 1983).

5. From this perspective, David Miller's *On Nationality* (Oxford: Clarendon Press, 1995) is the most thoughtful account.

6. In this discussion, I focus on the general question of heightened concern for one's compatriots, understood here as cocitizens of a nation-state. I therefore place no special emphasis on the distinction between conationals and cocitizens. Since the differences between these two types of group are potentially of great ethical importance, an adequate survey would turn to the issue of nationality as an ethical value for persons, as distinct from the value of shared citizenship, and would clarify the relation between nationality and global justice. I attempt this in *Global Justice*, chap. 6.

7. Ronald Dworkin, *Law's Empire* (Cambridge, Mass.: Harvard University Press, 1986), pp. 199–200.

8. A. John Simmons, "Associative Political Obligations," *Ethics* 106 (1996): 261. For an additional, related criticism of Dworkin's approach, accusing it of risking circularity by presupposing the justice of certain types of favoritism, see Simon Caney, "Individuals, Nations and Obligations," in Simon Caney, David George, and Peter Jones, eds., *National Rights, International Obligations* (Oxford: Westview Press, 1996), 133.

9. I am not denying that the granting of citizenship to immigrants can be, and often is, an extremely important matter, for both the admitting country and the applicants. My point is simply that its importance is not what it would be if, as the exclusionary patriot maintains, the granting of citizenship to a person were at the same time the recognition of that person as a moral subject.

10. Stephen Nathanson, "In Defense of 'Moderate Patriotism'," *Ethics* 99 (1989): 538, similarly rejects what he calls "extreme patriot-

ism," whose defining feature is its wholesale exclusion of noncompatriots from ethical concern.

11. Brian Barry, "Can States Be Moral? International Morality and
the Compliance Problem," in his *Liberty and Justice: Essays in Political
Theory*, vol. 2 (Oxford: Clarendon Press, 1991), p. 165.

12. See Hans Morgenthau, *In Defense of the National Interest: A Critical Examination of American Foreign Policy* (New York: Knopf, 1951), pp.
35–36. I am grateful to Simon Caney for reminding me of this realist
strategy.

13. Henry Shue, *Basic Rights: Subsistence, Affluence, and U.S. Foreign
Policy* (Princeton, N.J.: Princeton University Press, 1980), pp. 131–32.
Shue is not himself a defender of compatriot favoritism.

14. Samuel Gorovitz, "Bigotry, Loyalty, and Malnutrition," in Peter
G. Brown and Henry Shue, eds., *Food Policy* (New York: Free Press,
1977), p. 133.

15. One might think that it is only the patriot who needs to give
some account of the moral character of compatriot relationships. However, my view is that both sides have an interest in developing such an
account, since there are strong conflicting intuitions both for and
against impartial concern and compatriot priority. Moreover, in order
to evaluate their own position, cosmopolitans need to discover whether
patriotism has powerful moral credentials.

16. Stephen Nathanson, *Patriotism, Morality, and Peace* (Lanham,
Md.: Rowman & Littlefield, 1993), p. 67.

17. Cf. Marcia Baron, "Patriotism and 'Liberal' Morality," in D.
Weissbord, ed., *Mind, Value and Culture* (Northridge, Calif.: Ridgeview,
1989), pp. 269–300. I have also been influenced here by what is now
the best discussion of the partiality/impartiality dispute: Brian Barry,
Justice as Impartiality (Oxford: Clarendon Press, 1995), part 3.

18. Nathanson, *Patriotism, Morality, and Peace*, p. 27.

19. Gorovitz, "Bigotry, Loyalty, and Malnutrition," p. 135.

20. Alasdair MacIntyre, "Is Patriotism a Virtue?" Lindley Lecture
(Lawrence: University of Kansas Press, 1984), p. 6.

21. By using the word *fanaticism* here, I do not mean to engage in
argumentative bullying. In the following paragraphs I show why the
word is justified in this case. That is, I think that first-order impartial-
ists are overly enthusiastic about the admittedly important idea that the
virtue of impartiality is central to a defensible account of morality, and
their enthusiasm blinds them to the further distinctions it is necessary
to make.

22. William Godwin, *An Enquiry Concerning Political Justice and Its In-*

fluence on Morals and Happiness, 3d ed. 1798, in *Political and Philosophical Writings of William Godwin*, ed. Mark Philp (London: William Pickering, 1993), vol. 4. The attentive reader will recognize my debt to the discussion in Barry, *Justice as Impartiality*, chap. 9.

23. See Thomas E. Hill Jr., "The Importance of Autonomy," in Eva Feder Kittay and Diana T. Meyers, eds., *Women and Moral Theory* (Lanham, Md.: Rowman & Littlefield, 1987), pp. 131–33. As Hill says, the idea that "we should live with our eyes fixed on abstract, impartial principles seems quite the opposite of what autonomous [that is, impartial] moral legislators would recommend" (p. 132).

24. Bernard Williams, "Persons, Character, and Morality," in his *Moral Luck: Philosophical Papers 1973–80* (Cambridge: Cambridge University Press, 1981), pp. 1–19.

25. I should make it clear that I disagree with Andrew Belsey, "World Poverty, Justice, and Equality," in Robin Attfield and Barry Wilkins, eds., *International Justice and the Third World: Studies in the Philosophy of Development* (London: Routledge, 1992), pp. 40–42, who thinks that favoring one's wife in this case is necessarily a veiled form of selfishness.

26. See Barry, *Justice as Impartiality*, p. 219.

27. Williams, "Persons, Character, and Morality," p. 18. Just for the record, I think it is probably a moral requirement of a husband in such a case to save his wife (or for a wife to save her husband). My substantive conclusion would then differ from both Godwin (who says that wife saving is in this case forbidden) and Williams (who says that wife saving is in this case merely permitted).

28. Perhaps Williams would agree that calm, reasoned justification is indeed necessary, in which case I have no quarrel with him. The problem of interpretation here stems from a fundamental lack of clarity as to whether or not reasons are thought to be necessary in the decision-making situation itself and/or in the relative calm of one's study, when one is considering what it would be right to do if one were faced with such an unpalatable choice. I am here interpreting Williams as saying that reasons are unnecessary in either case. Thus interpreted, Williams and I disagree.

29. This point was emphasized by Samuel Scheffler in "Families, Nations and Strangers," Lindley Lecture 1994 (Lawrence: University of Kansas Press, 1995), pp. 9–12.

30. Nathanson, *Patriotism, Morality, and Peace*, pp. 118–19.

31. I am referring here to the handicapped to whom we correctly think we owe a duty of justice. I do not intend to defend the behavior of free riders who are able to contribute but choose not to do so.

32. Robert E. Goodin, *Protecting the Vulnerable: A Reanalysis of Our Social Responsibilities* (Chicago: University of Chicago Press, 1985), develops the vulnerability model at some length. However, he thinks it provides support for compatriot favoritism only within certain limits.

33. This was pointed out in, among others, Shue's *Basic Rights*, pp. 137–38; and George P. Fletcher's *Loyalty: An Essay on the Morality of Relationships* (Oxford: Oxford University Press, 1993), p. 58.

34. These potential foundations for compatriot priority are discussed by Shue in *Basic Rights*, p. 135.

35. MacIntyre, "Is Patriotism a Virtue?" p. 6.

36. Ibid.

37. See Nathanson, *Patriotism, Morality, and Peace*, p. 82.

38. Self-interest may dictate peace, but only when the state with whom one's own state's interests conflict is strong enough to withstand attack and to inflict damage on one's own state.

39. Fletcher, *Loyalty*, p. 20.

40. On the other hand, imagine how credible a commitment of "loyalty to everyone on the planet" might look as a response to an invasion of the earth by strange and violent extraterrestrials!

41. In *Global Justice*, chap. 6, I address a related point made by David Miller on the question of the relation between fulfilling duties at home and fulfilling similar duties to outsiders. As I point out there, the Scandinavian countries show more concern for fellow citizens and give far more international aid than do other countries.

42. Fletcher, *Loyalty*, p. 21.

43. Ibid.

44. Ibid.

45. These points are related to Terry Nardin's defense of international society as a practical, nonpurposive association in *Law, Morality, and the Relations of States* (Princeton, N.J.: Princeton University Press, 1983). International society might be understood to be committed to a common cause if by this we mean that the demands of justice must be met by every state. But if this is Nardin's view, it would seem to be a long way from an Oakeshottian account of international politics (that is, Nardin's aim), according to which, one would have thought, meeting those demands would constitute a commitment to an illegitimate enterprise. For further discussion of Nardin's views, see Chris Brown, *International Relations Theory: New Normative Approaches* (Hemel Hempstead: Harvester-Wheatsheaf, 1992), pp. 124 ff.

46. Shue, *Basic Rights*, p. 146.

47. Cf. Geoffrey Scarre, *Utilitarianism* (London: Routledge, 1996), p. 36.

170   CHARLES JONES

48. Fletcher, *Loyalty*, p. 35.

49. Daniel Bell, *Communitarianism and Its Critics* (Oxford: Clarendon Press, 1993).

50. Ibid., pp. 137–38.

51. Cf. Stephen Nathanson, "In Defense of 'Moderate Patriotism'," *Ethics* 99 (1989): 549.

52. Bell, *Communitarianism and Its Critics*, p. 150.

53. Richard Rorty, *Contingency, Irony, and Solidarity* (Cambridge: Cambridge University Press, 1989), p. 191, italics in original.

54. Bell, *Communitarianism and Its Critics*, pp. 150–51.

55. There is good reason to doubt the effectiveness of pointing out that "it is outrageous that an American should live without hope." If we maintain that this sort of claim is "morally as well as politically" persuasive, we would have to point to instances in which this strategy had a noticeable effect.

56. One of the problems with Rorty's view is that he does not think that the need to put one's arguments in terms of "us" rather than "human beings" suggests anything morally amiss with the prevailing condition of moral debate.

57. Cited in Howard Zinn, *Declarations of Independence: Cross-Examining American Ideology* (New York: HarperCollins, 1990), p. 234.

58. Ibid., p. 237.

59. Ibid., p. 232.

60. Richard Rorty, "Human Rights, Rationality, and Sentimentality," in Stephen Shute and Susan Hurley, eds., *On Human Rights: The Oxford Amnesty Lectures 1993* (New York: Basic Books, 1993), p. 133.

61. Ibid.

62. This point is well made in Marilyn Friedman's *What Are Friends For? Feminist Perspectives on Personal Relationships and Moral Theory* (Ithaca, N.Y.: Cornell University Press, 1993), p. 75: "We live in a world in which many people do not have adequate resources for caring for their loved ones effectively. Under these circumstances the social practices by which we each favor only our respective 'own,' if untempered by any methods for redistributing caretaking resources, would result in gravely inadequate care for many of the world's people."

63. I am grateful to John Baker, Brian Barry, Simon Caney, John Charvet, Will Kymlicka, Susan Mendus, David Miller, Stephen Nathanson, Ian Shapiro, and Alan Weir for helpful comments on an earlier version of this article. I also gladly acknowledge the indispensable financial assistance provided by the Social Sciences and Humanities Research Council of Canada and University College Cork's Boole Fellowship in Philosophy.

7

JUST TAXATION AND INTERNATIONAL REDISTRIBUTION

HILLEL STEINER

I. COMPOSSIBLE RIGHTS

What should we provide to other persons, and what do we morally owe them? Most people, I think, would agree that these two questions are not equivalent and that we can make little headway toward understanding the demands of justice unless we see the various items sought in the second question as forming only a subset of those sought in the first. There are many things—goods and services, including services of forbearance—that we ought to provide to others and that we would therefore do wrong to withhold from them. Their flourishing, their autonomy, their liberty, often their very survival, vitally depend on such provision. Yet only some of these things can be said to be owed to them. Only some of these correlate to rights in those persons. Only some of them are concerns of justice. Which ones?

Evidently, answers to this question vary substantially from one conception of justice to another: memberships in the set of owed things are notoriously contested, though some are more contested than others. Among the less controversial are those items that we owe as restitution; that is, no theory of justice that I know of treats the deprivation consequent on a rights violation simply as a regrettable piece of misfortune occasioning no claim in its victim.[1] Thus, the owed status of those items is due to their (sometimes imperfect) capacity to substitute for other owed things and to compensate for our failures to provide them.

A second type of owed thing—at least as uncontroversial as restitutions—consists of those items that we contractually undertake to provide.[2] Even so meager a conception of justice as Hobbes's seems to underwrite their inclusion. Hobbes's account of the matter also serves to remind us how problematic even contractual duties can be, how contracts can fail to be worth the actual or hypothetical paper they are written on. My contractual undertaking to supply you with the Brooklyn Bridge fails to vest me with a duty to do so (and fails to vest you with the right correlative to that duty) if I have already given such an undertaking to someone else or, more generally, if the Brooklyn Bridge is not mine to supply.

For what is true of both restitutional and contractual duties to provide is that they unavoidably presuppose rights on the part of the putative providers. They presuppose their antecedent rights to whatever it is that they owe. Thus we might usefully characterize these presupposed rights as *prior rights* and the rights doing the presupposing—the rights correlatively entailed by restitutional and contractual duties—as *posterior rights*.[3]

Even if what I owe you is (merely?) a forbearance, it is clear that others' noninterference with its provision is a necessary condition of my being able to provide it and, thus, of my having a duty to do so.[4] If, contrarily, others do interfere and, moreover, are at liberty, empowered, or even duty bound to do so, then the set of rules sustaining my forbearance duty and their liberty (power, duty) is incoherent. It generates a set of incompossible rights, and such sets imply contradictory judgments about the permissibility of particular actions.[5]

So if the set of restitutionally and contractually owed things is to be a possible set, if none of these duties to provide is to be deemed invalid because it cannot be fulfilled, it must be embedded in a larger set of owed things: a set that therefore includes *non*posteriorly owed things. As Hobbes correctly perceived, I cannot have a duty to forbear from blocking your exit if others, who have a right "even to my own body," install it permanently in the doorway. Nor can I owe you the corn I contracted to deliver if others, lacking a duty not to deprive me of it, do so.

This key feature of the logic of compossible rights is succinctly captured in Locke's remark that "where there is no property, there is no injustice."[6] Injustices, we are presuming, consist at least of nonfulfillments of restitutional and contractual duties. For such injustice to be possible, for such duties to exist, they must be fulfillable. A set of jointly fulfillable posterior duties presupposes a further set of duties that are thus nonposterior and that protect the domains—the action spaces—in which posterior duties can be fulfilled free from anyone's permissible interference.[7] And of course, those nonposterior, domain-protecting duties must themselves be jointly fulfillable ones. Hence and as Locke's remark suggests, it requires no great conceptual strain to see these domains—these zones of noninterference—as consisting of property rights.

II. THE GLOBAL FUND

If the set of owed things must include a core subset of forbearances—prior negative duties not to encroach on others' domains—what are the contents of those domains? The immediate answer is that these are bewilderingly variable. Who owns what or, conversely, who owes whom forbearance from interference with what activities, is plainly not a question that can be interestingly answered in the abstract. The contents of respective domains vary enormously both temporally and interpersonally, for the simple reason that domain owners have—and tend continuously to exercise—protected liberties to engage in multifarious activities amounting to transformations of those contents and/or transferences of them to the domains of others.

What can be answered in the abstract is what sort of rule can justly constrain the initial formation of those domains. Given their highly variegated contents and the corresponding variety of forbearances correlatively owed to their several owners, what sort of rule appropriately determines the initial conditions from which all this variegating activity then generates permissible

departures? In short, what must persons' initial domains be like
to be just?

It is a sufficiently agreed feature of justice that however varied
and complex its complete set of distributive demands may be
seen to be under different theories, there is some foundational
level at which equality is the appropriate norm. Precisely what
must be distributed equally and, consequently, what sorts of
thing may be distributed unequally remain a matter of philosophical dispute. But that something requires equal interpersonal distribution seems to be an intrinsic feature of justice,
however it is construed.[8]

According to the view being developed here from the requirements of rights compossibility, the items to be justly equalized
are persons' initial domains: the ultimately antecedent or prior
rights that they have and successively transform and transfer to
create posterior rights and duties for themselves and others. So
those ultimately prior rights look like being ones to *untrans*-
formed and *un*transferred things. Others' ultimately prior duties are to refrain from interfering with the varying dispositional
choices that each makes in respect of those things. If each person is justly vested with an equal initial domain, it follows that
each is justly bound by correlative duties of equal initial forbearance. What things, then, can count as untransformed and un-
transferred?

Here we could do worse than again to follow Locke's general
guidance and construe such things as being of two basic types:
our bodies and raw natural resources.[9] To say that persons have
the initial rights to their own bodies is not to deny that they are
at liberty to transform or transfer parts of those bodies or those
bodies' labor—or, more generally, to invest those things in pursuit of their several ends—and thereby successively to modify
those initial rights. It is to imply only that others' initial forbearance duties include not interfering with their doing so. These
various duties of equal initial forbearance—this foundational
bundle of entirely negative duties—can thus be compendiously
construed as correlating to the initial rights of self-ownership
vested in each person, initial rights against any form of enslave-
ment or lesser servitude.

But if equal initial domains—equal initial action spaces—give us each titles to our bodies, they must also give us titles to things external to our bodies, since unimpeded access to such things is a necessary condition for the occurrence of any action. And this is where raw natural resources come to figure as the other constituents of those domains. Part of our foundational set of duties of equal initial forbearance are duties to acquire no more than an equal portion of such resources, leaving (as Locke put it) "enough and as good for others."[10]

What if some persons acquire more than this, leaving others with less? Then presumably the former, having defaulted on their duties of initial forbearance to the latter, owe them restitution. This compensation, whatever form it may take, must be equivalent to the value of what has been overacquired. So here we have a case of noncontractual but nonetheless positive duties to provide goods: duties that, though noncontractual, are clearly in the owed category and correlate to rights vested in those to whom they are owed. These are not what Brian Barry aptly characterized as "duties of humanity," and indeed, their validity is in no way predicated on their beneficiaries being in a state of need.[11] These duties are ones of justice and they arise, posteriorily, as straightforward restitutional implications of the overacquirers' failure to comply with their prior negative duties of forbearance.

It is not hard to see how this line of thinking begins to approach the issue of just international redistribution. The world's raw natural resources are compendiously describable as constituting a set of territorial sites, and the value of any such site is the sum of the values of all the sub- and supraterranean resources, as well as the surface areas, it comprises.[12] The aggregate global value of these sites thus constitutes the *dividend* in the Lockean computation of what "enough and as good for others" amounts to. No doubt this aggregate global value fluctuates over time, as does the magnitude of the Lockean *divisor*, that is, the number of others that there are. Whatever these fluctuations may be, each person's initial domain includes a right to the *quotient*: a right to an equal portion of the aggregate global value of territorial sites.

Elsewhere, I have suggested that we can conveniently conceive of the rights and duties implied by this argument as jointly constituting a global fund.[13] Liabilities to pay into the fund accrue to owners of territorial sites and are equal to the value of the sites they own, and claims to equal shares of that fund are vested in everyone. The global fund is thus a mechanism for ensuring that each person enjoys the equivalent of enough and as good natural resources.[14]

An essential characteristic of nations is that they are actual or aspiring claimants of territorial sites. The scope of their jurisdictional claims extends not only to sections of the global surface but also to the resources found below them and the airspace, portions of the electromagnetic spectrum, and so forth located above them. Private persons and state agencies who control the use of these things usually have a fairly shrewd idea of what they are worth. They know that an acre on the Bangladeshi coast is worth less than an acre in the center of Tokyo. Accordingly, the global fund's levy on the ownership of the latter will be greater than on the ownership of the former.[15]

Of course, within the limits of what justice permits, nations are presumably licensed to determine their own domestic objectives and to deploy the range of redistributive measures appropriate to those ends. But what justice clearly does not permit is their determining the distributive entitlements of persons outside their respective jurisdictions. Thus, although the full value of that Tokyo acre is justly owed to the global fund, whether liability for its payment should fall exclusively on its owner or should be financed in some other way may be a matter for decision by Japanese political-choice processes. What cannot justly be a matter for such political choices is the amount owed to the global fund for Japanese territorial sites.

The core idea here, that just redistribution is to be funded by an egalitarian allocation of natural resource values, is not a novel one. Nor should its Lockean origins be allowed to obscure the fact that it has more recently come to figure—in one form or another—in a wide variety of conceptions of justice, many of which are distinctly un-Lockean in provenance. Indeed, several of these accounts have similarly extended this idea to the international plane. It is on the two most developed such accounts that I wish now to focus, since, in my view, their lack of Lockean foundations seriously impairs the coherence of that extension.

III. Against Beitz

Charles Beitz has advanced what must count as one of the first sustained attempts to derive an argument for international redistribution from a more general theory of justice.[16] His claim is that Rawlsian theory can underwrite the extension of the difference principle to the international plane in two ways. As is familiar, Rawls sees this principle as determining a fair distribution of the benefits and burdens produced by social cooperation. Rawls's mistake, in Beitz's view, is to assume that the boundaries of the cooperative schemes to which this principle applies are given by the notion of a self-contained national community. For the facts of contemporary international relations—in particular, the interdependence resulting from international investment and trade—indicate that the world is not made up of self-contained nations but imply the existence of a global scheme of social cooperation.[17]

But Beitz wants to go further and to privilege one kind of international redistribution by liberating the case for it from any reliance on these contingent facts of contemporary international relations. Accordingly, he argues that even if we counterfactually suspend the assumption of such functioning schemes of social cooperation and interdependence, the veiled parties to a set of Rawlsian international contractual deliberations would nonetheless know that natural resources are distributed unevenly over the earth's surface. Hence they "would view this distribution of resources much as Rawls says the parties to the domestic original-position deliberations view the distribution of natural talents."[18] That is, these contracting parties—each appropriately ignorant of their comparative territorial circumstances—would regard this natural resource distribution as a morally arbitrary fact and, consequently, the benefits derived from these resources as justly subject to redistribution.

Beitz is not slow to acknowledge the problematic aspects of Rawls's view that the natural talent distribution is morally arbitrary. These problems have been well rehearsed in the literature and include such considerations as the fact that

> natural capacities are parts of the self, in the development of which a person might take a special kind of pride. A person's decision to develop one talent, not to develop another, as well as his or her choice as to how the talent is to be formed, and the uses to which it is to be put, are likely to be important elements of the effort to shape an identity. The complex of developed talents might even be said to constitute the self.[19]

Because talents are tied to persons as identity-constituting elements, their location and consequent relative interpersonal distribution do not seem best described as morally arbitrary. Indeed, it is plausibly suggested that persons' claims to their talents are protected by considerations of personal liberty, that is, by Rawls's lexically prior first principle.[20]

Moreover, this line of reasoning suggests another important respect, unremarked by Beitz, in which differential talent distribution may be an unlikely candidate for moral arbitrariness. For even if—at some cost to the standard interpretation of his principles—Rawls were thus to concede nonarbitrariness to the distribution of self-developed talents, he might still wish to insist on the arbitrariness of the distribution of pre-self-developed ones. Indeed, it is precisely this distinction that is underwriting his attribution of arbitrariness to talent differentials, in his insistent imputation of those differentials to individuals' differential genetic endowments and background social circumstances.

Yet even this concession would not suffice to sustain his thereby modified arbitrariness claim. For if my talent's being constitutive of my self is conceded to be a matter of moral relevance, the fact that its initial development occurred at the hands of others—notably, my parents—rather than my own, does not obviously deprive it of that relevance. Parents typically choose whether to attach considerable value to, and invest considerable sacrifice in, the development of their children's talents or, more generally, their capacities.[21] Consequently, it is misleading to characterize the level of talent we possess when we arrive at the threshold of adulthood and moral agency as fully imputable to chance contingencies, insofar as this is suggested by a phrase like "background social circumstances," a phrase that implausibly leaves delinquent parents morally blameless.[22]

In any case, Beitz argues—and however problematic may thus be Rawls's construal of talent differentials as arbitrary—no such difficulty attends the claim that nations' natural resource differentials are similarly arbitrary. "The natural distribution of resources is a purer case of something being 'arbitrary from a moral point of view' than the distribution of talents."[23] The two cases are said to be importantly *dis*analogous and for two reasons. First, and unlike talents, natural resources cannot be understood as constitutive of selves. Hence the denial that they are tied to persons in morally relevant ways does not engender the sorts of problem associated with the corresponding denial in regard to talents. Second, and unlike talent acquisition, natural resource appropriation is a rivalrous affair: "The appropriation of scarce resources by some requires a justification against the competing claims of others."[24] There must be principled reasons that the latter should bear the opportunity cost of refraining from the beneficial use of resources that are no one's product and of which the former's appropriation deprives them. The only plausible such reason for that forbearance appears to be that, by so doing, forbearers become entitled to a share of those benefits.

Consistent as this conclusion is with the Lockean one advanced previously, two serious difficulties beset Beitz's manner of reaching it. In the first place, it is unclear that postulating the competing claims of others, as a warrant for the presence of Rawlsian distributive concerns, is consistent with his counterfactual suspension of the assumption that the world is not made up of self-contained nations and that international relations therefore exhibit functioning schemes of social cooperation and interdependence. For situations in which some persons' appropriative claims compete with those of others and these groups are each (members of) different nations, are unmistakably situations in which the nations involved cannot be described as "self-contained." One group's self-denying respect for the claims of the other, whose otherwise unattainable level of prosperity thereby depends on that forbearance, would surely be an instance of what Rawls often refers to as the "burdens of cooperation."[25] This implies the presence, not the absence, of international cooperation and interdependence.

Equally significantly, it is unclear that Beitz is correct to claim that natural resources lack the identity-constituting quality of natural talents. It would be patently absurd to think of them as constitutive of individuals' selves: a resource's owner is fully identifiable without any reference to that resource. But within the Rawlsian framework, that is not the relevant point of comparison. Nor, therefore, does it support Beitz's disanalogy claim. For on his own reading of it, the Rawlsian forum for fashioning principles of international justice is a second original position: one that, unlike the first, is populated not by individuals but, rather, by nations.[26] And it would be difficult, to say the least, to think of any single feature—or combination of them—that is less controversially constitutive of a nation's identity than its territorial site.[27]

So I am driven to conclude that Beitz is unsuccessful in his attempt to use the Rawlsian framework to underwrite the international redistribution of natural resource differentials. The charge of distributional arbitrariness, which is what usually occasions redistribution in Rawlsian theory, is not made to stick. And since the special case—for privileging the redistribution of those differentials as noncontingently just—is one that relies on the inconsistently sustained heuristic assumption of noninterdependent nations, that case also fails.

IV. AGAINST POGGE

More recently, Thomas Pogge has been similarly engaged in constructing an international extension of Rawlsian principles for just redistribution.[28] But his enterprise begins with an explicit caveat on what Rawls actually says about the basis for that extension, although it is a caveat that Pogge sees as amply warranted by more fundamental Rawlsian commitments. Rawls, as was noted, conceives of the principles of international justice as chosen in a second original position, the parties to which are nations, not individuals. Pogge—persuasively in my view—argues that the arrangements that would emerge from such a situation "would be incompatible with Rawls's individualistic conviction that in matters of social justice only *persons* are to be viewed as ultimate units of (equal) moral concern."[29] In support of this claim about Rawlsian justice and individualism, he quotes a passage that might well have come straight out of Nozick's *Anarchy, State and Utopia* but that, in fact, is Rawls's own methodological statement that

> we want to account for the social values, for the intrinsic good of institutional, community, and associative activities, by a conception of justice that in its theoretical basis is individualistic. For reasons of clarity among others, we do not want to rely on an undefined concept of community, or to suppose that society is an organic whole with a life of its own distinct from and superior to that of all its members in their relations with one another. . . . From this conception, however individualistic it may seem, we must eventually explain the value of community.[30]

A person's nationality, Pogge suggests, is just one more deep contingency (like genetic endowment, race, gender, and social class) that is present from birth and operates as a morally arbitrary factor in generating interpersonal inequalities. Accordingly, it is more consonant with the individualistic spirit of the Rawlsian project that parties to the second original position be persons, not nations—and even more consonant that there be only a single (person-populated) original position that generates a single set of norms for global application.[31]

All this seems to be going in the right direction as far as the Lockean view, advanced previously, is concerned. Leaving aside their deep differences over the foundationalism of contracts,[32] both the Lockean and Poggean positions conceive just principles as generating a set of egalitarian individual redistributive entitlements of global scope. Moreover, Pogge, too, sees natural resource values as especially eligible to fund these entitlements. My complaint, as with Beitz's argument, is that the case for this eligibility is not convincingly made out—though for different reasons.

Pogge's mechanism for this egalitarian redistribution is one that he dubs the *Global Resources Tax* (GRT).[33] Like Beitz, his claim for its privileged plausibility rests on its alleged nonreliance on several highly defensible theoretical and empirical assumptions that would lend it even greater support. Specifically, he believes the case for it can be made even if we accept (1) that the forum for choosing international principles is to be a second original position populated only by nations; (2) that each of these nations is a "people," that is, is a linguistically, ethnically, culturally, and historically homogeneous unit; and (3) that no injustice has attended the emergence of current national borders. Although Pogge himself accepts none of these propositions—ones that he finds present in Rawls[34]—his project is to vindicate GRT despite this "self-imposed triple handicap."[35]

So what, then, is GRT?

> The basic idea is that, while each people owns and fully controls all resources within its national territory, it must pay a tax on any resources it chooses to extract. The Saudi people, for example, would not be required to extract crude oil or to allow others to do so. But if they chose to do so nonetheless, they would be required to pay a proportional tax on any crude extracted, whether it be for their own use or for sale abroad. This tax could be extended, along the same lines, to reusable resources: to land used in agriculture and ranching, for example, and, especially, to air and water used for the discharging of pollutants.[36]

Pogge argues that although the incidence of such a tax would fall exclusively on resource owners, its burdens would not, inasmuch as it would raise prices for consumer goods and services in proportion to their natural resource content, that is, in proportion to "how much value they take from our planet." The cost of gasoline would contain a higher proportion of GRT than would the cost of a museum ticket.

In another passage, Pogge suggests that the theoretical appeal of this tax ought to be very wide indeed:

> The GRT can therefore be motivated not only forwardlookingly, in consequentialist and contractualist terms, but also backward-lookingly: as a proviso on unilateral appropriation, which requires compensation to those excluded thereby. Nations (or persons) may appropriate and use resources, but humankind at large still retains a kind of minority stake, which, somewhat like preferred stock, confers no control but a share of the material benefits. In this picture, my proposal can be presented as a global re-

sources dividend, which operates as a modern Lockean proviso. It differs from Locke's own proviso by giving up the vague and unwieldy condition of "leaving enough and as good for others." One may use unlimited amounts, but one must share some of the economic benefit. It is nevertheless similar enough to the original so that even such notoriously antiegalitarian thinkers as Locke and Nozick might find it plausible.[37]

Pogge then offers a perceptive discussion of the moral, political, and economic problems of both setting the Rawlsian-optimal rate of GRT and ensuring the intended redistribution of its proceeds. Some of these problems are indeed ones facing any redistributive global tax. However, the issue I wish to address is the prior one of whether GRT, as described, actually does possess the broad theoretical appeal Pogge attributes to it.

Clearly, and leaving aside the disputable claims about Locke's antiegalitarianism and the vagueness and unwieldiness of his own proviso, GRT at first glance appears to come very close to the Lockean-inspired global fund proposal advanced earlier. It, too, sponsors a global resources dividend by entitling everyone to a share of the benefits from natural resources that only some unilaterally control. The difference—and it is one of the utmost theoretical relevance here—lies in their respective identifications of the tax base to be used.

In Pogge's account, that base is the aggregate value of only *used* resources, with only some proportion of that value to be taxed. Whereas for the global fund (and, I think, for Beitz), that base is the aggregate value of *owned* resources—whether used or not—with that value to be taxed at a rate of 100 percent.

To see the significance of this difference, let's return to Pogge's example of Saudi oil. Suppose there is a large oil deposit located beneath the Ka'aba mosque in Mecca. If, as Pogge is heuristically assuming, each nation is to be taken as a fully homogeneous unit; if it owns and fully controls all resources in its territory and is not required to extract, or to allow others to extract, any of these resources; and if it is required to pay GRT on only those resources that it does choose to extract, then we can be reasonably certain that the Ka'aba oil will not be extracted. Nor, therefore, will it be GRT taxed, whereas the ownership of that site, like any other, would be global fund taxed to the full extent of its natural resource value. This does not imply that under the global fund, the Saudis would be required to defile that sacred site and sink wells to extract the oil it contains. It implies only, in Pogge's own terms, that in unilaterally appropriating that site, they must compensate those thereby excluded. What they choose to do with that site is justly up to them.

The more general theoretical point here is simply this: If nations are presumed to be homogeneous in the way Pogge is counterfactually stipulating and if they are to be fully sovereign over the natural resources in their territorial sites, then some set of what Pogge calls "collective values and preferences"—some common conception of the good—will inform the domestic rules regulating the use of those resources. For some nations, these regulations will be far less restrictive and will allow far more extraction or varieties of use than are permitted by other nations' value sets. Rules regulating the extraction of American oil will, we might assume, be less restrictive than their counterparts in some other places. And one question thus is: Who should justly bear the costs of each nation's value set? For of any two nations with equal resource endowments, the more restrictive one will contribute less GRT than its counterpart does. Yet other things being equal, both will receive the same share of the total revenue thereby yielded. From an egalitarian perspective, from a global fund perspective—perhaps from *any* perspective— it looks as though the value set of the former is being subsidized by the latter. And this seems sufficient grounds to eliminate at least Lockeans and Nozickians from Pogge's list of theoretical constituencies who will find GRT attractive.

It is true that the question for Pogge is not directly the one just posed: Who should justly bear the costs of each nation's value set? Rather, it is, What natural resource tax would the nations, which are the veiled parties to the second and international original position, rationally choose? This is how that former, more direct question must be couched in the broad Rawlsian contractualist framework that Pogge embraces. More specifically, would they choose GRT or the global fund?

How should we approach the answer to this question? I assume that each nation's being veiled in ignorance means that it is crucially unaware of two things. It does not know whether and to what extent it is resource rich or resource poor, that is, above or below average in its resource endowment. Similarly, it is ignorant of the content of its value set, that is, whether and to what extent it is use restrictive or use permissive with regard to natural resources. With these two variables in play, all that each nation can know is that when the veil is lifted, it will find that it occupies one of four positions: (1) it is resource rich and use restrictive; (2) it is resource rich and use permissive; (3) it is resource poor and use permissive; or (4) it is resource poor and use restrictive. Being use restrictive lowers one's liability to GRT but not to the global fund, whereas being resource rich raises one's liability to the global fund but not to GRT. Thus, as we have seen, under GRT but not the global fund, a resource-rich nation whose value set is strongly informed by, say, "green" concerns or location-based religious ones, will contribute less to international redistribution than will an equally resource-rich nation whose value set assigns less prominence to such restrictive concerns.

In general, the global fund promises a higher tax yield for this redistribution than does GRT, for two reasons. The first is that it taxes owned resources rather than used resources and the latter are only a subset of the former. Second, in taxing only use, GRT rate setters must consider the disincentive effects of setting that tax rate too high. Whereas the global fund rate is invariable at 100 percent, the GRT rate must not be so high as to discourage the use of those (fewer) resources that are not subject to use restrictions. It is, of course, a matter of empirical investigation as to what higher tax rate will deliver a lower total tax yield than some lower tax rate. But we know almost certainly that a GRT rate of 100 percent on what is in any case a lower maximum tax base will strongly discourage the use of all those resources. So compared with the global fund, GRT labors under a double handicap in seeking to maximize funds for global redistribution and is bound to deliver less. And this seems sufficient grounds to eliminate consequentialists, as well, from Pogge's list of theoretical constituencies who will find it attractive.

Can GRT retain some appeal for, at least, Rawlsians? Would rational choosers behind their veil of ignorance prefer it to the global fund? I think that although there are strong reasons to

suppose otherwise, nevertheless and under Pogge's heuristic assumptions, the answer is ultimately yes—but at a significant cost.
Let us first look at those strong reasons against it.

From a Rawlsian perspective, the global fund also labors
under a redistributive handicap, namely, that it must distribute
its proceeds equally to all and cannot target them to the worst
off. Although an equal share of global fund proceeds is bound to
be greater than an equal share of GRT proceeds, Rawlsian *maximin* does not require such proceeds to be distributed equally.
Hence whether it would be GRT or the global fund that maxi-
mizes the receipts of the worst off would depend entirely on the
aggregate yield of GRT, which in turn depends on both the proportion of global resources that are not subject to domestic use
restriction and the optimal tax rate that can be levied on them.
In some circumstances, it would be GRT that maximins; in others, it would be the global fund. However, a resource tax that
would invariably trump both of these in the maximinning stakes
would be one that imposes the global fund's levies but discards
its equal distribution of them in favor of a maximinning one. So
on the face of it, GRT should have no appeal for Rawlsians, either. Fortunately for Pogge's argument—though unfortunately
for the worst off—this is not true. Why not?

As we have seen, the global fund is no respecter of nations'
value sets: it taxes all their resources indiscriminately and regardless of whether or not domestic value sets permit their use.
Now a plausible suggestion is that the relation between nations
and their value sets is not unlike the relation that Beitz previously found between individuals and their talents: that is, that
its value set is constitutive of a nation's identity.

I myself have no definite view on this suggestion. But if we
take it to be true—and it is not made less plausible by Pogge's
heuristic assumption that nations are each completely homogeneous entities—then it looks like the liberty-protecting appara-
tus of Rawls's first principle must again swing into play in an
original position populated, as Pogge also heuristically assumes,
by nations and not by individuals. For as Beitz noted, the possession of identity-constituting items is not appropriately viewed as
an instance of moral arbitrariness and is protected by lexically
prior considerations of liberty. Accordingly, to tax use-restrictive

nations as heavily as equally resource-endowed nations whose value sets are use permissive—as the global fund would do—is akin to taxing talented individuals purely for having those talents and regardless of whether or not they use them to secure benefits. The Rawlsian first principle clearly prohibits this: it does not penalize potentially successful neurosurgeons for becoming mediocre poets instead. Hence, citing Rawls's remark that "greater natural talents are not a collective asset in the sense that society should compel those who have them to put them to work for the less favored," Pogge himself observes that "this much is enshrined in Rawls's first principle"[38] and insists that

> Rawls simply takes for granted [that] persons have their natural endowments in a thick, constitutive sense and are fully entitled to (exercise control over) them. There is no question that Genius's talents must not be destroyed or tampered with or taxed and that she must not be coerced to develop or exercise them.[39]

So GRT, despite its lower maximinning capacity, looks like the best resource tax that the worst off can hope for. Ironically perhaps, it thus appears that what Pogge described as self-imposed handicaps on his argument for GRT—namely, the heuristic assumptions of national homogeneity and a nation-populated second original position—turn out to be key supports for that argument.

This is not the end of the matter, however. For since Pogge himself offers convincing reasons for rejecting those assumptions, an obvious question is how the case for GRT would fare in that event. What if—consonant with the individualism that he finds at the core of Rawlsian theory, though not in Rawls's own international extensions of it—the contract situation were instead Pogge's favored single global original position populated by individuals rather than nations and, moreover, individuals whose nationality is simply one more of those nonconstitutive deep contingencies that are hidden from them behind the veil of ignorance? Would these choosers still prefer the resource-use base of GRT, or would they opt for the resource-ownership base of the global fund? The latter but not the former would exact the value of their oil deposit from whoever chose to acquire the ownership of the Ka'aba mosque site. But it would also yield a greater maximin. Which would be chosen?

Here we need only recall that a defining feature of Rawlsian contractors is their ignorance of the contents of their value sets. Moreover, individuals' respective conceptions of the good, being revisable without a loss of personal identity, are nonconstitutive of them. In Rawls's famous phrase, "the self is prior to the ends which are affirmed by it."[40] These contractors are similarly ignorant of their respective natural resource holdings, which are similarly nonconstitutive of them. So individuals, unlike nations, are not constrained by the first principle's lexical priority in their choice of resource tax. Hence the same risk-averse reasoning that leads them to prefer maximin distribution ought to induce a preference for the global fund's tax base over that of GRT.

If this is indeed the warranted conclusion for Rawlsians, it nonetheless remains an open question as to whether Rawlsian maximin or Lockean equality is the appropriate norm for distributing the proceeds of that tax. Elsewhere I have argued that a comprehensive understanding of what counts as natural resources—along with consistently factored culpabilities, and the corresponding redress, for individuals' adversities—imply that those who remain worse off under Lockean resource equality do so because of their own choices.[41] But since that is another whole story in itself and one that raises much larger issues about the foundations of these two conceptions of justice, it is probably best left unaddressed here.[42]

NOTES

1. This is not to deny either that many restitutional claims are difficult to substantiate or that even if sufficiently substantiated, fulfilling them may be undesirable from the perspective of values other than justice.

2. At least, under appropriate conditions of voluntariness—with these being variously implied by the different conceptions of justice in question.

3. And hence their respective correlatives as *prior* and *posterior* duties.

4. On the principle that "ought implies can." That is, another person's preventing my doing the dutiful action A is a sufficient condition for denying any delinquency on my part. The same is true with regard to preventing my doing B, when the latter is (1) permissible and (2) a necessary condition of my doing A.

5. See Hillel Steiner, *An Essay on Rights* (Oxford: Blackwell, 1994), pp. 74–101.

6. John Locke, *An Essay Concerning Human Understanding*, ed. Peter Nidditch (Oxford: Oxford University Press, 1975), p. 549. Similarly, Hobbes: "It is consequent also to the same condition [that is, the absence of the possibility of injustice], that there be no propriety, no dominion, no *mine* and *thine* distinct" (*Leviathan*, ed. Michael Oakeshott [Oxford: Blackwell, 1946], p. 83).

7. That is, they protect these domains or action spaces in the normative sense of precluding permissible encroachment on them—not in the empirical sense of precluding actual encroachment.

8. See Amartya Sen, *Inequality Reexamined* (Oxford: Oxford University Press, 1992), p. ix: "A common characteristic of virtually all the approaches to the ethics of social arrangements that have stood the test of time is to want equality of *something*. . . . They are all 'egalitarians' in some essential way. . . . To see the battle as one between those 'in favor of' and those 'against' equality (as the problem is often posed in the literature) is to miss something central to the subject" (italics in original).

9. Locke himself believes that our bodies are owned not by ourselves but by God. Cf. John Locke, *Two Treatises of Government*, ed. Peter Laslett (Cambridge: Cambridge University Press, 1967), pp. 289, 302.

10. I interpret this as a duty that, like all correlative duties, can be owed to only those who share some element of contemporaneity with us. For an argument as to why future generations lack rights against present ones, see Steiner, *An Essay on Rights*, pp. 259–61. It is also argued (pp. 250–58, 273) that symmetrically, past generations lack rights against present ones and that accordingly, the estates of the dead are subject to this same egalitarian distributive norm.

11. See Brian Barry, "Humanity and Justice in Global Perspective," in J. Roland Pennock and John W. Chapman, eds., *NOMOS XXIV: Ethics, Economics and the Law* (New York: New York University Press, 1982).

12. That is, the value of a territorial site is equal to the difference between the aggregate market value of all its contents and the aggre-

gate market value of those of its contents that constitute improvements made to it by human activity.

13. See Steiner, *An Essay on Rights*, chap. 8.

14. In this sense, the global fund is a source of what is currently called "unconditional basic income."

15. Too many accounts of natural resource values continue to take an unduly "geological-cum-biological" view of their subject and fail to appreciate—as persons in real estate markets do not—that portions of sheer (surface and aboveground) space also possess value.

16. Charles Beitz, *Political Theory and International Relations* (Princeton, N.J.: Princeton University Press, 1979).

17. Ibid., pp. 143–53.

18. Ibid., p. 137.

19. Ibid., p. 138.

20. Ibid., p. 139.

21. Such investment strongly reflects parental ambitions. And theories denying its moral relevance thereby lack what Dworkin aptly labeled "ambition sensitivity" in his argument that just distributions are ambition sensitive and endowment insensitive. See Ronald Dworkin, "What Is Equality? Part 1: Equality of Welfare, and Part 2: Equality of Resources," *Philosophy & Public Affairs* 10 (1981): 185–246, 283–345.

22. To impute it to chance contingencies is problematically to imply that our identities are invariant with respect to the identities of our parents. It is true that what is more adequately so characterized is the factor of our talents that is supplied by their genetic endowments. In *An Essay on Rights*, pp. 237–49 and 273–80, I suggest how and why that factor may be construed as an element of natural resources without impairing self-ownership and what the just redistributive implications of this are. On the just liabilities of delinquent parents, see also my "Choice and Circumstance," *Ratio* 10 (1997): 296–312.

23. Beitz, *Political Theory and International Relations*, p. 140.

24. Ibid., p. 141.

25. There are many degrees of cooperation. In Hobbesian states of nature, to refrain from predatory activity is to be a cooperator. Any denial that such scenarios constitute the relevant baseline for identifying cooperation itself presupposes an alternative precontractual baseline that must consist of a distributive norm prescribing a set of inviolable domains whose owners' interactions would then count as cooperation.

26. Ibid., pp. 133–34. See John Rawls, *A Theory of Justice* (Oxford: Oxford University Press, 1972), p. 378.

27. It is under the description *territorial site*—rather than in terms of "x gallons of crude oil, y hectares of arable land, etc."—that nations

designate the object of their jurisdictional claims. That is, not just any old *x* gallons and *y* hectares will do.

28. See Thomas Pogge, *Realizing Rawls* (Ithaca, N.Y.: Cornell University Press, 1989), and "An Egalitarian Law of Peoples," *Philosophy & Public Affairs* 23 (1994): 195–224.

29. Pogge, *Realizing Rawls*, p. 247 (italics in original).

30. Rawls, *A Theory of Justice*, pp. 264–65; cf. Pogge, *Realizing Rawls*, p. 247.

31. Pogge, *Realizing Rawls*, pp. 246 ff.

32. As suggested previously, the core of one argument against foundational contractualism is simply that a necessary condition of the joint performability—the possibility—of the set of contractually undertaken duties is the joint exercisability of the liberties they presuppose: an exercisability that is guaranteed only by a set of prior (compossible) rights. For recent debate on locating the foundations of justice in contracts, see the exchanges among Brian Barry, Neil MacCormick, and myself in "Brian Barry's *Justice as Impartiality*: A Symposium," *Political Studies* 44 (1996): 303–42.

33. Pogge, "An Egalitarian Law of Peoples," p. 199.

34. See John Rawls, "The Law of Peoples," in Stephen Shute and Susan Hurley, eds., *On Human Rights* (New York: Basic Books, 1993).

35. Pogge, "An Egalitarian Law of Peoples," p. 199.

36. Ibid., p. 200.

37. Ibid., pp. 200–1.

38. Pogge, *Realizing Rawls*, p. 64.

39. Ibid., p. 79.

40. Rawls, *A Theory of Justice*, p. 560.

41. See Steiner, *An Essay on Rights*, and "Choice and Circumstance." That their adversities are self-incurred certainly does not imply any absence of duties to relieve them. It implies only that such duties are ones of humanity rather than justice and hence are not justly enforceable.

42. This chapter has greatly benefited from comments and criticisms supplied by Jerry Cohen, Katrin Flikschuh, Ian Shapiro, and Andrew Williams.

8

REALISM REVISITED: THE MORAL PRIORITY OF MEANS AND ENDS IN ANARCHY

LEA BRILMAYER

The taste for simpleminded moralism is a luxury that most state leaders feel they are not in any position to indulge. It is a luxury, they feel, that is reserved for those who make a living moralizing (like academics) and for those (like human rights activists) who are far enough removed from having any influence that they need not seriously worry whether their proposals might be seriously naive. The men and women who make decisions on behalf of sovereign states feel that they cannot afford to choose a plan of action by whether it would please philosophers. The responsibility that comes with leadership puts them always in a position of having to make difficult choices, and the sorts of things they weigh are not well captured by simpleminded moral rules that have appeal in the academy.

Are state leaders cynical to feel this way? Does this rejection of moralism mean a rejection of morality? Are state leaders who take a skeptic's view of international legalities any worse because of that? Are they fooling themselves when they tell themselves that as leaders, they have a right (or duty) to turn away from moral recipes of right and wrong? If they are—if they are merely cynically rationalizing their immoral conduct with high minded talk about state interests and international realities—then how is it that apparently decent and obviously committed people feel this way when put in that position? What is there about being in a position of leadership that makes a decent human being doubt moral rules?

We know that some state leaders are truly cynical and immoral, and at the other end of the spectrum are the occasional saintly figures who never deviate from what strict principles require. But between the polar opposites of Machiavelli and Gandhi fall the large majority of persons making international decisions. They tend toward realism—toward a school of thought that emphasizes practicalities and state responsibilities instead of moral rules of right and wrong—but are often strongly influenced by ethical considerations. While realism often masquerades as moral skepticism, flaunting its contempt for naive idealism, many "realists" in fact consider themselves more truly moral than the "idealists" they castigate. This chapter is an examination of the moral compass that guides them in their better moments.

My sympathies are increasingly with these morally sensitive realists, but the point here is not to show that they are right and idealism is wrong. Their ethical position must first be constructed, for their affirmative position has been obscured by their louder negative rhetoric, condemning simpleminded moralism. Two philosophical arguments are central to this reconstruction. The first is that the moral appeal of realism lies in the fact that as a species of consequentialism, it is well situated to meet the problems that all deontological approaches inevitably confront. Realism is an ethic of consequences, and because it chooses means solely with an eye toward their accomplishment of those chosen ends, it need not in theory worry that it is paving the road to hell with good intentions. That is a worry in practice only, because in theory if the road leads to hell, then the intentions are the wrong ones. The second is that the reason that it can sell itself as a distinctively international theory is that it is in the international context that the problems posed by deontology appear most glaring. In well-governed domestic societies, deontological reasoning and consequentialism tend to converge; we can act, in most instances, with the moral confidence that "right" actions will have "good" results. This is not true, however, in the international setting, where the hell to which good intentions lead is terrible and not unlikely.

This chapter concludes with some suggestions about how these arguments point toward a reconstruction of realism that highlights its ethical dimensions. It starts with a short discussion of which "realism" it is we seek to reconstruct.

I. WHICH REALISM?

Realism is the "bad boy" of international jurisprudence. The realist perspective has come to be equated with scientific cold-heartedness, with a Machiavellian disregard for moral decency, with a ruthless focus on one's own interests, and with a calculating willingness to do whatever must be done to advance those interests. When international moralists set about the task of arguing for ethical principles of international relations, the preliminary target usually is international realism, for realism is seen as antithetical to moral principles. It is hard to deny the appeal of setting about things in this way; there are enough realist statements to the effect that "moral argument has no place in international relations," that the temptation to take them at face value—and to shoot them full of holes—is virtually irresistible. Here, however, we resist that temptation and try to distinguish those varieties of realist thought that exhibit complete moral skepticism from those that are more sympathetic to the moral point of view.

There are several important strands of realist thought, each with different moral characteristics. An important one is neorealism, which focuses on a supposedly objective analysis of the interaction of different state units in an anarchical state system. Neorealism professes a lack of interest in normative questions, and instead it focuses on "scientific" analysis. It is not a moral interpretation of realism and does not aspire to be. What interests neorealists is more the mechanics of the structure of the international system than the quandaries and dilemmas that statesmen and stateswomen face. The loudest voices in the "morality has no place in international relations" chorus are neorealists, who are not interested enough in taking moral argument seriously to acknowledge the space that ethics leaves for a nuanced balancing of pragmatic considerations. Neorealists are not interested in moral argument, and although they are entitled not to be, they would be better off simply leaving it at that rather than insisting that no one else should be.

Classic realism provides a more nurturing environment for moral reasoning than neorealism does, because it lacks neorealism's overblown pretensions to scientific purity. Classical realism—the realism of Morgenthau, Niebuhr, and Kennan—is the school of thought that best captures the sympathies of statesmen and stateswomen. Two themes coexist in classical realism, one that might be called *national interest realism* and one that might be called *realist morality*. National interest realism may perhaps be the dominant thread, although it is not the one of dominant interest here. It emphasizes the duty statesmen have to their own nations, as opposed to duty to the interests of the global community at large. National interest realism has moral overtones because it speaks of duty. But it does not overtly incorporate any duty to outsiders. There are many reasons to think that it in fact leaves room for such consideration and that it is therefore entirely compatible with realist morality. For this reason, I will briefly mention national interest realism once again at the end of this chapter. They are different threads, however, and need to be untangled.

The thread from which national interest realism must be separated—the one of primary interest here—is realist morality. Realist morality emphasizes that in order to be truly ethical, realist diplomats should take a hardheaded look at the long-term effects of what they are doing, rather than acting on narrow moralistic principles. The defining characteristic of this realist morality is the conviction that simplistic moralism tends to backfire in the long run, that it is counterproductive in terms of its own announced goals. This version of classical realism shares some characteristics of "national interest" realism: the sense of responsibility to those who are affected by one's decisions, and the elevation of this responsibility over commitment to abstract moral principle. We will see that a defining element of both is their consequentialist character: they concern themselves more with the actual effects of a decision than whether the decision is made in accordance with some preconceived set of moral rules. But if national interest realism is taken at face value, it sees the statesperson's constituency as including only conationals. Realist morality need not be limited in this way, however; the consequences of a statesperson's actions generally may also matter.

It would not be wise to claim that this realist morality is the best (most accurate) interpretation of realism or that inconsistent versions of realist thought are somehow not authentic. Even to the extent that realist morality is authentic, it probably does not encompass all the different positions that realist thought covers. For example, realism is typically understood to focus exclusively on the actions of states (as opposed to private individuals or nongovernmental organizations), and some versions of realism go as far as insisting that only the systemic interactions of states (as opposed to their internal workings) are of interest. This position is not a consequence of realist morality; it is entirely beside the point in our discussion. Further adding to these difficulties, realist writings are often unclear about their moral positions, making it difficult and probably unproductive to stake out claims to authenticity. In any event, such debates about what "realists" as a group believe are of interest mainly to intellectual historians. There is probably no single "most authentic" interpretation of realism, and even if there were, appropriating that title would not be my objective. A better way to describe the enterprise here is that we are trying to determine whether a morally appealing version of realism can be constructed. If many realists choose not to adopt it, that is their business.

The morally appealing construction of realism that I offer here is grounded in the conviction that the consequences of a diplomat's actions are morally more important than whether those actions are right in some isolated and abstract sense. Stated perhaps too simply, it rests on the premise that diplomats must sometimes be willing to employ morally unattractive means when these are necessary to achieve morally desirable ends. Consider some examples of arguments usually thought to exhibit realist characteristics. Realists sometimes observed that Jimmy Carter erred in withdrawing support for the shah of Iran on the grounds of the shah's human rights abuses. The long-term consequence (so the realist argument goes) was a far more repressive government's coming to power, one over which the United States did not have as much moderating influence. Similarly, boycotts of Chinese products or economic sanctions against South African goods were sometimes said to be counterproductive because boycotts tend to isolate outlaw regimes, simply driving the governments in question to take an even harder-line stand. In addition, it is claimed, such boycotts backfire because it is the poor and helpless of society that they hurt the most.

Similarly, a realist might argue for nuclear deterrence, knowing very well that nuclear weapons are terrible and that deterrence creates some probability that they might be used. He or she might argue that nuclear deterrence by "responsible" powers is the best way to avoid an even greater catastrophe, such as a despotic power acquiring nuclear weapons and using them to intimidate the rest of the world into submission. A realist might argue that one should support certain regional powers rather than others because in the long run a balance of power is the most stable and therefore the best situation that can realistically be achieved. Or a realist might argue that it is sometimes necessary to violate international legal principles of nonintervention because a nearby nation is having a seriously destabilizing effect on the region as a whole.

These are realist arguments, even though they clearly contain moral elements. They are realist in the sense that they try to take a "realistic" look at what will actually happen as a result of taking a moral stand. They contain moral elements because the actual consequences are then evaluated from a moral point of view. In all these cases, the "realist" point of view is characterized by both pragmatic analysis of the likely results of actions and sensitivity to the moral overtones of the likely results. The realist morality places priority on ends rather than means and on the goodness of the consequences rather than the abstract rightness of the actions viewed in isolation.

This is the thread of realism that we want to focus on here.

1. Realism's main complaint against idealism is its lack of concern with the consequences of actions. Idealism backfires. The attractions of realism are precisely the

difficulties of deontological forms of moral reasoning, and vice versa.

2. Comparable problems arise in any situation in which deontological reasoning and consequentialist reasoning diverge; they are not limited to cases involving international decision making. The tension between "realism" and "idealism" is endemic to all leadership and is not peculiar to international relations.

3. The realists nonetheless are not completely wrong to see international decision making as distinctive, because it is in international decision making that deontological reasoning about means and consequentialist reasoning about ends are most likely to diverge. Although the same moral dilemmas can arise in either domestic or international decision making, they are actually more likely to occur in the international context, and when they do arise, they are more often intractable.

4. The reason for this is precisely the feature of international politics that realists find so compelling: the fact that there is no centralized power to enforce international law.

In sum, realist morality is based on the proposition that in situations of anarchy—international affairs being one such situation—the consequences of one's actions should be given higher moral priority than the moral attractiveness of the means that one employs.

II. REALISM AND "MORAL RECIPES"

Although this is not the place for elaborate digressions into the finer points of moral philosophy, it is helpful to situate the disagreement between the realists and those they criticize in the broader context of moral debate. The disagreement can usefully be understood as an example of the familiar debate between consequentialist and deontological moral theory. The mood of realist morality is one of impatience with simplistic moral rules and, therefore, with morality as a whole (with which simplistic moralism is erroneously equated). This can easily be appreciated if one keeps in mind the sort of idealism that realists object to.

The idealism that is the chief target of the realist scorn involves a simpleminded application of moral rules, what one might call *moral recipes*. This label, though dismissive, is an apt one because realists are, in fact, dismissive of moral reasoning as they understand it. Precisely the thing that realists object to is that (in their view) morality attempts to impose preconceived and oversimplified conceptions of how to act. In response, it is entirely appropriate to point out that morality is not necessarily the set of preconceived simplistic "dos" and "don'ts" that realism seems to think it is. Morality has room for exceptions, for subtlety and doubt, for rebuttable presumptions, and for a balanced consideration of a variety of factors depending on the circumstances. The naive moralism that realism attacks is more or less a straw man. But if what we want to understand is how the realists see their own moral vision, it helps to start by contrasting it with what they see themselves rejecting. Even if what they reject is a straw man, understanding what that straw man looks like and why they find it so upsetting is instructive.

Take, for example, the realist rejection of absolute principles of human rights. Idealists (according to the realists) make blanket statements that violations of human rights ought to be condemned in every case or that it is always immoral to lend one's support to governments that violate their citizens' human rights. Another example is the use of chemical weapons or land mines . Is it always wrong? Idealists (the realists fear) wish to say so categorically. What about violations of international law, for instance, principles prohibiting armed aggression? Realists expect idealists to counsel that international law must always be obeyed. Should countries sometimes repudiate their treaty obligations or, even worse, violate their treaty obligations secretly? Again, the idealist is painted as one who addresses issues of this sort dogmatically and categorically.

What makes such positions "deontological" is that the actions in question are judged by some intrinsic moral quality instead of in terms of their consequences. Using chemical weapons or violating human rights is wrong regardless; it is intrinsically wrong. In some circumstances, it may improve things overall if chemical warfare is used or armed aggression is initiated. The reason is that the opponent one faces may be so evil that the benefits outweigh the suffering caused by the means that one engages. But those means are not, for that reason, any less the source of suffering, and this suffering may be inflicted on innocent people. Someone who is inclined to see things in deontological terms looks at the act itself—starting a war, supporting human rights abuses, engaging in deceit or spying, employing destructive weapons, killing innocent civilians, violating one's treaty obligations—and condemns it without taking into account the countervailing long-term reasons that might be offered in the action's defense. These long term-reasons would be relevant from the point of view of the consequentialist, who wants to know all the effects (long and short term) that a particular action will have.

The realist's scorn for what is seen as simpleminded and naive insistence on absolute compliance with moral rules does not necessarily arise out of any lack of respect for human well-being and human rights. Certainly, most classical realists would prefer a world in which there was more respect for human rights rather than less, for both themselves and the rest of the human race. The disagreement lies instead in the realist belief that human well-being and human rights are further advanced in the long run if the effects are calculated pragmatically and in the realist belief that this long-term calculation is what matters. A simpleminded application of moral recipes (in this view) backfires because it does not take into account the complexities of international relations.

We gave some examples earlier. Withdrawing political support for the shah of Iran (it was argued) backfired because the end result was the coming to power of a regime that was an even worse violator of human rights. Boycotting the goods of countries with repressive regimes will backfire if it causes economic dislocation and injury to the least advantaged in the boycotted country or if the boycott simply isolates the human rights offender (or fails to work altogether because other countries do not observe it). A country that refuses to employ certain types of weapons or tactics can put itself at a disadvantage, with the end result being the systematic extinction of exactly those nations that behave most scrupulously. These are the sorts of arguments that realists are willing to consider and (when appropriate) to make. The realist position is not that it never pays to take principles into account, but that there is no guarantee that deciding on principle will have the desired effect. One should always be aware that others may act out of self-interest. One should always make a clear-sighted calculation of how best to achieve the goals one has in mind and act on these clear-sighted calculations rather than on naive assumptions about how one wishes the world to be.

One might view calculations of this sort as cynical, and indeed, they are the opposite of the fuzzy-headed romanticism usually ascribed to Woodrow Wilson or Jimmy Carter. The realist would argue that it is necessary to see people and international events for what they are and not for what one might like them to be. If it is cynical to be realistic about the sort of motivations present in international relations, then the realist is a cynic. But the realist should not, for this reason, be assumed to be immoral. The realist may see herself as simply making the morally best choice under morally difficult circumstances. It is the idealist (according to this view) who is immoral. The idealist is self-indulgent and shortsighted, self-righteous and smug. The idealist is more concerned with maintaining his own moral purity, with keeping his moral hands clean. The idealist (according to this view) cares less about the welfare of the world around him than with some abstract rightness of his own actions.

The realist, in contrast, congratulates himself on his willingness to confront the tragic fact that sometimes well-intentioned actions are not enough. Sometimes for the general and long-range benefit of all, it is necessary to face unpleasant reality and do things one would rather not do. Acting in a way designed to bring about good consequences lacks the moral certainty of acting in accordance with simple moral principles. There is an obvious appeal to simply following the moral recipe, even knowing that "the heavens may fall," that if things go wrong, it is not one's own fault, because one has kept one's own hands clean. This appeal is the intuitive appeal of deontological reasoning. But it is a temptation that realists resist, and they feel themselves superior for having refused the easy moral choice.

Realism feeds on the divergence between deontology and consequentialism. If we could always act in confidence that following simple moral recipes would lead to good results, then why should we turn anywhere more complicated for assistance? Calculating the consequences of our actions is a difficult and uncertain business. It can require that we do unpleasant things, things we find morally unsavory. If we had reassurances that if we did the "right" thing, then "good" would always follow, we would have little reason to take risks and, in particular, little moral reason to engage in the regrettable.

Except for those of us with appropriately equipped religious convictions, such reassurances do not exist. The source of realist morality's appeal lies in our lack of moral confidence, in the uneasy belief that if we do care about consequences, we cannot simply follow the commandments and then leave the rest to divine power. There are too many circumstances in which we know that obeying the rules means playing into evil hands. Moral dilemmas of this sort are fertile ground for realists because they give a moral motivation for departing from moral formulas.

III. THE ESSENTIAL COMMONALITY OF INTERNATIONAL AND DOMESTIC MORALITY

To find examples of such dilemmas, we need only look as far as domestic moral theory. Moral dilemmas force us to confront the sad fact that we cannot necessarily satisfy all our moral intuitions with a single course of action. Circumstances in which every moral theory leads to the same conclusion are unlikely to be interesting, for theory craves dilemmas, and dilemmas arise when strongly held moral intuitions point in opposite directions. For instance, a stock example involves being captured by bandits and taken to a remote area. The head of the gang of bandits has been planning to kill a number of innocent hostages and offers to strike a deal with you. You can select one of the individuals who is about to be killed and shoot that person at point-blank yourself. If you do this (you are told), the rest of the hostages will be allowed to go free. Or you can refuse to get involved, in which case the gang will shoot all the hostages. The dilemma is that if you agree to participate, fewer innocent people overall will be killed, but you will have killed an innocent person. If you stick to your moral principles and refuse to pull the trigger, you can tell yourself that the killing that takes place in consequence was not of your doing. But your actions will result in the murder of several extra innocent people.

The stock examples of realist morality have a similar flavor. A certain regime, for instance, has an abominable human rights record. It not only refuses to hold popular elections, but it also represses its own people through torture and gross political intimidation. It requests assistance, and your state knows that any support it gives will only enable the repression to continue. But waiting in the wings is an even more evil regime; one like Pol Pot's or the ayatollah's. Should your state keep its hands clean, refuse assistance, and let the current government go down? Or should it "choose the lesser of two evils," "look to the long run," follow a policy of "constructive engagement" or "containment"? The dilemma is more common than we would like to suppose.

One thing that should immediately be apparent is although the examples of Pol Pot or the ayatollah have an international flavor (they involve regimes in other countries), this is not deeply important to the dilemma they present. If the United States faces a dilemma in deciding whether to support oppressive regimes, in what way is that dilemma theoretically so different from the dilemma of a domestic political opponent? An ordinary Iranian ought to be just as concerned about the long-run consequences of refusing to support the shah as would an ordinary American taxpayer. In both cases, there is a moral question arising from the fact that the probable alternatives are even worse. The "international" flavor of the problem is entirely coincidental because the moral problem confronting the United States is theoretically identical to the moral problem posed domestically.

Indeed, the stock example that philosophers use to drive a wedge between consequentialist and deontological approaches—our example of the bandit gang—itself illustrates that such dilemmas are not peculiar to the international arena. Here, also, a domestic situation provides a dilemma regarding whether one ought to keep one's hands clean by applying simple moral rules or whether one ought, instead, to face unpleas-

ant realities and act to bring about the best set of consequences.
The parallels between the "bandit" and the "totalitarian
regime" examples are quite striking. In both cases, someone else
will behave in an unscrupulous and destructive way if you do not
do the morally unpleasant but necessary thing.

The realist condemns moral prissiness, naive beliefs that others can be counted on to follow moral rules, and misplaced confidence that doing the "right" thing will lead to "good" results.
But such realism cannot be limited to international morality. If
one is convinced that it is better to look at things this way in in-
terstate relations, it is hard to see why one does not do so in domestic moral reasoning as well. In what sense, then, is international morality distinctive? Realists persist in the belief that
their approach is somehow most compelling where no central
government exists. They cite the absence of world government
as somehow justifying the rough-and-tumble practical morality
that idealists reject. The belief that "the ends justifies the
means" is more appropriate, they think, in international relations. But why, when one can see that conflict between acceptable means and desirable ends is just as much a feature of domestic moral theory as it is of international decision making?

The answer, it seems, lies in an important feature of consequentialism. Consequentialism does not, in theory, rule out any
factual circumstance of a moral problem as *a priori* irrelevant.
Anything that might affect the calculation of consequences is
potentially of moral importance. One such factual circumstance
of potential importance is the fact that others cannot be expected to comply with moral rules. From a consequentialist
point of view, it certainly matters what the conduct of others in
response to one's own decision is likely to be. To the extent that
such responsive conduct affects consequences, it will affect the
calculations of what is right or wrong. If the possibility of such
conduct systematically sways calculations in one way or another
and if others' conduct is likely to be different internationally
than domestically, then one might expect international and domestic moral calculations to work out differently. International
conseqentialism, in other words, must include in the moral
equation the fact that other actors may not comply with legal
and moral norms. This can also happen domestically, but in

well-governed domestic societies, such occurrences, though possible, are rare. International and domestic morality are, in theory, identical, but since the practical circumstances of application are different (speaking probabilistically), the results of applying moral theory tend (again speaking probabilistically) are different as well.

It is interesting in this regard that the bandit hypothetical involves an important element of "anarchy," of having to take into account the imperfect nature of other actors' compliance with moral rules. There is a sense in which the situation in this (admittedly far-fetched) hypothetical is "anarchical," just as international relations are. What animates the example is the picture of a group of lawless individuals who are prepared to do evil things. The moral dilemma is a direct result of the facts that others are not prepared to follow moral rules and that there is no effective power for enforcing those moral rules. One wishes that the situation could be resolved by some police force that would rescue all the innocent people and punish those who caused the problem, but the hypothetical is designed to make that resolution seem unlikely. It is precisely to make the situation more "anarchical" that the hypothetical is situated in a remote area where help is likely to be unavailable. Under such circumstances are you supposed to take an action that seems intrinsically immoral, in order to save as many lives as possible? Or to refuse to accommodate yourself to an intrinsically immoral situation? In theory, the question is not very different from the problem of whether statesmen and stateswomen should take into account unpleasant and immoral realities when deciding what to do.

In practice, though, there is a difference. The hypothetical just described is fairly ridiculous. It has to be, for philosophers must go to some extremes to offer domestic "anarchical" situations in which one cannot resolve the tension by simply turning to the state. The reason that the hypothetical problem is located far out in an inaccessible area, where no prospect of help is likely, is to make the chance of intervention as remote as possible. The situation of anarchy must be built into the hypothetical in a rather artificial way. The difference between international and domestic moral theory, then, is that philosophers need not go to such absurd lengths to hypothesize cases in which authori-

tative intervention is unlikely. In the international arena, it is all
too likely that no one will come to the rescue when evil-minded
people threaten. In the international arena, hypothetical examples are all too plausible. Indeed, they are hardly hypothetical;
real examples come easily to mind.

What makes realism seem attractive as a theory of international relations—even to people who have little attraction to
consequentialism as a matter of domestic morality—is that the
actual cases in which a consequentialist approach to moral reasoning appears compelling are more common internationally
than domestically. Internationally, there are more cases (and,
more important, more credible cases) in which the consequentialist stakes are high, that is, when following deontological
moral rules risks serious harm to others. The gulf between deontological reasoning and consequentialist moral reasoning is
much wider in international theory than in domestic theory. In
domestic theory, one must strain to think of hypotheticals in
which the tension between deontology reasoning and consequential reasoning is acute, for in domestic situations, the state
is present in the background. In domestic situations, one can
usually "solve" the tension by controlling the evil and aberrant
behavior of others through state action. Since realist morality
feeds on the divergence between consequentialist and deontological ethics, it gains appeal in international affairs, but that
appeal shrinks in importance in ordinary domestic times and
situations.

IV. MORAL CONFIDENCE AND INTERNATIONAL ANARCHY

The reason that the divergence is greatest in international affairs is related to a characteristic of international politics that is
frequently cited by realists as an explanation for the reduced importance of ethical reasoning: the supposed "anarchy" of international relations. I have argued elsewhere[1] that this notion of
"anarchy" is poorly understood and it should be clear from the
preceding discussion that even if it were better understood, it
would not (in my view) be correct to say that its existence elimi-
nates the need for moral reasoning. However, if by "anarchy" we
mean simply the absence of an institution that enforces interna-

tional moral norms, then this absence does play an important role in moral analysis. When the institutions for enforcing moral norms are imperfect (or absent), it is harder to have confidence that engaging in "right" actions will have "good" consequences. The consequentialist cost of obeying deontological norms is high, and therefore the allure of realism is strongest. In international anarchy, moral confidence is lacking.

What is it about the existence of a well-governed political society that makes it less likely that individuals will face difficult moral dilemmas of choosing between obeying moral precepts concerning legitimate means and the advancement of morally desirable ends? Put in another way, why is it that individuals acting in domestic society can behave according to deontological moral principles without worrying too much about consequences, without worrying that their well-intentioned actions may backfire? Why in most domestic cases do deontological reasoning and consequentialist reasoning tend to converge? What, conversely, is it about international society that deprives people of their moral confidence that doing what seems right also leads to morally acceptable results?

The answers to these questions lie in the ways that good governments actively set out to achieve desirable social states of affairs through the structuring of individual conduct. Governments advance toward social goals by reducing them to their components of individual action and then requiring compliance with those individual standards of conduct. Assume, for example, that a reduction in infant mortality is desired. To achieve this, a government may identify the various causes of infant mortality: premature births due to poor medical care of or substance abuse by the pregnant woman, poor nutrition due to ignorance or poverty, environmental threats such as poor sanitation or polluted water, and so forth. In pursuit of its goal of reducing infant mortality, the government may provide better prenatal care, counseling for substance abuse, improved sanitation, nutritional information, and the like. It does so by requiring certain things of its citizens in an effort to marshal resources to solve the problem. Taxpayers are asked for financial support; the sale of certain drugs is criminalized and warnings are required for others; water quality control is imposed; and so forth.

Virtually every social goal that a government seeks to achieve requires it to break down the problem into its constituent elements, to develop effective means to achieve those ends it finds
desirable. Good governments identify morally desirable goals
and find means for bringing them about, and a good government uses the coercive power of the state as a way of inducing
compliance with the means that it has selected. It reasons backward, from good consequences to effective deontological rules.

Conversely, when a state is considering a rule that seems desirable from a deontological point of view, it is likely to look forward into the future to determine its likely consequences. It assumes the responsibility of evaluating the consequences of the
rules of conduct it imposes. If it seems that the rule is likely to
backfire, it may either reconsider or take preventive measures to
avert the undesirable side effects. If it does its job well, its citizens should be able to trust those rules and comply with them in
the relative security that the long-range consequences have been
considered. Thus, whether one views political decision as either
a forward- or a backward-looking enterprise, good governments
act in a way that tends to bring together behavior according to
deontological rules with the achievement of overall social benefits. Good governments bestow on their citizens an important
moral benefit: the moral confidence that they can do as they
think right, viewed deontologically.

Good governments also provide moral confidence in another
respect. Not only are its citizens relatively secure in the knowledge that the consequences have been taken into account, but
they also act with the confidence that others will also be comply-
ing. This is more a question of the government's strength than
its moral vision or its policymaking skills. Strong and effective
governments are able to discourage disobedience of the rules
and remedy the violations that do take place. If a government is
not sufficiently effective to provide this moral environment for
action, then individuals will lack the moral confidence that others will also do their part. They must be concerned that their
well-intentioned actions will fail to be effective or will even backfire. The consequence of noncompliance by others may be that
the desired goal is not achieved or that the consequence may actually be that attempts to achieve the goal make things worse.

Take the case of gun control. Probably everyone (even members of the National Rifle Association) agrees that there would be fewer deaths from gunshot wounds if no one possessed guns. But there is disagreement over whether it is possible to achieve this goal (zero gun ownership) by banning guns. Gun control opponents claim that criminals will still be able to get guns: "When guns are outlawed, only outlaws will have guns" as the bumper sticker says. They raise the possibility that we all will be worse off by requiring law-abiding citizens to hand in their guns, because we will then be prey to those few elements of society that still possess them. Not only do we have to worry that some will simply fail to do their part—by not handing in their guns—but we also have to think about the possibility that some may actively and perversely take advantage of the situation (those who prey on the now unarmed populace).

The gun control example is an interesting one because of the analogues in international relations. There is widespread agreement, for example, that it would be a better world if we could eliminate nuclear weapons, land mines, and chemical warfare. Proposals are continually made to ban these methods of destruction, and the perennial realist reply is that this would be utopian. Outlaw states would get access to these weapons. Not only would we have failed to achieve our objective of banning them, but we also would have actually made things worse because outlaw states would have greater power over the states that did comply. In a world of perfect institutions, individuals would not have to worry about such consequences of their own good-faith compliance with deontological rules. When institutions are imperfect, however (and they admittedly are imperfect internationally), only a deontological "true believer"—or someone with complete confidence in God's plan for the world—is willing to "do right, though the heavens may fall."

Whether internationally or domestically, a well-ordered political system gives individuals moral confidence, assurances that if one acts individually according to the system's rules of action, the consequences will generally work out for the best. This moral confidence comes from the secure belief that by and large, others will act predictably and according to generally accepted moral standards. The structures of political decision making promulgate norms that effectively integrate individual responsibility with the overall social good, with deontological rules, that is, those that are also acceptable consequentially. These structures also assume the responsibility of making sure that others act according to these rules—they enforce the general rules of behavior—and the task before the individual himself or herself is simply to carry out his or her own part of the bargain, to behave according to those principles in his or her own conduct. The individual who behaves according to moral rules and is well intentioned need not be overly concerned that good intentions will go seriously astray. It is the task of government to control the sort of perverse and aberrant behavior that makes morally well-intentioned actions backfire.

When the government is strong and good, behavior in accordance with its rules of conduct usually produces good results. The reason is that a good government formulates rules of conduct that produce good consequences for society at large and a strong government is able to put them into operation despite the efforts of ill-intentioned persons to evade or frustrate them. There is no ironclad guarantee that behaving according to social and legal rules will never backfire, but there are assurances that circumstances of this sort are exceptional so that the individual who relies on individual standards of behavior can act in moral confidence. Deontology and consequentialism are still in theory quite different ways of approaching morality, and in some circumstances, the two diverge. But as a general and a practical matter, the tension is not acute. The individual who wishes to do what is morally right according to simple rules of conduct can rely on the ability of the government to make sure that others do this also, and he or she can avoid the uncertainties and anxious calculations caused by the awareness that those with whom one interacts may be perversely planning to take advantage of one's own commitment to moral standards.

V. THE MORAL VISION OF REALISM

From the moral realist's point of view, the problem with international society is the absence of political institutions that are both good and strong. Some international institutions are relatively strong; the Western alliance, for example, is at this point strong enough to force its will on the rest of the world in most instances. But the international institutions that have the strength to structure state conduct do not necessarily do so in the most moral of ways; instead, they tend to advance the state interests of the small number of powerful states that dominate them. Because one cannot count on them to force other actors to comply with moral rules, one must always plan for the possibility that other actors will behave illegally and immorally.

But if the institutions that are strong are not necessarily good, it is also the case that the institutions that are good are not necessarily strong. Some international institutions consistently try to enforce international norms of conduct. Although they are far from perfect, the International Court of Justice, the regional courts of human rights, and various development-oriented institutions of the United Nations come to mind. However, such international institutions that adopt a legal or moral point of view are frequently not strong enough to put that point of view into practice. Even though they might wish to throw their weight behind international principles, they are not in any position to guarantee compliance. This is the source of the diplomat's moral dilemma.

From the realist point of view, statesmen and stateswomen cannot safely assume that "someone else" is providing assurances that individual moral conduct will have good consequences. In domestic society, individual actors assume that if they do their part, they need not worry any further. The lack of assurances along these lines forces every international decision maker to make his or her own strategic consequential calculations. Each time a national leader acts, it is with the knowledge that no moral "safety net" exists. Good intentions and decision according to individual moral principle are not enough. The world is an unpredictable and dangerous place, say realists, with other states poised to capitalize on one's weakness. According to the realist way of thought, this factor must always be taken explicitly into account, unless one simply wishes to throw the consequences to the winds and follow moral recipes.

Caring about the consequences of one's actions internationally inclines one in the general direction of realism. Consequentialism explains the distinctive characteristics of international realism, but it does so in a way that makes realism consistent with morality. These characteristics are its cynicism, its fatalistic resignation to the occasional necessity of doing what seems to be immoral, its emphasis on the duties of leadership, and its condemnation of what it sees as naive self-indulgence on the part of the idealists.

The *cynicism* of realism comes from the willingness to recognize that others cannot be counted on to behave according to principle. Realism is not necessarily cynical in the sense that its practitioners are themselves amoral or immoral, that they themselves are moral skeptics. But realism is skeptical about the purity of others' motives. Realists feel this cynicism to be a prerequisite to any evaluation of the effects of one's own conduct. Naive idealism is condemned for its rosy assumptions about other states' motives. To be cynical, according to the realist, is merely to be clear-sighted. And being clear-sighted is the first prerequisite to being moral.

The *fatalistic resignation* of realism to the occasional necessity to do "immoral" things comes from a belief that what matters about one's actions is the results that they produce, not their intrinsic moral nature or the good intentions behind them. No matter how well intentioned one's actions are or how consistent they seem to be with moral strictures, if at the end of the day they have produced human misery, then the realist diplomat will feel that he or she has not done his or her job well. Accordingly, unpalatable means may sometimes have to be employed to reach desired ends. The moral realist is not happy that this is so; ordinarily he or she would prefer that it were not necessary to cause injury, to engage in deceit, or to violate his or her solemn commitments. But the realist accepts the necessity of occasionally doing these things as the price of assuming leadership.

This emphasis on the *duties of leadership* is the third distinctive attribute of realism. Many realists have remarked that with leadership comes responsibility for others, and this means sometimes having to do things that would be abhorrent to a private party. The truth of this remark lies in the fact that exercising a leadership role means being consequentialist. The duties of leadership include caring about the effect of one's behavior on others. The leader must be "public regarding," as opposed to obsessed with maintaining his or her own moral purity. The tragedy that realists see in leadership is that a true leader may sometimes have to be willing to sacrifice his or her own moral scruples out of a sense of responsibility to others.

Finally, realism scorns the *self-indulgence of idealism*. Idealism is seen as the easy way out. Not only does the idealist insist on keeping his or her moral hands clean, at the expense of the interests of others, but the idealist wants to see things as easier than they really are. Moral recipes are cheap and easy to apply (in the eyes of the realist), whereas true moral responsibility requires making decisions in the face of great uncertainty. Not only must one be willing to do the dirty work of leadership, but one also must be willing to do it without any assurances that the consequential calculations that one makes will be proved correct. The realist believes that a leader must be willing to live with the personal uncertainty and insecurity that comes from knowing that having done his or her best is no guarantee. Uncertainty is a fact of life, and those who cannot deal with life's complexities had better avoid the role's responsibility.

These basic characteristics are only the first steps toward an outline of what a realist morality would look like. We have described it is a kind of consequentialism. But what kind? One thing that should be clear is that it cannot be as dogmatic as realist rhetoric sometimes seems to be. Such a morality cannot, of course, dogmatically reject the idea of ethics in international relations; it cannot, in other words, equate "morality" with "moral recipes." It must also remain willing to consider the beneficial consequences of idealism and of respect for legal and moral rules. Sometimes there are strategic advantages over the long run to promoting international norms. By acting consistently and according to moral principles, one might set a good example, encourage compliance by other states, assure others of one's good intentions, and alter the tenor of international discourse. Such phenomena are sometimes dismissed out of hand as idealistic nonsense. For a consequentialist, however, they cannot be dismissed out of hand. It cannot be taken as an article of faith that principles are always silly or counterproductive; realist morality must be more open-minded to the possible pragmatic benefits of observing legal and moral norms. This seems clear from what has been said already.

But on other issues, what we have said does not take us very far. In particular, we have said nothing about how the consequences of actions are to be evaluated. Is realist morality a sort of consequentialism that places value on human happiness, so that actions are to be chosen according to some principle of utility maximization? Or is realist morality intent on maximizing something else, such as respect for human rights? Is the objective the promotion of individual liberty? Social equality? The rights of states? Does realist morality even require the maximization of something? Or does it take consequences into account in some other way?

Another open question is how the statesperson is supposed to balance the interests of his or her own state against the interests of others. A predominant concern with one's own interests is not necessarily immoral if, for example, there are moral limitations on which of one's own interests one is allowed to promote. One possibility is that realist morality requires only that a statesperson limit policies to those designed to further legitimate state interests but that as long as a state leader is advancing a genuine state entitlement, any means might be employed. Or one might hold that realist morality actually sees the pursuit of legitimate self-interest as a means to the greater end of promoting state interests generally, that there is some "invisible hand" mechanism in which the pursuit of individual legitimate interests produces the best results overall. Or one might hold that realist morality requires a direct pursuit of the general good, but in a hard-headed and clear-sighted way.

Still another open question is whether to differentiate between the consequences of one's actions for innocent states, as opposed to those that are actually responsible for norm violations themselves. Perhaps there are limits on the means that might be employed when the costs fall on states (or individuals) that obey the rules but no limits on states (or individuals) that have forfeited protection of the rules because of their own illicit conduct. What we have said so far does not help distinguish these positions from one another or to sort out which are the more appealing (or the more consistent with traditionally realist views).

We noted at the beginning of this chapter that realism has many different threads. The realist morality we have described is only one of them. Some realists (predominantly neorealists) may truly believe that morality has no place in international relations because morality is not "objective" and "scientific." Other realists may genuinely believe that nothing matters besides aggrandizement of the national interest, defined only in terms of whatever is of advantage to a state in its own view and whatever the cost to outsiders. The version of realism investigated here allows for moral analysis and for the possibility that that moral analysis includes giving weight to the interests of others. It merely insists that the interests of others are often not advanced by following simpleminded moralistic recipes. This is an ethical position, with its own distinctive ethical vision. Although it may be wrong—a question that cannot be pursued here—it cannot be dismissed out of hand as incoherent, amoral, or immoral.

NOTE

1. In *American Hegemony: Political Morality in a One SuperPower World* (New Haven, Conn.: Yale University Press, 1993), esp. chap. 2.

INDEX

217